THE GEODESIC MANIFESTO

Essentials of Software Development
for the Post-Agile World

Bob Erickson

Version 1.3
Cover art by Nicholas Erickson.
All photos taken by the author.
All figures created by the author, except as noted.

Contact me at bob@GeodesicManifesto.com.

This first edition needs feedback. Contact me with your comments or visit my blog at https://www.GeodesicManifesto.com. I would appreciate honest reviews on Amazon, or anywhere else reviews are posted.

Printed in the United States of America
First Printing: 2019
ISBN of print version: 9781797459028
ISBN of e-book version: TBD

This book is dedicated to all the software developers and managers whom I worked for, who worked for me or who worked with me. They all made this book possible.

TABLE OF CONTENTS

FOREWORD

Some early readers had some trouble getting going. They got through the first chapter, then tried to continue linearly and got stuck. I added this foreword to help you navigate through the book in the way that works best for you.

When I first saw a document in pdf format, I was very disappointed that it was organized in pages. Computers should have freed us from the constraints of the page. Pages made perfect sense as an organizing principle when we distributed documents on paper. But a page is not the natural organizing principle for text-based information. Text is a stream of words composed into sentences composed into paragraphs composed into . . . and finally, into a document. And that ". . ." represents the meta-organization of the document that authors impose to best convey their ideas.

Linear text streams have been the organizing principle for literature since Genesis. And for most books, we start at the beginning, go through the middle, and stop at the end – in the order that the Author intended. This is certainly true of fiction – it's difficult to imagine understanding "Huckleberry Finn" by reading its chapters in some other order. Twain's organizing principles were time and the Mississippi River that both flow inexorably onward.

However, text books and books like the Bible are different. Professors often use a text book in nonlinear order, skipping chapters and sometimes assigning chapters in a different order from the book's order. The Bible is seldom read from cover to cover. It has a simple hierarchical organization: Testament, Book, Chapter and Verse. Bible students wander about the text, delving into small pockets one day and another pocket the next that may be related in some way other than by proximity in the text.

Linear reading relies on the Author's organization. Nonlinear reading typically relies on an expert guide to lead the reader along a path. The guide understands the dependency relationships among the sections– you can't understand section B if you haven't read section A. And they understand other relationships – section D is related to section B in a way that the professor wants to emphasize, so come back to section C later.

The Geodesic Manifesto is organized in a linear stream of text, because there isn't a good alternative. But the story I'm telling isn't a linear story; it's a collection of related essays. There are a lot of potential paths from the Chapter 1's introduction to Chapter 11. The path I've chosen for my linear stream attempts to make sure that concepts are presented before they are used, and that the diversionary material is spread out so that the book stays interesting. But that means there isn't a Mississippi River-like flow. If the Architecture chapter, for example, seems out of place, you can trust that it's there for a reason and read it in order, or you can come back to it later when it's clear that you should have already read it.

Here a couple recommended paths through the book that emphasize different aspects of software for different types of readers. For context, here is a simplified table of contents:

1. Bridges to Software
2. The Agile Manifesto – the Good, the Bad and the Ugly
3. The Role of the Software Manager
   - 3.2. Leadership
   - 3.3. Organization
   - 3.5. Planning
   - 3.6. Control
4. The Role of the Software Developer
5. Architecture
6. Challenging Problems
7. Software Quality
8. Common Processes
9. Methodology Frameworks
10. Creating a New System
11. Hope

The Casual Reader
Read chapter 1, and the introduction to each of the other chapters and all the non-sequiturs. Check out the key concepts section at the end of each chapter to see if there's something you want to explore deeper. The Leadership, Organization and Control sections of chapter 3 have broad appeal as do the Teamwork and Customer Interaction sections of chapter 4.

The Software Manager
Read chapters 1-4. Skim chapters 5 and 6. Read chapter 7. Read the introduction and the first two sections of chapter 8 (Software Processes, and Limits to Agility) and use the rest of the chapter as a reference. Read chapter 9, skimming after the XP section. Read chapters 10 and 11.

The Software Developer
Read chapters 1, 3-7, especially 5 (Architecture) and 6 (Challenging Problems) and 10. You can skim the Planning section of chapter 3. Skim the rest.

The Agile Aficionado
Read chapters 1, 2, and 8-11. If that converts you, then read the rest of the book.

Part 1:
FOUNDATION

Temple of Olympian Zeus, Athens, Greece

1 BRIDGES TO SOFTWARE

Humankind has built bridges for thousands of years. I don't mean the metaphorical bridges that span the gap across our political divide; I mean real bridges that make it possible to walk across water without getting that squishing sound in your Converse™ high tops. In Paris there are 37 bridges across the Seine. In London, 32 bridges across the Thames. There are dozens of bridges that cross the Rubicon. We build rope bridges, stone bridges, suspension bridges, railway trestles, and covered bridges with year-round autumn foliage. We build bridges over rivers, canyons, lakes, railroads, roads and the English Channel. Whoops! that's a tunnel.

Bridges don't fail.

OK, occasionally they fail, but we can name the failures because they are so rare: the spectacular Tacoma Narrows bridge failure (look it up on YouTube if you haven't seen it); the Interstate 35W bridge in Minneapolis; the San Francisco Bay Bridge (but there was an earthquake involved). And London Bridge has been "falling down, falling down" for ages. Bridge failures make the news.

But mostly, they don't fail. Cars, trains and people cross them every day without a moment's thought concerning whether this will be their last crossing. If they're about to fail, the authorities close the bridge until it can be repaired. If we measured bridge failures compared to the number of crossings, it would be in the parts per billion. Or less.

Software fails every day.

Like bridges, there are big failures that make the news – the Facebook and Yahoo data breaches, for example – but mostly, software failures are so commonplace we hardly notice them. When our Words with Friends™ app suddenly quits, or our PC spontaneously reboots, or Excel™ freezes in the middle of a calculation, we shake it off, briefly wonder if it was something we did, and then start over, hoping we can pick up where we left off. The coffee machine at the office reminds me every day – I push the buttons for a double decaf (I know – why bother?), the machine pours the first shot, then displays "Ready. Take your Cup," while proceeding to pour the second shot. I guess the decaf QA engineer was too sleepy to notice.

Why is software so bad? Do we need thousands of years of practice before we can get it right? Or is there something inherent in the software problem that makes it harder than building bridges or cars or airplanes? More practice will help, but the software problem is exceedingly more complex than bridge design. And in many cases, the economics don't make it worthwhile to build better software. And software is so easy to change that it's never complete and the next version isn't better, just different. And as the software system grows, it becomes harder and harder to make the next version, until finally we give up and start over, knowing that we have the same chaotic life cycle ahead.

In this book, I will explore the problem of software development – not from an academic perspective, but from the viewpoint of someone who has spent thirty-plus years immersed in software development. My career has gone back and forth between software development and software management, and with each transition, I have learned more about what I should have done better in my previous role. I have made a lot of mistakes and I learned from that. I have done a few things right and I learned from that. I have seen it done well and I've seen it done poorly, and I learned from that. And I learned from writing this book – the act of expressing your ideas will often lead to better ideas.

This is not a book about how to write code – there are plenty of those and I have nothing significant to add. This is not a book about algorithms – how could I hope to out-algorithm Donald Knuth?

This is not a book about Agile, which is an incomplete and often inadequate way of thinking about software that has caught our attention because the Old Way was so bad, and because the founders chose a perfect name. I will play the role of the guileless boy in *The Emperor's New Clothes* who is the only one with the audacity to declare that the Emperor is naked.

I propose a new manifesto, the Geodesic Manifesto, that supplies a wardrobe for the Agile vision and addresses the problems that have blocked the way for many Agile hopefuls. The Geodesic Manifesto forms the backbone of this book. It's short – fits on one 8½ x11 page, but it's dense, with many concepts that take long chapters to describe.

This is a book about why. This book discusses how to think about software. It sets forth several models for evaluating software development and discusses the philosophy I have forged during my career for how to apply those models. It looks at many facets of the problem of software development and attempts to abstract each facet into a few key concepts.

After you've read the book, you will be able to apply the concepts to your own software problem, or at least console yourself with the knowledge that you have a very hard problem. If I could give this book to my twenty-five-year-old self, the entire course of history would have changed. A little.

This book is targeted at anyone who wants to improve how software is developed. Managers will learn about leading their team but also about designing architectures and solving challenging problems. Developers will learn about development processes and their role in the organization.

For the structure of this book, I have chosen this conversational, first-person style. The "you" I am talking to is usually a software manager, but sometimes you're a software developer. I'll try to make it clear when I switch.

The book has a main set of sections that discuss facets of the software problem, and, interspersed throughout the text, are sections that I label "*Non-Sequitur*" that consider related topics that are only loosely connected to the main sections. You can skip these if you want or read them in a different order or you can skip the main thread and only read the non-sequiturs. If you bought, borrowed or stole the book, I thank you. You owe me nothing more.

Each chapter starts with a *non-sequitur* and concludes with a "Key Concepts" section that reviews the material in the chapter and provides cross references back to the discussion. The book is heavily cross-referenced using hyperlinks. If you're reading on paper, you'll have to traverse the hyperlinks the old-fashioned way – use the index.

In this chapter, I will introduce some of the key concepts that serve as background for the rest of the book. Some concepts are pervasive in software development such as requirements and a brief overview of graph theory. I present three models for understanding software that later chapters will reference frequently. I present the Geodesic Manifesto and provide a brief explanation with references to further information in the rest of the book Finally, I list the characters in this story.

A Note on Gender

For years, the pronoun 'he' represented a person of unspecified gender when its antecedent was a person of unspecified gender. In the sixties this usage started to unravel as women rightly objected to the default masculine pronoun. Over the last fifty years we have become increasingly aware of gender to the point that today even assuming that there are only two genders can trigger objection.

But the English language has not evolved. The only singular pronoun with unspecified gender is 'it'. You and I would both object to being referred to as 'it'. Common usage is evolving to use the word 'they' as a singular pronoun referring to a person of unspecified gender. I'm sorry, but the training I received from Sister Eucharia's ruler and Mrs. Hurd's red pen is too deeply embedded for me to adopt that usage. So, until we add a new pronoun (I recommend the word 'che', rhymes with 'the'), I'm stuck.

So, when I have to use a singular pronoun to refer to a person, I randomly choose one of my fictional characters: Jack and Jill, Bonnie and Clyde, or Victoria and Albert. Then I use 'she' or 'he' as appropriate. I hope you can abide that.

1.1 *Non-Sequitur*: Lessons from "The Imitation Game"

Part of my inspiration for this book came from the movie, "The Imitation Game". After watching it, I felt sympathy for Commander Denniston, the poor bastard who was responsible for managing the team of mathematicians, chess masters and puzzle solvers breaking the German Enigma code at Bletchley Park during WWII. Alan Turing, the brilliant mathematician, played by Benedict Cumberbatch, has built a machine that he claims is Britain's best hope to crack the code. The machine impressively whirrs and spins and ka-chunks away but has yet to crack a single coded message. Commander Denniston, played by Charles Dance, is the frustrated manager of this early software project. Of course, he doesn't call it software because the word wasn't applied to computer code until much later, but it has all the earmarks of a software project:

- It's late.
- No one can predict when it will be done.
- All previous predictions have been wrong.
- No one can define the next milestone – in fact, no one thought to ask.
- The system architect (Alan Turing) is a notoriously poor communicator.

Commander Denniston is a successful leader trained in Britain's military. He is an expert in command-and-control organizations and in logistics. He expects that when he gives an order it will be obeyed. He considers that all members of his staff are equivalent -- after all, one soldier is much like another. In fact, uniformity is a requirement; a soldier who is different will infect the entire brigade. The discipline of the British military formed the backbone of the Empire.

Now he finds himself in charge of a mission that everyone thinks is impossible. He has a few thousand people intercepting and decoding messages one by one, and he has a small team trying to break the code. He has never encountered anything like this, where the best efforts of his staff are inadequate to carry out his orders. Command-and-control organizations depend on the leader's understanding of the strategy. The strategy of applying a machine to defeat another machine is not part of his training. He does what he was trained to do – when things aren't going well, he goes back to basics. He pounds the team with the only hammer he knows – he issues orders. First, he delivers a deadline ultimatum. When that fails, he turns to the time-honored tactic of finding someone to blame.

Alan Turing does not match Commander Denniston's idea of a soldier. Turing is not like anyone else, and is not deferential to his commanding officer. Turing's idiosyncrasies both annoy and baffle the commander, and his best model for understanding Turing is a soldier who drinks too much or goes AWOL. The accepted standard for dealing with such a soldier is to throw him in the brig, and if the bad behavior continues, discharge him. So, he tries to remove Turing from the project.

Which brings us back to the earmarks of a software project.

- The manager does not understand the computer, the mathematics behind the solution or the architecture of the system.
- His best tactics for improving things are to re-organize and to apply more brute force, a strategy that clearly (at least in hindsight) can only make things worse.
- He also employs the oft-failed strategy of setting an impossible deadline.

Despite all this, the project succeeds because upper management (Winston Churchill) believes that the best hope is to put the cleverest man in England on the problem, and because the team, fueled by ale and shepherd's pie finds the required breakthrough at just the right time to save the movie and win the war.

Poor Commander Denniston! If only he had read this book, he would have learned:

- That a clear vision and an empowered team are more effective than uninformed orders
- Why software projects are complex and how to overcome their inherent difficulties
- The importance of software architecture and methodology
- How to help the cleverest man in England come to that breakthrough as soon as possible

1.2   Requirements

The term *'requirements'* is ubiquitous in the realm of software development. So, before I start bandying about the word, let's discuss what requirements are, where they come from, and how seriously we need to worry about them.

Requirements are statements about what the software needs to do without regard to how it does it. The term has been used in software development for a long time, and, as you might guess, there are various factions about how precisely they should be specified and how important they are to the development process. I have seen requirements documented with many pages of numbered and cross-referenced statements. I have seen requirements summarized in one PowerPoint slide with big font. Neither of those extremes meets the needs of software development.

The term 'requirement' implies 'necessity', but if some of the requirements are not met at the time we need to ship, we will ship anyway. The requirements are really guidelines with degrees of necessity. I would prefer to use the term 'capability' instead of 'requirement', but the term is so ingrained in the culture that I will continue to use it with this modified definition.

Some requirements are truly critical, and some are so peripheral that only left-handed aardvark keepers need them. Most are somewhere in between. Any product has sets of requirements that are sufficient – multiple sets, because {a,b,c,d} might be sufficient, but also {a,b,e,f}. Agreement on which sufficient set is the primary implementation target is important for the development team.

Some requirements are Boolean – either met or not met, for example, accepting a specific input file format. Other requirements are parametric, with a measurable attribute, for example, the time it takes to process a transaction. Requirement authors often try to transform parametric requirements into Boolean requirements by specifying a threshold. But don't believe it, that threshold is fuzzy at best and will continually move toward zero or infinity, whichever is harder to implement.

Requirements are essential to guide the development team. They define what developers will implement. They help the team set priorities. They guide testing. They provide a vocabulary for the team to use when talking among themselves and with customers.

But because requirements are written in natural language, they are ambiguous. A developer needs to interpret the text and implement the requirement into code. Once implemented, the ambiguity is gone, but there is no guarantee that the developer's interpretation matches what the user meant. Add to that the high probability that the implementation has bugs, and you can see where quality problems come from.

The most common way of reducing requirement ambiguity is to break down requirements into a set of user stories. For example, the requirement for a C++ compiler to have clear error messages – a very ambiguous statement – might include this user story:

- When code illegally references a private member of a class, I want to see both the calling code and the declaration of the private member.

This is a much less ambiguous statement. The clear-error-message requirement might break down into hundreds of these user stories. Although ambiguity is reduced by the user stories, there is no guarantee that the set of stories completely covers the requirement.

Because requirements are often wrong, and always incomplete, software developers must continually make uninformed guesses to answer the question, "What would the user want?" The best practice is for developers to learn to think like users. Then the question transforms to "What would I want?" which is much easier to answer.

Old-style software development expected requirements that were supposed to magically appear at the exact moment they were needed with answers to any question that might be posed. *Should I make the Grpbxtz widget configurable?* The requirements were called "Marketing Requirements" although no one in the Marketing Department would ever use the product. For years, I tried unsuccessfully to get my teams to call them "Market Requirements," and to instill the notion that everyone is responsible for understanding the market. But the term lived on and they continued to be late and inadequate, and I continued to get questions like, "Why can't Marketing tell me the marginal benefit of the Grpbxtz widget?" And I wanted to reply, "Because they haven't got a clue. No one has a clue. And they're busy putting lipstick on the pig you shipped last year! Just make it configurable." But I didn't.

One of the key outcomes of the Agile revolution is that we now recognize that it is impossible to know the complete set of requirements at the beginning of the project. It may be impossible ever to know them. But we need something to guide the team, so, the team should make the best guess they can about the requirements using whatever resources are available, and they should assume the requirements are wrong. Later when they have limping software, they can get feedback from users, refine the requirements and feed the new requirements into the product development.

Assuming the requirements are wrong is the best assumption the team can make. First, it's unlikely that the team can guess the requirements out of thin air. But more importantly, it creates a mindset that whatever software they write will need to adapt quickly as they discover better information about the requirements.

Since the requirements are wrong, anything that depends on the correct, complete requirements, will also be wrong. In particular, early estimates of software schedules and development cost will always be optimistic because so much of what's needed has yet to be defined.

The requirements need to be pretty good by the time you release the system or you run the risk of shipping a Clydesdale when you needed a thoroughbred.

1.3   Models for Software Development

Software development is complex, and every development project is different. But there are common themes that apply to all projects. The synthesis of those common themes into models helps us to understand our complex problem.

A model is a metaphor for some aspect of the whole. A good model helps you understand one or more facet of the problem at hand and guides you to make good decisions.

Unfortunately, software development is too complex to be guided by a single model. In the following sections, I present three models for software development:

- The Yin-Yang Model explains why software development is difficult, and gives some guidance on how to combat the forces of evil that cause software problems.
- The Software Thermodynamic Model draws a parallel with classic thermodynamics and explains how software rots.
- The Complexity Model explains how to characterize a software development problem and the best method for solving that problem.

These three models, plus the Geodesic Manifesto that follows this section, form the backbone of the book, which will often refer to them.

1.3.1   The Yin-Yang Model

Software development reflects the classic battle between Good and Evil, light and dark. The forces of Evil do everything they can to make development difficult. But with courage and perseverance, the forces of Good can improve the process and help you create better software sooner.

In this section, I introduce five pairs of Yin-Yang terms. One side of the pair, the Yin, refers to an Evil feature of software that makes the problem hard, and the other side refers to its Good counterpart. Sometimes you can make a conscious tradeoff between them, but often the dark side dominates and your job is to minimize its impact.

1.3.1.1   Complexity vs. Simplicity

Bridge-building is a complex undertaking. A bridge has lots of components - the Golden Gate Bridge has over a million rivets. Bridges interact with the environment – painting the Firth of Forth Bridge took almost 30 years. They often need to be enhanced while remaining open to traffic – widening of a local bridge took over a year, but it was closed for just a few hours.

Software is *complex.* A typical system depends on thousands of code statements, sometimes millions. A bridge may have a million rivets, but there are only a few different types of rivets. Every code statement is unique. Each of those statements interacts with other statements, sometimes directly but often indirectly, in ways that are not readily apparent.

To implement that complex system, you need a complex organization of developers, software validators and many others. Coordinating all these activities is also complex.

While there's nothing you can do about the fact that you have a lot of code to manage, you can impose *simplicity* to parts of the code and to the process of creating it. You manage complexity with *Architecture*, that organizes code statements into manageable chunks, and with *Methodology*, that provides processes and guidelines for the developers who write those statements.

In the section The Complexity Model of Software Development, I will offer a pseudo-formal definition of complexity. Much of the book is dedicated to discussions of architecture and methodology.

1.3.1.2 Opacity vs. Visibility and Clarity

Golden Gate Bridge, from Lincoln Park, San Francisco, California

When I look at the Golden Gate Bridge, I can see how it was built. Its two massive towers of steel and concrete provide the bases of support. The main cables are anchored in concrete at both ends. The suspension cables hang from the main cable and support the roadway. If I move closer, I can see the rivets that hold the steel together. Even though some parts of it are encased in concrete, or hidden from view, it's clear that the design and the embodiment of the bridge are similar.

Software is *opaque.* The embodiment of a software system is extremely different from the code that implements it. By observing what it does and how it operates, I can only guess at the high-level architecture of the system. And the details are completely obscured.

The opacity of software makes it difficult to diagnose problems. What you can observe is a mere shadow of the cause of the problem. Not even a shadow – the thermal profile of the shadow.

The opacity of software makes it difficult to enhance. Each enhancement must begin by some developer coming to a new understanding of that part of the implementation – even if that developer was the original author. The code may be unambiguous, but the intentions and interactions are lost in the complexity of the software.

It takes work to overcome opacity with *visibility*. The purpose of software debuggers is to provide complete visibility, but they're only practical for use by developers. You can add diagnostics that provide a window into the internals of the code; diagnostics are useful for developers and validators. And you can make sure that your architectures and processes encourage *clarity* of the code, again only useful for developers.

When users encounter a problem, they are doomed to workarounds based on black magic incantations.

1.3.1.3   Vulnerability vs. Reliability

Bridge builders are acutely aware of what happens if a component fails. Wherever possible, they avoid the possibility of a single point of failure – a place in the design where a single component could fail and bring down the bridge. If a girder could be held in place by two bolts, the designer might use four or six bolts to ensure it never moves. If the designers can't avoid having a single point of failure, like the towers of the Golden Gate Bridge, then they overdesign those components.

Software is *vulnerable*. Every code statement is a potential single point of failure for a software system, although the severity of the failure may range from annoying to fatal. Since each code statement is written by a human, the likelihood of failure is significant.

To get high-quality software despite its vulnerability, we rely on testing through the opaque interface. The opacity obscures the vulnerability so much that we can't even measure software bugs until after they have been observed. If a bug fails in the forest of code without making any noise, then it doesn't exist.

It is possible to build highly *reliable* subsystems, but the cost is very high, so only critical subsystems, for example, the core of the Linux Kernel, can get the required scrutiny. You need to identify the parts of your system that need extra attention and come up with strategies that overcome the vulnerability.

Reliable software has few potential bugs lurking in the code waiting to happen. Developing reliable software is the main theme of the chapter Software Quality.

1.3.1.4   Rigidity vs. Flexibility

As you drive down the interstate, you will observe that most bridges look alike. The highway department has a few flexible designs that they reuse over and over. The design process for a highway bridge is to choose the design type, and then to adjust the parameters to adapt the design to the specific situation. Design reuse saves money and time, and the highway department can concentrate on making those few designs extremely robust.

It's somewhat ironic that software, the most configurable thing in the world, is *rigid.* Most software systems are built for a particular purpose and tested for that purpose. Any attempt to use a piece of that system for another purpose is likely to expose problems in the design or implementation. When requirements change, you can't bend the software to comply with the new information, you need to bolt on something new because modifying the existing system will cause it to shatter.

Building *flexible* software subsystems that can quickly adapt to changes requires a different mindset from the more common single-use development. You have to think ahead to know what kinds of changes are likely, and then you need to design the software to make those kinds of changes easy, even though you have no idea of the details of those potential changes. Building flexible software may take a little more work at the beginning, but the payback could be huge because often the alternative is starting over.

1.3.1.5   Chaos vs. Repeatability

At six AM, traffic sails across the San Francisco Bay Bridge. At seven AM, it crawls. Somewhere between, a driver tapped the brakes, a bird hit a windshield, a gust of wind pushed a car near the other lane. That perturbation, together with the increased number of cars slowed traffic until later in the day when lighter traffic could clear the bridge. But at seven AM, all you can see are a couple cars in front of you and you wonder what happened.

Chaos theory studies the behavior of complex systems. In a chaotic system, cause and effect are only loosely linked. The famous "butterfly effect" illustrates how a small change in one parameter can lead to an enormous change in the later state of the system.

In a deterministic system, if we know the entire state of the system it is possible to predict the next state of the system. But most of the time, we can only observe a subset of the state of the system, and so the next visible state often appears to be random. I call this the "iceberg effect". When we're caught in a traffic jam, we tend to blame the cars we can see, but they are victims the same as we are.

Software is *chaotic*; it is subject to the software butterfly effect and the iceberg effect. Small changes to the software, or to the input data, can lead to big changes in the resulting state of the system.

To clarify, chaos and complexity are not the same thing. *Complexity* refers to the code itself and the process for creating that code. *Chaos* refers to the state of the system while the software is running.

The software butterfly effect can have two kinds of manifestation. First, the final state of the program's data can be different. This is common in systems that use complex numerical analysis or optimization algorithms. Second, the modified program state can trigger bugs that have lain dormant for years.

Software users expect *repeatability*. When they do the same thing over and over, they expect the same result; any other result causes insanity. The opacity of software hides a lot of information from users. When you add the iceberg effect, sometimes software can appear to be non-deterministic.

As an example, the other day, my wife was on the phone with a colleague reviewing a complex spreadsheet used to manage the attendees at a Boy Scout adult training event. They were each looking at the same file on their separate personal computers. My wife referred to the "menu on the right." Her colleague replied, "I don't see that. I used to see it, but I don't anymore." They spent a few minutes trying to figure out how to get that menu, and then gave up. Something in the state of their computers caused them to see different results from the same input.

It takes thought and effort to overcome chaos to meet the expectations of users.

1.3.2   Software Thermodynamic Model

Usually, we think of software at the microscopic level, one code statement at a time. Of course, that's how we develop it and how we modify it. But the system will quickly reach a level of complexity that will benefit from understanding it at a macro level. In this section, I will draw an analogy between software and classical thermodynamics that provides a useful model for understanding software, even though the mathematical rigor is missing.

Classical Thermodynamics

Thermodynamics is a branch of physics that studies the behavior of systems that are too complex to analyze at the component level. It relates heat and temperature to other forms of energy and work. We may not be able to analyze a balloon full of helium at the atomic level, but the statistical behavior of those atoms is consistent, and we can treat the helium in the balloon as a single object with a temperature and pressure, and use that macro-behavior to understand why the balloon rises.

Thermodynamics has four laws, numbered from zero to three. They start at zero not because the scientists who formulated them were computer scientists, but because the well-established laws (one to three) depend on a definition of temperature, so scientists tacked on a zeroth law to rectify that omission. Here is a layman's version of the laws. In these laws, I distinguish between an object, which might be a balloon full of helium, from a system, which includes all the objects in the limited universe of your observations.

0.   If two objects are each in thermal equilibrium with a third object, the two objects are in thermal equilibrium with each other. By definition, two objects in thermal equilibrium have the same temperature.
1.   Energy can change forms, for example, from kinetic energy to heat energy, but the total energy of a system never changes.
2.   The entropy of a system never decreases. Entropy is a measure of the energy of a system that has been lost to heat and can never be converted to another form. It is analogous to disorder. A gas has more entropy than a liquid, which has more entropy than a solid. It's a measure of the energy that's lost and no longer usable.
3.   At a temperature of absolute zero, an object has zero entropy. (It's not exactly zero, but zero is close enough for software.)

Software Thermodynamics

Software changes every day. Bug fixes, enhancements, refactoring – they all contribute to the continuous change. And after every change, there's more code. The figure below shows how the amount of code in the Linux Kernel has grown over time.

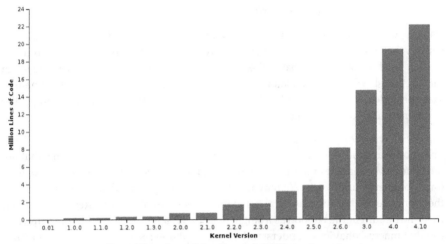

From https://en.wikipedia.org/wiki/Linux_kernel

With more code there are more bugs. If you search the web for "bugs per line of code", you will find various estimates from 0.1 to 50 bugs per thousand lines of code, depending on lots of factors, including the difficulty of the code, the ability of the developer, and the level of testing. The exact value of the number doesn't matter except that it's not zero. More code means more bugs.

A useful metaphor is to think that all those changes increase the *entropy* of the software. But we need to understand what entropy means in the context of software.

It takes work to create and maintain software. Let's define a unit of work, the *swerg* (a portmanteau of SoftWare erg), to be one staff hour of work – one average software developer working for one hour.

A software module, some logical collection of code like a function, a class, a source file, a library, etc., has some amount of *latent work* W_L needed to make it meet the current requirements of that module with zero bugs. Of course, the requirements will change, but for the definition of latent work, assume the requirements are frozen. The latent work includes work required to meet the requirements W_R and work required to fix all real and latent bugs W_B.

(1) $\quad W_L = W_R + W_B$

A *real* bug must be both triggered with the right conditions, and observed. A *latent* bug is bad code that is waiting for the trigger and observation to happen.

Suppose that a module M has 100 swergs of latent work (W_L). An average developer, Jack, applies 20 swergs (W_D) to improving M. You would think that M now has 80 swergs of latent work, but while Jack worked, he created new bugs, so M now has 85 swergs of latent work. It's useful to think of the difference between the expected value and the true value as an increase in the entropy E of module M.

$$(2) \quad \Delta E = W_{L2} - (W_{L1} - W_D) = 85 - (100 - 20) = 5$$

From this we can define the **entropy** of a module to be the amount of work needed to fix all the latent bugs in that module. This definition is intuitively close to thermodynamic entropy since disorder breeds bugs.

Next, we need to define a temperature. Temperature is a property of the module. Conceptually, a **hot** module is difficult to modify. Any change to that module will create lots of new bugs and increase the entropy. A **cool** module is easier to modify. To be consistent with our conceptual understanding, I will define the module temperature:

$$(3) \quad T_M = \frac{\Delta E}{W_D}$$

where ΔE is the increase in entropy in the entire system (not just module M), and W_D is the developer work applied to the module. This definition depends on an average developer making an average change, and of course that never happens, because in your organization, all the developers are above average.

One of the factors that determines the temperature of a module is the amount of coupling of that module to other parts of the system. In a hot module, a single software change can greatly increase the entropy. That is because in a hot module, code often has convoluted relationships to other parts of the system. That one change can cause (or expose) new bugs in unchanged parts of the system. The entropy doesn't just add, it multiplies. This is sometimes called, "Software Rot", a common term for the phenomenon that, over time, parts of the system, that previously worked just fine, start to fail even when they have not changed.

In a cool module, software changes are isolated and do not propagate entropy beyond the boundaries of the module where the change is made. When new code is added, entropy is increased, but it doesn't multiply. In a cool system, software rots much more slowly.

Let's look at the extremes. When entropy increase is greater than the developer work applied, you have a poison module. Everything you do to it makes the system worse. Perversely, high temperature modules are both the ones you want to change the most, and are the hardest to change. They become extremely stable because no developer will touch that module, and you are stuck with the current implementation.

On the other hand, you can imagine changes that decrease the system entropy by more than the effort applied – a module with a negative temperature. These changes are rare, and modules with negative temperature don't last very long. Usually, they are removed from the system by re-architecting parts of the system to remove inter-module coupling, or re-writing a critical module that has had a lot of problems. I fondly remember the deep sense of satisfaction I experienced when one of these changes worked.

Fixing the bugs found by testing can decrease the entropy of a system, but testing can't reduce the temperature of the module. If the module is hot, once you've recovered from one change, then the next change you make is likely to introduce new bugs. The only way to reduce the temperature of a module is to improve the architecture to isolate the effects of changes.

There are no laws of software thermodynamics, but there are tendencies that parallel the laws of classical thermodynamics.

0. A software system won't come to thermal equilibrium, but a hot module is likely to increase the temperature of the modules it interacts with.
1. Software is not a zero-sum game. All the work that goes into making software creates value in the software system. The value of the software is much more than the cost of the swergs that went into it.
2. The entropy of a system always increases. That's because the amount of code in a system always increases. Those rare changes that remove code are offset by many more changes that add code. Less code may have fewer bugs, but most bugs are caused by writing not quite enough code.

This is not a law. It is possible to reduce the entropy of a system, but it takes work. It is much easier to design a cool system that will have low entropy than to fix a hot system that has high entropy.
3. The latent work of a software system never reaches zero. Changes in the requirements cause changes in the code, which create new bugs. Software is only stable when it's dead.

1.3.3   The Complexity Model of Software Development

The Complexity Model of software development has served me well over the past twenty years. It is simple enough that most people can quickly understand it, yet rich enough that it can be applied to a wide range of problems.

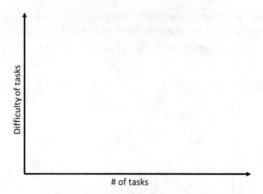

Software problems can be characterized by the number of tasks it takes to solve a problem and the difficulty of the tasks. I will divide this space into four quadrants.

1.3.3.1   Trivial Problems

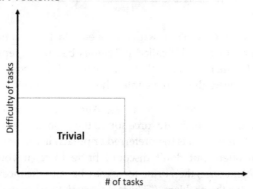

The lower-left quadrant, problems that can be solved with a few easy tasks, is named *Trivial*. It's a nice place to work, but it doesn't pay very well. However, it is the goal of software development to transform a problem from the other quadrants to the Trivial quadrant. When people talk about "Ease of Use" for a software product, they are really evaluating how close to the origin did the product get.

For example, consider fingerprint security for the iPhone®.

Once it is set up, the use model is trivial – put your finger on the button. But behind the scene, there's a lot of stuff going on. The sensor outputs an array of pixels. Then image processing transforms the pixels into something that represents the fingerprint. And then the fingerprint must be matched to the master fingerprints you set up. And if it finds an acceptable match it lets you use the phone.

On the other hand, the setup of the master fingerprints is a process that takes quite a few tasks. You must follow instructions and respond to arcane feedback before the phone accepts your master fingerprint. This process is tedious and thus, leads us to the next quadrant in the model.

1.3.3.2   Detailed Problems

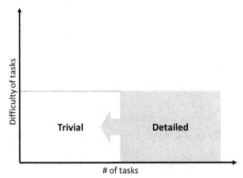

The lower-right quadrant, problems with lots of easy tasks, is named *Detailed*. When I first came up with this model, I called it *Tedious* because it represents the kind of problem I despise. But then I realized that any organization needs people to solve these problems and that, indeed, there are people who love solving these problems.

Detailed problems are solved in two ways. Automation transforms the Detailed problem into a trivial problem. Brute force solves the problem by applying lots of time and/or resources. Automation is the preferred approach if you are going to encounter the same problem often. But don't discount brute force; if you're only going to encounter this problem once, then brute force may be both the most efficient and most expedient way to solve the problem. ("There is no such thing as ineffective brute force, only insufficient." – attributed to Lou Scheffer) And even for problems you plan to automate, using the brute force approach at first may help you understand how to automate the process.

Consider the problem of the Postal Service. They need to deliver millions of items each day. They use automation for a lot of the processing, but the final mile is still served by thousands of postal workers who physically deliver the mail.

1.3.3.3   Challenging Problems

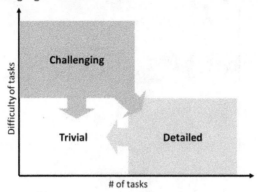

The third quadrant, problems with a few difficult tasks, is named *Challenging*. This is the reason I became a software developer in the first place. This is the realm of the NP-complete problem, of the problems that are closely tied to mathematics, of statistical analysis, of numerical analysis, of optimization, of cryptography. This is the realm of the PhD dissertation, of the technical journals, of professors who have dedicated their lives to one Challenging problem.

A Challenging problem is solved by transforming it into one or more Detailed or Trivial problems. The key to the solution is invention. The solution may be in the literature, or it may never have been encountered before. The solution may require applying techniques from many sources. The best software developers for these problems understand a wide range of techniques, and are willing to experiment with these techniques until they find the combination that works best for the problem.

Consider Alan Turing's problem with the Enigma code. Let's assume that I needed to solve that problem today (so I don't have to build a computer from scratch). I might try the brute force technique first to understand how bad it is. I would read papers on cryptographic cracking. I would try a few of the techniques in the papers. I would sleep on it and sometimes wake up with new ideas. And eventually, I would have an acceptable solution. I might be able to improve the solution over time.

An important characteristic of Challenging problems is that they are inherently unpredictable. Before starting on the Enigma decryptor, I could fairly accurately predict how long it would take to develop the code to try to decrypt the message. But I would almost certainly be hopelessly optimistic about any guess about when the code would succeed at decryption. And after the acceptable solution is in place, I would be hopelessly wrong about a prediction for when the code would run ten times faster.

There is a later chapter dedicated to a discussion of Challenging Problems.

1.3.3.4   Complex Problems

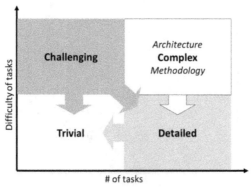

The final quadrant, problems with lots of difficult tasks, is named **Complex**. Most problems worth solving fall into this quadrant. No one person can solve a Complex problem – it takes a team. To make the team effective requires two things: an architecture that provides a framework for breaking tasks into manageable chunks, and a software development methodology that makes sure that when those chunks are completed, they will work within the whole.

The essence of software leadership is the ability to develop architectures and methodologies. These two aspects of software development are co-dependent. The best methodology in the world will fail if the architectural underpinnings aren't strong enough to hold it up. The best architecture won't get off the ground without a solid methodology to make sure the pieces can come together to form a useful whole.

There is a later chapter dedicated to Architecture. Most of the rest of the book discusses various aspects of Methodology.

1.4   The Geodesic Manifesto

Unless you studied topology, you probably have only heard the word 'geodesic' applied to Buckminster Fuller's dome. In topology, a geodesic is the shortest path between two points in a generalized space. On a Euclidean plane, it is a line segment. On the surface of a sphere, it is a segment of a great circle. The geodesic from Sacramento to Reno, given the constraint of driving an automobile, goes through the Donner Pass. Dijkstra's algorithm can find a geodesic in a graph, the shortest path between two nodes. In software, the geodesic is a metaphor for the way that a productive software team starts with nothing but a twinkle in someone's eye, and ends up with high-quality working software.

The Geodesic Manifesto describes the Geodesic Philosophy at a high level. Like Agile, it aims to help software development teams quickly create high-quality software in a world where requirements are vague, incomplete and changing. Whereas the Agile Manifesto (discussed in the next chapter) focuses on what not to do, the Geodesic Manifesto describes what to do to achieve your goals. Agile's negative views of process, documentation, planning and leadership have led many development teams into one-way, dead-end tunnels. I hope that the Geodesic Manifesto can free them to use the ways that work, even if they're not "Agile."

This section presents the Manifesto, followed by the annotated Manifesto. On first read, you may want to skip to the annotated version that includes brief discussions with links to the parts of the book that expand on the key concepts.

THE MANIFESTO OF THE GEODESIC PHILOSOPHY OF SOFTWARE DEVELOPMENT

ASSUMPTIONS

We assume these truths:

- Our goal is to create software-based solutions that do what the user wants in the way the user expects.
- Requirements are an inaccurate abstraction of what customers and users want. Requirements cannot be known completely and will change even after they are known. The only true specification of the solution is working software.
- People who develop software have a wide range of ability, motivation and temperament.
- Our problem is to help those people overcome software's inherent difficulties: complexity, opacity, vulnerability, rigidity, and its chaotic nature.

PRINCIPLES

To overcome the limitations of requirements:

- We have frequent interaction with customers and users.
- We frequently deliver working software and actively seek feedback.
- Developers must learn to think like their customers.

To overcome the limitations of people:

- We build synergistic teams that improve the performance of every individual.
- We establish a methodology that fosters creativity and encourages interaction.
- We encourage frequent and open communication among team members.

To overcome the inherent difficulties of software:

- We seek out change from as many sources as possible.
- We plan for change, and change the plan when necessary.
- We embrace change through constant measurement, analysis and improvement of the software and methodology.
- Developers strive for the highest level of technical excellence and assume responsibility for quality.

PILLARS

Success depends on:

- Leadership that:
  - Creates a vision for the solution we're trying to create
  - Organizes the development team to maximize the contribution of each member
  - Develops dynamic plans that answer three questions: When will it be done? What will it contain? What do I do next?
  - Establishes processes and controls that maximize productivity and creativity
- An architecture that organizes the solution into modules and their interactions that is modular, flexible, consistent and sufficient.
- A methodology that defines common processes and controls that foster innovation, empower the development team to create the best solution, and maximize efficiency while minimizing risk
- A decision-making ethos to guide us as we change the vision, plan, architecture and methodology.

1.4.1 The Annotated Geodesic Manifesto

THE MANIFESTO OF THE GEODESIC PHILOSOPHY OF SOFTWARE DEVELOPMENT
- ❖ *Now that's a pretentious title!*

ASSUMPTIONS

We assume these truths:
- Our goal is to create software-based solutions that do what the user wants in the way the user expects.
    - ❖ *The Manifesto primarily addresses software, but software is often part of a larger solution that may include hardware, data and other stuff.*
    - ❖ *The Quality chapter defines high quality software with this statement: "High Quality Software does what the user wants in the way the user expects."*
- Requirements are an inaccurate abstraction of what customers and users want. Requirements cannot be known completely and will change even after they are known. The only true specification of the solution is working software.
    - ❖ *See the Requirements section earlier in this chapter.*
- People who develop software have a wide range of ability, motivation and temperament.
    - ❖ *The Organization section of the Software Manager chapter discusses these traits of software developers.*
- Our problem is to help those people overcome software's inherent difficulties: complexity, opacity, vulnerability, rigidity, and its chaotic nature.
    - ❖ *These are the five Yin traits from the Yin-Yang Model.*

PRINCIPLES

To overcome the limitations of requirements:
- We have frequent interaction with customers and users.
    - ❖ *The Agile Manifesto's principles recommend daily interaction with "business people", whom I refer to as "customer advocates".*
- We frequently deliver working software and actively seek feedback.
    - ❖ *The chapters on Methodology, starting with Common Processes focus on software delivery.*
- Developers must learn to think like their customers.
    - ❖ *There is a brief discussion of how to think like a customer in Think Like a Customer*

To overcome the limitations of people:
- We build synergistic teams that improve the performance of every individual.
    - ❖ *The Agile Manifesto talks about self-organizing teams. But self-organization is not enough. A team needs leadership and direction to make the transformation from a bunch of people who work together into a team that can move mountains. When that happens, it's a wonder to watch.*

❖   *In Teamwork, I present four values essential to synergistic teams: Mutual Success, Mutual Ownership, Common Understanding and Continuous Improvement.*

- We establish a methodology that fosters creativity and encourages interaction.
  - ❖   *The chapter Common Processes discusses what processes are needed for an effective methodology.*
  - ❖   *See the Methodology Frameworks chapter for examples of high-agility methodologies.*
- We encourage frequent and open communication among team members.
  - ❖   *Organize teams and office space to maximize communication efficiency.*
  - ❖   *Avoid unnecessary documentation; write only what's needed for the use and development of the software.*
  - ❖   *The formality of communication must increase with physical and organizational distance.*

To overcome the inherent difficulties of software:

- We seek out change from as many sources as possible.
  - ❖   *Changes come from customers, users, testing and the creativity of the development team.*
- We plan for change, and change the plan when necessary.
  - ❖   *We need a plan, but only if it can adapt to the changing environment.*
- We embrace change through constant measurement, analysis and improvement of the software and methodology.
  - ❖   *The continuous improvement cycle – measure, analyze, implement – forms the core of every Agile methodology. Lean thinking provides a framework for doing that.*
- Developers strive for the highest level of technical excellence and assume responsibility for quality.
  - ❖   *Technical excellence is one of the principles of the Agile Manifesto.*
  - ❖   *Write code that is easy to understand, easy to extend, and easy to change.*
  - ❖   *In the Quality chapter I propose that developers must assume responsibility for quality because they are the only ones who can affect it. Validators identify problems, but developers created the problems.*
  - ❖   *Quality is achieved through effective development processes that include code review, high coverage test development, frequent measurement, and quick feedback about problems.*

PILLARS

Success depends on:

- Leadership that:
  - o   Creates a vision for the solution we're trying to create
  - ❖   *The Vision section of the Software Manager chapter discusses how to create and communicate a vision.*
  - o   Organizes the development team to maximize the contribution of each member

❖ *The Organization section of the Software Manager chapter discusses management of the team.*
   o Develops dynamic plans that answer three questions: When will it be done? What will it contain? What do I do next?
❖ *The word 'dynamic' implies that the plan needs to change as the project evolves. We can't expect to plan once and then execute. Plan for change and change the plan when necessary*
❖ *The Agile Manifesto devalues planning and has given a lot of lazy managers the excuse to avoid it. But planning is necessary because at any point, you need to be able to answer these three questions. See the section of the Software Manager chapter.*
   o `
❖ *See the Common Processes chapter and the Control section of the Software Manager chapter.*
- An architecture that organizes the solution into modules and their interactions that is modular, flexible, consistent and sufficient.
  ❖ *The Architecture chapter briefly discusses how to think about architecture. These five attributes help distinguish good architectures from bad.*
- A methodology that defines common processes and controls that foster innovation, empower the development team to create the best solution, and maximize efficiency while minimizing risk
  ❖ *The Methodology Frameworks chapter provides examples and analysis of common methodologies.*
- A decision-making ethos to guide us as we change the vision, plan, architecture and methodology.
  ❖ *The primary purpose of this book is to help you build an ethos – a guide to tell right from wrong in software development.*
  ❖ *Decision making is discussed in the Leadership section of the Software Manager chapter.*
  ❖ *As the Agile Manifesto states, "At regular intervals, the team reflects on how to become more effective, then tunes and adjusts its behavior accordingly."*

1.5   Graphic Details

I occasionally use concepts from graph theory to describe parts of the software development process. Since I realize that some of you are unfamiliar with graph theory, this section is a very basic introduction with the definitions of the terms I use. If you are confident in your knowledge, you can skip this section, but you'll miss all the graph theory jokes.

Two nodes, Neil and Sheila, walk into a bar. Why didn't Sheila duck?

A **graph** is a set of **nodes** (sometimes called vertices, but not by me) and **edges** that represent the relationship between nodes. When using a graph, the nodes will represent something, like the corners of a polygon or the modules in a software architecture. The edges may also represent something, like the edges of a polygon or the dependencies in a software architecture. In *directed graphs*, edges have direction – they point from one node to another. In an *undirected graph*, edges just represent a relationship without the notion of from-to. The name, "undirected graph", is distinctly unimaginative, but you can see why they didn't call it the "any-which-way graph".

A graph has a *loop* (mathematicians prefer 'cycle') if you can leave a node and find your way back to the same node without repeating any edges.

> *The bartender says, "You're looking a little edgy." Sheila replies, "My edge points to him and his edge points to me. I'm feeling a little loopy." Neil says, "That's a cyclical argument."*

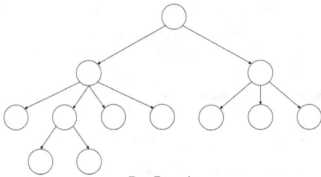

Tree Example

A *tree* is a directed graph where every node has at most one input edge. There is one root node of the tree that doesn't have any inputs. The outputs of a tree node connect to the child nodes. Nodes without any children are often called *leaf nodes*. If you draw it carefully, a tree looks like an oak, with all the nodes branching from the root. If I draw it, you can think of it more as a hydroponic tree, because I always draw the root node at the top.

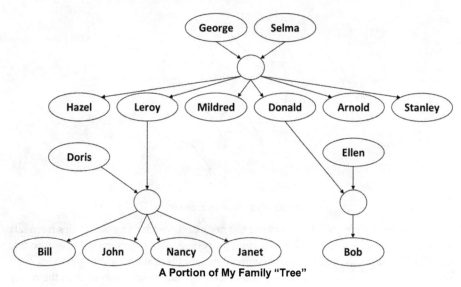

A Portion of My Family "Tree"

There's a special kind of directed graph that has no loops. It's called a **Directed Acyclic Graph**, or **DAG**. Your family tree is not a tree; it's a DAG with two kinds of nodes. One node type represents an individual, Uncle Leroy; and the second node type represents a union that produces children, Uncle Leroy married Aunt Doris and they had four children. We know it's a DAG because a loop would mean that you are your own ancestor, which can only occur in bad time travel science fiction.

> *"Do you have any children?" asked the bartender. "Just one boy," said Sheila. "We call him Dagwood."*

There are two common ways to search a graph: depth-first and breadth-first.

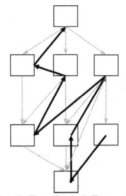

Depth-First Search Example

In *depth-first search*, you start from the top node and search successor nodes from left to right. If the successor node has not been processed, then search its successor nodes. Once all the successor nodes have been processed, or there are no successor nodes, then process that node. In the example graph above, the nodes are processed in the order shown by the red lines. The advantage of depth-first search is that when you process a node, you know that all its successors have already been processed. One of the uses of depth-first search is to find the longest path from the start node to any leaf node.

"Dagwood is in the navy, specializing in depth-first charges," said Neil.

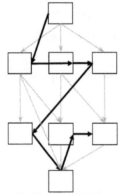

Breadth-First Search Example

In *breadth -first search*, you start from the top node, process it, and then put all its successors in a queue. Take the node from the head of the queue, process it, and then put all its successors in the queue, skipping the ones that have already been processed or are in the queue. In the example above, the nodes are processed in the order shown by the red lines. One of the uses of breadth-first search is to find the shortest path from the start node to any leaf node.

"You've gained a little weight, dear," said Neil. *"Maybe you should stand a little taller."*
"Breadth first, dear," replied Sheila.

I didn't say they were good jokes.

1.6   Dramatis Personae

Software development has a large cast of characters. In this section, I list the characters and the names I use for them throughout the book. Beware that in some organizations these names mean something else.

Software Developer – A person who writes software for a living. Also known as programmer, coder, hacker, software engineer, computer scientist, and many other names.

Software Validator – A person who verifies that software does what it's supposed to. Software must be tested to validate that it delivers the intended reliability and functionality. Developers are responsible for some of the testing, but independent system testing is done by the validation team. I use this term instead of the more traditional "quality assurance" (QA) because over time QA acquired a bad reputation as a job where failed developers ended up.

Architect – A developer who is responsible for maintaining the integrity of the architecture.

Tech Writer – a person who writes product documentation. Users require documentation to effectively use the product. The required amount and quality of documentation depends on many factors like the complexity of the product, the sophistication of users and level of support that's available.

Manager – a person who manages a group of software developers. This person is responsible for making sure the software gets done with all the required features, on the committed schedule, and with high quality. The manager is also responsible for the welfare of his team.

User – a person who uses the software.

Customer – the person (or entity, if it's a company or other organization) who pays for the software. Sometimes this is the user. More often, this is an entity who provides the software to the users. For example, if I buy PhotoShop™, I am both the user and the customer. If IBM buys photoshop, IBM is the customer. There will be many users within IBM who have no idea how much, or under what terms, IBM paid for PhotoShop.

Customer Advocate – someone within your organization who can speak for the customer. This might be someone in marketing, sales, or support.

Executive – someone up the chain of management from the Manager, typically the Manager's boss's boss or higher. Also known as upper management.

Knobs, Inc. – a purveyor of door handles that have well known requirements and never need an upgrade.

1.7   Key Concepts

Requirements

- Requirements are an abstract specification of what the software should do.
- Requirements aren't required; they are guidelines for capabilities that have a degree of necessity.
- Requirements cannot be known completely and will change over time.

The Yin-Yang Model

- The Yin-Yang Model presents five pairs of good vs. evil traits of software:

Yin	Yang
Complexity	Simplicity
Opacity	Visibility and Clarity
Vulnerability	Reliability
Rigidity	Flexibility
Chaos	Repeatability

Software Thermodynamics

- The Software Thermodynamics Model is an analog to classical thermodynamics that attempts to define entropy and temperature of software.
- Entropy represents the development work that is wasted because it creates bugs or needs to be redone.
- The temperature of a module represents the tendency of work done on that module to create entropy. Work done on low temperature modules tends to create little entropy, while work done on high temperature modules tends to create a lot of bugs, and therefore a lot of entropy.

Complexity Model

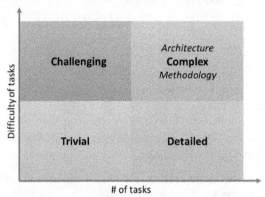

Complexity Model

- The Complexity Model partitions software problems into four quadrants based on the number of tasks required to solve the problem, and the difficulty of those tasks.
- Complex problems are solved with a combination of Architecture and Methodology.

The Geodesic Manifesto
- The Geodesic Manifesto presents the key concepts that will be addressed in this book.
- It presents a way to achieve the agility that organizations want, together with the predictability and quality that they need.

2 THE AGILE MANIFESTO –
THE GOOD, THE BAD AND THE UGLY

When I started work on this book, several people questioned my sanity. "Why write a book about software development? We already have Agile." If you've been anywhere near software in the last decade, you've heard about Agile. Maybe you worked on a team that used Scrum. Maybe you were even on a team that used Extreme Programming (XP) and achieved Agile enlightenment – or you heard of such a team.

Many good books describe the essence and details of Agile. In preparation for this chapter, I read and referred to:

> Learning Agile – Understanding Scrum, XP, Lean and Kanban
> Andrew Stellman & Jennifer Greene, 2015.

It is an excellent resource with clear writing and many illustrative examples. If you are not familiar with Agile, I recommend that you refer to this book or another, or at least the Wikipedia articles, before continuing with this chapter.

Most of what follows is criticism of Agile because I think we can do better. But we can only do better because Agile has led the way since its inception in 2001. We have learned a lot in the past two decades of applying the values and principles of Agile. For the most part we have abandoned the Old Way of managing software projects that expected unchanging predictability. We have stopped trying to fit software development into the management frameworks of other engineering disciplines. We have reduced our dependence on the heroism of key employees and set reasonable expectations for long-term effort levels. We expect requirements to change.

On the other hand, much has changed in those two decades. We now expect that software will be developed with teams that span two or three continents. The sheer quantity of software that's needed has strained the ability to staff projects with highly skilled developers. The widespread application of machine learning has changed the nature of much software development. Many development teams that have tried to implement Agile have failed to get the hoped-for improvements.

Agile has become a religion with many adherents to its established dogma. They treat the Agile Manifesto as if Moses brought it down from Sinai with the Commandments. It's time for a reformation. I won't present ninety-five theses, but I will apply the principles of Agile to Agile itself.

> At regular intervals, the team reflects on how to become more effective, then tunes and adjusts its behavior accordingly.

Principles behind the Agile Manifesto, various authors
http://agilemanifesto.org/principles.html

In this chapter, I will review the key points of Agile – with a capital A – and include editorial comments regarding where it works well, and how it needs to improve to achieve the agility – with a lower-case a – that its name implies.

2.1 *Non-Sequitur:* Software Creationism

Parable

In the beginning the venture capitalist turned on the lights and the software developers created the Tree of Life. On the first day they built the roots, and then the trunk and then the branches and finally, by the end of the week, it bore fruit – peaches, which were not forbidden. And they saw that it was good. And when the snake wanted apples, they surgically removed old code and grafted new code until the new tree bore both peaches and apples – and plums, because they could, although no one asked for plums. And it was still good. But then the raccoon wanted chicken pot pie, and they could not get chickens from the same root stock, so they hacked in another set of roots and another trunk that was a little like the old trunk, and branches that were a little different from the old branches, and there were chickens. But they were scrawny little chickens that didn't lay eggs. Meanwhile the plums were falling to the ground because no one wanted them, and the rats were eating them, but leaving the skins and pits, which attracted fruit flies that cast a blight upon the peach and apple crops. But all their efforts went to coaxing the chickens to lay eggs, so they couldn't improve the yield for the peaches and apples, or even take the time to stop producing plums. And the snake said, "Give me apples or you're all going to hell." But they were already there.

Sermon

What went wrong? Which temptation should they have avoided? The apples? The plums? The chickens? What if the raccoon will pay a lot more for chickens than the snake will pay for apples? Maybe the peaches were the real problem, and they should have focused on chickens all the while.

Almost everyone believes that software is a product of intelligent design; that it's created by a group of individuals who know the purpose of their endeavor, and who implement exactly the required functionality in the optimal way. That's a good metaphor for the peaches, and maybe the apples. But after that, the process looks more like evolution – random mutations trying to survive in the wild. Modules change. Some are destroyed. Whole branches get neglected. New branches are created. Soon the system is a chicken tree that yields legacy apples, which was not at all what they intended to build.

We can't think of software the same way we think of door handles. When Knobs, Inc. sells a door handle, it's finished. They will never see it again. If the customer wants an enhancement to the door handle – maybe a textured surface – Knobs will build a different door handle and sell it.

A software system is a kind of living being. It grows to adapt to its environment. It grows new branches that yield new fruit. It changes to make more fruit faster, or to make better tasting fruit, or fruit that won't rot. When I sell software, I sell (actually, license) its current capabilities, but in many cases, the customer thinks they bought not what it is, but what it should be; and they believe they are entitled to what it could be. So, software continues to change long after the sale has closed.

Living beings are entropy-reducing machines, using energy to push entropy out into the environment. The software system's energy comes from its developers. We can use that energy to grow the system, but we also need to use some of that energy to reduce the entropy. The health of the system depends on how we make changes, because without controls on how we evolve the code base, entropy will win. The system will become fat and slow and unable to adapt and it will die. In other words, software rots.

The Agile revolution has showed us that change is not the enemy. We can respond to change in ways that make the system stronger, or we can choose the expedient path – hacking the system to please the racoon. That is Faust's bargain, the path to perdition.

2.2   The Old Way

In the 80s, it became clear that software development was both difficult and different from other engineering disciplines. From the common results – late, buggy software – the industry decided that the problem was lack of discipline. So managers tried to apply rigid processes to the software problem. They started with the kind of process that worked for tangible deliverables like doorknobs and transistor radios. The form of the process was called Waterfall, because each step needed to complete – metaphorically, fill up the reservoir – before the next step could begin.

Proponents of the Old Way hoped that a lot of work up front in requirements gathering, specification, design and planning would remove uncertainty from the project. The implementation should be a simple matter of writing down in code what was already decided.

As an example, here is a summary of the process steps that were the standard at one company I worked for in the 90s. Each of these steps came with a predetermined delivery date.

1. MRD – Marketing Requirements Document: someone in the marketing department was supposed to write down what the software was supposed to do. This never happened. Usually someone in software development would write something so we could get past this step.
2. FS – Functional Specification: from the user's view, explain how the software will meet the requirements. There would be some meetings where we discussed this, and we would write something that we knew was wrong. We would never look at it again.
3. DS – Design Specification: explain how the software will implement the functional spec. I never wrote one of these, and the ones I saw were completely incomprehensible.
4. ES – Engineering Start: after steps 1-3 were complete, you could write the first line of code. Of course, since most of the software developers didn't participate in requirements gathering or specification writing, they were busy writing code and locking the project into decisions that were made without adequate information.

[Note that there are no milestones between ES and CF. This was supposed to be the easy, predictable part of the project.]

5. CF – Code Freeze: everything is done; don't change anything except to fix a few bugs. Usually this was the first time that all the pieces of the project came together, so there were lots of "bugs" that required major changes. The developers' euphemistic expansion of CF was "Code Faster".
6. CFA – Code Freeze Approval: all coding and testing is complete and ready to ship. The euphemistic expansion of CFA was "Code Faster, A-----e".

We knew that the Old Way was a farce. The requirements were never complete. Specifying functionality and design without writing code was impossible. Constraining both schedule and functionality always led to poor quality that we had to patch later in a series of dire emergencies.

My most successful projects abandoned the process. They started with a vision – a few pictures, some key concepts, some lofty goals – and discovered the details on the fly. We had a general picture of an architecture. We defined a few milestones. And, when things started to work, we got users in a room, watched them work with the software, made changes immediately and got feedback before they left the room.

Twice in my career I saw teams that had been slogging along within the process suddenly transformed into super-teams by the power of a vision and the freedom to build what they believed in using whatever means they saw fit. Each of those teams delivered a complex new product in less than a year, and both of those products were able to evolve rapidly as the market changed around them.

That transformation into a super-team is what Agile is trying to deliver.

2.3   The Agile Manifesto

> We are uncovering better ways of developing software by doing it and helping others do it. Through this work we have come to value:
>
> **Individuals and interactions** over processes and tools
> **Working software** over comprehensive documentation
> **Customer collaboration** over contract negotiation
> **Responding to change** over following a plan
>
> That is, while there is value in the items on the right, we value the items on the left more.

The Agile Manifesto, various authors – http://agilemanifesto.org

At the turn of the twentieth century, the literary form called the manifesto moved from politics (Jefferson's *Declaration of Independence*, 1776; and Marx & Engels' *Communist Manifesto*, 1848) to the world of art (F.T Marinetti's *The Founding and Manifesto of Futurism*, 1909). Now in the twenty-first century, with the Agile Manifesto, it has moved into the world of software.

Transformations of slogging teams to super-teams, like the ones I described above, inspired the authors of the Agile Manifesto. It came out of a meeting of a few software thought leaders in 2001. They were in the middle of breaking out from traditional process-heavy, over-documented, always-late software development methodologies – the Old Way. They were advocating several different alternative methodologies, and wanted to identify the common traits of their alternatives. They agreed on the "Agile Manifesto," a statement of the values and principles behind Agile software development.

Julian Hanna, in his 2014 article for *The Atlantic* magazine, reviews the history of the manifesto in the political and art worlds (somehow, he missed the Agile Manifesto ☺) and finds ten traits common to the best ones.

1.	Manifestos usually include a list of numbered tenets.
2.	Manifestos exist to challenge and provoke.
3.	Manifestos are advertisements.
4.	Manifestos come in many forms.
5.	Manifestos are better very short than very long.
6.	Manifestos are theatrical.
7.	Manifestos are fiction dressed as fact.
8.	Manifestos embrace paradox.
9.	Manifestos are always on the bleeding edge.
10.	Manifestos are magic (almost).

"Manifestos: A Manifesto: The 10 traits of effective public declarations, an Object Lesson", Julian Hanna, as originally published in The Atlantic, June 24, 2014. Used by permission.
https://www.theatlantic.com/entertainment/archive/2014/06/manifestos-a-manifesto-the-10-things-all-manifestos-need/372135/

The Agile Manifesto challenges the Old Way and provokes change by devaluing the things you thought were most important. It served as an advertisement for some of the authors who were software consultants and needed validation for their work. It's short – 68 words. The "X over Y" statements are inherently paradoxical. (Although the last sentence denies the paradox, as if suddenly a lawyer appeared.) At the time of its writing, the Old Way was still strong and Agile was the bleeding edge.

The Agile Manifesto is both fiction and magic. It's meant to make you think about what's wrong with software development and how to fix it. But in doing so, it presents a future that is too good to be true, and a philosophy that is too simple to work in practice.

Manifestos are temporary vision statements that start a movement, but need to be supplanted by new visions as the movement matures. "Like all good manifestos," Hanna wrote of the Futurists, "they built in their own obsolescence, clearing the way for the next vision of the future." If Agile is truly about responding to change, then the Agile Manifesto also built in its own obsolescence in its continuous-improvement principle. Let's clear the way and see how the Geodesic Manifesto can become the next logical step in software development.

2.3.1   Agile Values

The value statements certainly "embrace paradox," but I find them unsatisfying. Each of the four value statements contrasts two aspects of software development. In most cases, the items on the left and right aren't even related. You can't trade off working software against comprehensive documentation. These statements are like saying I value apple pie over sunshine because that sunburn I got last summer was nasty.

The statements devalue the aspect on the right without providing criteria to evaluate how much. They are reactions against the Old Way more than they are a vision for the future. You can only get the 'items on the left' with a good portion of 'items on the right'.

History moves in extremes. The Old Way needed to end. While moving away from the Old Way, Agile moved too far in the direction of anarchy, so that any attempt to use documentation, planning or processes often meets with the objection: "That's not Agile!" The Geodesic Philosophy tries to balance the need for agility with the need for control and predictability.

Individuals and interactions over processes and tools

This statement reacts against the Old Way's focus on process. The problem with processes in the Old Way was that there were too many unproductive processes and processes that were inappropriately rigid. Processes that required writing specifications that no one would read, or that required following steps that delayed the work needed to solve a problem sapped productivity and removed creativity from software development.

Not all processes are bad. Common processes standardize mundane tasks so developers don't have to think about them. They let developers concentrate on solving the problem at hand. Tools like source control systems, and processes like continuous integration remove burdens from developers and let them concentrate on writing better code. A code review process or a project status process, like a daily standup meeting, encourage interactions in a standardized way. Good processes improve the results of low-skilled developers' efforts while enabling high-skilled developers to contribute at peak efficiency.

This statement has led many to believe that any process is bad. Ironically, the Scrum methodology, the poster-child methodology of Agile, has a very rigid process. The Scaled Agile® Framework (https://www.scaledagileframework.com) presents an elaborate system of processes, but it feels as if their documentation strives to avoid the word 'process' because of this Agile value.

Individuals, if left to themselves, will create a hundred different processes that change every day. Standardizing common processes is a necessary part of software development. The Geodesic Philosophy encourages common processes, and encourages the development team to periodically review processes to ensure that they continue to promote creativity, productivity and quality.

The left side of this statement, individuals and interactions, is diminished by binding it to the right side. People are the engine that drive software development. The statement makes us think of people primarily as executors of processes, but they are much more than that. The Geodesic Philosophy recognizes the diversity of people and encourages finding the best way that each individual can contribute.

Working software over comprehensive documentation

This statement reacts against the Old Way's mandate to specify everything up front. Written specifications are always incomplete and quickly out of date. I agree that working software is the best specification, but some documentation is necessary, and the statement doesn't provide criteria to judge how much. Today's global development puts such a burden on communication that a lot needs to be written to avoid misunderstandings and incomplete communication.

Like the previous statement, the left side is diminished by the right. The statement focuses on software's role as the canonical documentation of the system rather than on its broad role as the goal of software development. The many aspects of software, such as quality, maintainability and evolvability, are hidden in the word 'working'.

The Geodesic Philosophy is more explicit. The first truth of the Geodesic Manifesto states that high-quality software is the goal. Limited and effective documentation is part of the Communication principle.

Customer collaboration over contract negotiation

This statement also reacts against specifying too much up front. Contract negotiation can commit you to things that don't make sense by the time they arrive. But if you are developing or customizing software for the Department of Defense, you may have no choice but to commit to deliverables in writing.

Customer interaction is critical to creating high-quality software. But collaboration is often inappropriate and sometimes impossible. If you are developing a product that will have a million customers, which ones do you collaborate with? Getting input from customers is essential to good software development, but how you do that depends on the nature of the customers. Collaboration is only one of the ways to achieve that.

The Geodesic Philosophy encourages customer interaction, using working software to get feedback from customers and users, and having developers learn to think like their customers.

Responding to change over following a plan

The final value statement is a reaction to over-constrained projects. The Old Way tried to plan projects without having all the information, and then tried to stick to the plan even as new information became available. It's like planning a trip from Boston to New York by first planning to go south for 115 miles and then west for 150 miles – it works in theory, but in practice it requires a lot of swimming.

The solution is not to devalue planning, but instead to encourage a different type of planning. No software gets done without a plan. A project without a plan will never be funded. Even a plan based on incomplete information can guide you on the first steps.

Responding to change and new information is the core tenet of Agile. The key to agility is to change the plan when more information is available.

The Geodesic Philosophy recognizes that plans need to be dynamic, and to react to the external and internal changes that are inevitable. At any time, the plan needs to answer three simple questions: When will it be done? What will it contain? What do I do next? Early in the project, the margin of error will be large, and we need to live with that. The Geodesic Manifesto's Change principle includes the statement: "Plan for change and change the plan when necessary."

2.3.2 Agile Principles

Together with the values, the Agile Manifesto lists the principles behind the values.

1.	Our highest priority is to satisfy the customer through early and continuous delivery of valuable software.
2.	Welcome changing requirements, even late in development. Agile processes harness change for the customer's competitive advantage.
3.	Deliver working software frequently, from a couple of weeks to a couple of months, with a preference to the shorter timescale.
4.	Business people and developers must work together daily throughout the project.
5.	Build projects around motivated individuals. Give them the environment and support they need, and trust them to get the job done.
6.	The most efficient and effective method of conveying information to and within a development team is face-to-face conversation.
7.	Working software is the primary measure of progress.
8.	Agile processes promote sustainable development. The sponsors, developers, and users should be able to maintain a constant pace indefinitely.
9.	Continuous attention to technical excellence and good design enhances agility.
10.	Simplicity--the art of maximizing the amount of work not done--is essential.
11.	The best architectures, requirements, and designs emerge from self-organizing teams.
12.	At regular intervals, the team reflects on how to become more effective, then tunes and adjusts its behavior accordingly.

The Agile Manifesto, various authors – http://agilemanifesto.org/principles.html

Wow! Twelve principles! Few of us can remember the names of the seven dwarfs or the seven deadly sins, so we have no hope of remembering a list of twelve anythings. And the statements are neither orthogonal nor complete. Three of them mention "working software". Some of them are vacuous platitudes: "Simplicity … is essential." None of them mention quality or leadership. They read like the result of a brainstorming session that ended without an analysis phase because it was time to catch a plane.

Dictionary.com lists thirteen definitions for the word 'principle'. None of those definitions quite matches the intention of the Agile or Geodesic principles. Let me present a synthesized definition of what I expect from a principle.

A principle is a rule of behavior that establishes a guideline for one aspect of a philosophy. It helps distinguish right from wrong. Good principles have these characteristics:

- A principle is general. A rule that is too specific will not be applicable in many situations.
- The set of principles for a philosophy should be complete, that is, it should guide you in all aspects of your philosophy.
- Within the set of principles, the individual principles should be independent and self-consistent. That is, no two principles should profess guidelines on the same aspect of the philosophy, and especially, no two principles should guide you in different directions.

The Agile principles don't follow those characteristics. They are full of redundancy and contradictions. Some are overly specific. And they don't cover the spectrum of what's needed to develop complex software systems. In practice, Agile adherents pick and choose the few Agile principles that apply to their version of Agile and ignore the others. In the rest of this chapter, I will explore the themes implied by these statements to find the essence of the Agile principles and adapt them as part of the Geodesic Philosophy.

2.4 Relating the Agile Principles to the Geodesic Philosophy

In this section, I go through the twelve Agile principles one by one and discuss how they are related to the Geodesic Manifesto. Note that the order of the evaluated principles is different from the original list.

2.4.1 Working Software

1. Our highest priority is to satisfy the customer through early and continuous delivery of valuable software.
3. Deliver working software frequently, from a couple of weeks to a couple of months, with a preference to the shorter timescale.
These two statements are almost the same. The first mentions the customer. The second includes specification of a timescale, which has no business in something called a principle, especially after the first calls for continuous delivery, which I assume is more frequent than two weeks. I guess redundancy emphasizes the importance of valuable, working software.

7. Working software is the primary measure of progress.
Except for the word 'measure', this statement adds no additional information. Measurement is an important part of the Geodesic Philosophy. Measurement is the way that changes are generated internally.

The Geodesic Manifesto makes software one of its assumptions, and includes frequent delivery as one of its principles.

2.4.2 Managing Change

2. Welcome changing requirements, even late in development. Agile processes harness change for the customer's competitive advantage.
This is a beautiful statement that contains the essence of Agile software development. Change is both the norm and the goal. My only criticism here is the phrase, "for the customer's competitive advantage". I think this reflects the bias of the authors of the Agile Manifesto who were mostly software consultants whose customers were the ones who built and owned the software. Software teams need to embrace change to increase the value of the software.

4. Business people and developers must work together daily throughout the project.
This statement seems important, but it has a couple serious problems.

First is the definition of the term "business people". From my reading about Agile, I inferred that "business people" are some amalgam of customers, customer advocates (like customer support), software sales people, marketing people and upper management – anyone who has an opinion about the priorities of software features. Most likely their opinions are conflicting, and they have a weak understanding of how particular software development tasks relate to software value.

Second is the frequency, "daily", which is probably a much higher change frequency than the software team can handle. As I mentioned above, the specification of a time should not appear in a principle. To manage change effectively, someone needs to integrate the opinions of all the business people to seek out the changes that are necessary, and then present them to the development team at a rate that will keep the team productive. See the discussion on Limits to Agility.

The Geodesic Manifesto includes changing requirements as one of its assumptions, and several of the principles discuss how to embrace and manage change, from customer interaction, feedback from working software, and planning for change.

2.4.3 Leadership

For working software and managing change, the Geodesic principles are merely restatements of the Agile principles. The next Agile principles we consider, however, revolve around people, communication and leadership. This is where the Geodesic Philosophy diverges from Agile.

The Agile founders seem to have had a general mistrust of management. In his "About the Manifesto" essay (http://agilemanifesto.org/history.html), Jim Highsmith refers three times to "Dilbertesque" organizations. Most of us have experienced the pointy-haired manager whose processes and demands subvert the efforts of his staff. A large part of the Agile manifesto is aimed at finding ways to succeed despite incompetent management. Ironically, Agile has provided a new tool in the arsenal of point-haired managers; they can now, in the name of Agile, waste your time with a daily standup meeting.

On the other hand, many of us have had great bosses who provide vision and direction, deepen motivation, take away excuses, and lead teams to produce things that they believed were impossible. Great managers find ways to succeed with the teams they have.

The Geodesic Philosophy is aimed at helping software managers become great software managers. The first step is to dissolve the adversarial barrier between managers and developers; that requires a deeper understanding of the problems each of them face. The next step is to identify the role that managers play in the software development process. Developers need to understand how managers who don't write code still provide a lot of value to the team.

11. The best architectures, requirements, and designs emerge from self-organizing teams.

This is a conjecture offered by the authors of the Agile Manifesto without proof. First, this definition might help us understand the statement.

> **Self-organization**, also called (in the social sciences) spontaneous order, is a process where some form of overall order arises from local interactions between parts of an initially disordered system. The process is spontaneous, not needing control by any external agent. It is often triggered by random fluctuations, *amplified by positive feedback*. The resulting organization is wholly decentralized, distributed over all the components of the system. As such, the organization is typically robust and able to survive or self-repair substantial perturbation. Chaos theory discusses self-organization in terms of islands of predictability in a sea of chaotic unpredictability.

https://en.wikipedia.org/wiki/Self-organization

Let's evaluate self-organizing teams for architecture. The lessons here will equally apply to requirements and design.

Instead of the Agile principle, I could alternatively state, "The best software architectures are designed by a single person with a vision for how the system should operate and evolve." Certainly, the architecture for Linux could not have spontaneously arisen from a randomly chosen group of software developers. It took the vision of Linus Torvalds to create the framework that could evolve into the Linux of today. And that evolution is now mostly self-organizing.

The positive feedback that I highlighted in the above definition is person-to-person communication. If left uncontrolled, that positive feedback can have disastrously negative effects. I have seen excellent architectures evolve into chaos because the self-organizing team decided that global variables and 30,000-line files were the best ways to solve architectural problems. Once a problem was solved with a global variable, that form of solution quickly became the norm.

Self-organizing teams can work well for architecture if:

- There is an architectural framework from which to evolve. Usually this was designed by a single person or a small group. It's easier to evolve from a context than from a blank slate.
- The team has an ethos for how to make decisions about architecture. That ethos can evolve over time as the self-organizing team learns more about its problems.
- Disruptive changes are quashed immediately and not allowed to become part of the self-organization's norms. I learned in control theory that a stable system requires negative feedback. If things are going out of whack, the negative feedback tries to pull it back toward the center. The cruise control in your car decreases the throttle when you're going downhill to maintain a constant speed. Self-organizing teams also need negative feedback loops to quash disruptive changes. That negative feedback loop comes from the leadership of the team – the managers and the technical leaders.

Architecture is one of the foundational pillars of the Geodesic Philosophy.

5. Build projects around motivated individuals. Give them the environment and support they need, and trust them to get the job done.
People come in many levels of experience, capability and motivation (and many other dimensions). Most of the time, you don't get to choose which individual to put on your project. You don't even get to choose which ones you don't want. You have a team; you need to do your best with the team you have. (Of course, you may be able to hire one or two additional team members, but new hires rarely affect the current project.)

Motivation comes from many things, including respect, belief in a vision, feeling of belonging, and confidence that one's efforts impact the results. A great manager understands how to grow the motivation of each individual on the team.

The environment and support that promote productive software development include tangible things like compute farms and file servers, intangible things like development processes and coding standards, and touchy-feely things like group openness. Software managers are responsible for all of these.

Some individuals have earned the right to be trusted. Others are on their way to earning trust, and others never will. Great managers give each individual all the freedom they can handle, and put controls in place to make sure they don't misuse their freedom and fall off a cliff.

Leadership is another of the foundational pillars of the Geodesic Philosophy. The Role of the Software Manager chapter discusses how managers succeed using leadership, organization, planning and control.

2.4.4 Effort

8. Agile processes promote sustainable development. The sponsors, developers, and users should be able to maintain a constant pace indefinitely.[1]
A steady pace with occasional bursts of extra effort is the norm for high performing teams. For some people, that steady pace is forty hours; for some it's fifty; for others, it's thirty-six. You're not going to get forty-five hours from a thirty-six-hour person. Deal with it!

I never minded putting in extra effort if I felt that I was the cause of the problem. Putting in extra effort to solve a problem someone else created annoyed me. That's fire-fighting.

Fire-fighting saps the energy from a team. There will always be emergencies – a customer will encounter a show-stopper bug and will need a fix immediately, or a competitor will suddenly support a new feature that you need to match. But if fire-fighting dominates the team's workload, you have a big problem. Agility can't help you. Only a time machine could help. You need to go back and fix the high-temperature modules that are causing the fires.

Since time travel hasn't been invented – and if it's going to be invented in the future, one would hope that the inventors would come back and tell us how to do it – the best way to avoid fire-fighting is to build high quality code the first time. To do that, you need to code and test at the same time, to have multiple eyes look at every software change, to thoroughly measure quality, and to provide near-instantaneous feedback when there are problems.

I've seen many teams that sacrificed quality in favor of schedule or functionality, and paid the price for it later. The Geodesic Philosophy strives to avoid problems rather than to fix them. That's why the Geodesic Manifesto focuses on technical excellence rather than effort levels.

---

[1] If a constant, steady pace is what's desired for Agile teams, why is the development cycle for Scrum called a sprint?

2.4.5   Communication

6. The most efficient and effective method of conveying information to and within a development team is face-to-face conversation.
This is a platitude that's so obvious it's useless because it doesn't say what to do when face-to-face communication is impractical.

In 2001, at the time of the writing of the Agile Manifesto, most software teams were co-located. It was rare to have geographically dispersed teams. Since then, multi-site development has become the norm, often with groups on three continents spanning twenty-four hours of time zones. In many cases, there is no mutually convenient time to meet, so even if you consider Skype to be equivalent to face-to-face, you can't meet the letter or the spirit of this principle.

The efficiency of communication decreases with distance, where the distance metric includes physical distance and other factors like organizational distance. The decrease in communication when a colleague moves up one floor is astounding.

With distance and the corresponding decrease of efficiency comes a need for more formality in communication. Groups from different buildings probably need scheduled meetings. Groups from different organizations within a company may need written documents. Groups from different companies may need legal contracts.

The Geodesic Philosophy encourages person-to-person communication, either face-to-face or electronically, when possible. Write things down when specificity is required or when physical or organizational distance is large.

2.4.6   Coding

9. Continuous attention to technical excellence and good design enhances agility.
This is a beautifully simple statement about how to write good software. I would replace the word 'design' with 'architecture'. I believe that architecture is the primary reason that software succeeds or fails. Good architecture is easy to understand, easy to extend and easy to change. Bad architecture can lead to rapid increase in entropy and will need big coding changes to implement small feature changes.

One of the implications of this statement is that you should fix problems as soon as you see them. Whenever I encountered a bug, I would almost always debug and fix it immediately because if I waited until tomorrow or next week, I could forget or might not be able to reproduce it. If I saw code that should be refactored, I refactored it. I created a lot of code check-ins, which I'm sure were annoying to some other team members, but the code was always improving.

10. Simplicity--the art of maximizing the amount of work not done--is essential.
Everything should be made as simple as possible, but not simpler.

Generally attributed to Albert Einstein

> I'm not a great programmer; I'm just lazy and I find lots of creative ways to avoid writing code.

Heard in a lecture at Synopsys, but I forget who said it.

I've already pointed out that this statement is nearly content-free. Out of context, the word 'simplicity' is too broad to have much meaning. And the negative, work-not-done definition should be switched around: "the art of minimizing the amount of work". But let's explore the spirit of the statement and try to understand why it's here.

One of the values of the Extreme Programming (XP) methodology is Simplicity. In that context, 'simplicity' has several aspects.

- Writing code that is easy to understand. For example, taking a few lines of code, extracting them into a function and giving the function a descriptive name is one of the best ways of writing clear maintainable code.
- Starting with the smallest possible subset of functionality and then expanding from there means that you have earlier working software and you avoided writing code for requirements that may disappear later.
- Design for today's requirements and update the design later if the requirements change.

The last two bullets essentially define the term "maximizing the work not done" in the Agile principle. While the first bullet above is essential to all software development, the others are one way to develop good software, but not the only way. Whether the smallest possible subset is the best starting point will depend on the project, and incremental design can lead you to an impasse that will require an expensive, risky rewrite. Just like you need a plan that you know will change, you need an architecture that can act as a guide even though you know it will change.

The Geodesic Philosophy has a strong emphasis on technical excellence, quality and architecture. Technical excellence means writing clear, maintainable code and continually trying to improve it. Software developers taking responsibility for quality means that they must test their code both with small unit and integration tests, but also in the context of the system. A good architecture requires a good architect (or architecture committee) who, like a great chess player, is always looking several moves into the future.

2.4.7 Continuous Improvement

12. At regular intervals, the team reflects on how to become more effective, then tunes and adjusts its behavior accordingly.

Continuous improvement is the key to Agile methodologies and to the Geodesic Philosophy. The measure-analyze-improve cycle is central to good software development. You can apply it to algorithms, to systems, to methodology and to the measure-analyze-improve cycle itself. A team that wants to measure everything is a team that wants to improve.

2.5 Manifestation

The Agile movement drove software development down the path of embracing change by using incremental methods and low-level decision-making. Like all great ideas, in retrospect it seems obvious.

But the authors of the Agile Manifesto did not define an Agile software methodology. They coopted the word 'agile' without defining what agility means in the context of software development. There is no document that explicitly defines what Agile means – the 262 words of the manifesto aren't nearly enough. There is no Agile certification program. Instead, a few of the authors defined frameworks, such as Scrum and Extreme Programming, and declared them Agile. Proponents of frameworks point at other frameworks, hold their noses, and declare them not-Agile (e.g., the rant about SAFe™ by Scrum founder Ken Schwaber:

https://kenschwaber.wordpress.com/2013/08/06/unSAFe-at-any-speed

Agile is defined implicitly; any methodology that is reasonably consistent with the Agile Manifesto can call itself Agile. But the Manifesto values and principles are incomplete, ambiguous, redundant and, in many ways, inconsistent.

The Geodesic Manifesto is an attempt to summarize the most important aspects of software development that are necessary to achieve agility. It includes major ideas that are missing from the Agile Manifesto, including leadership, architecture and quality. It deemphasizes other ideas, such as simplicity and face-to-face communication. I tried to fix the consistency and redundancy problems, but I'm pretty sure it's still incomplete and ambiguous.

The Agile Manifesto is frozen in time. The authors have declined to let the Manifesto evolve. This has led various people to make their own versions, such as the brutal rewrite that is the Geodesic Manifesto, and the gentler modifications of the Disciplined Agile Manifesto:

https://www.disciplinedagiledelivery.com/disciplinedagilemanifesto

To make sure that the Geodesic Manifesto remains viable, I have put the text of the Manifesto in the public domain. At some point, I will find a way for it to evolve without me, but until then, I will act as arbiter. Send your suggestions for improvement to me at bob@GeodesicManifesto.com.

The Geodesic Manifesto now belongs to the industry.

2.6   Key Concepts

The Old Way

- The <u>Old Way</u> of managing software projects tried to treat software like other mature predictable technologies.
- It depended on up-front planning and design, and expected that the act of coding was as simple as paint-by-numbers.

The Agile Manifesto

- The Agile Manifesto consists of four value statements and twelve principles.
- Agile software development uses incremental and iterative methods to adapt to changing requirements, and to react to the learning that occurs while writing code.
- The Agile Manifesto, however, doesn't do a good job of defining what Agile means.
- To avoid the problem of having a frozen, but inadequate, definition of Agile, the <u>Geodesic Manifesto</u> has been put in the public domain to allow for evolution.

3 THE ROLE OF THE SOFTWARE MANAGER

Lots of software developers aspire to become software managers. At one point, almost everyone in my team expressed a goal to be a manager within a year. If that happened, I would have had to buy a flock of pigeons so that each of them had something to manage. There's some prestige in being a manager. There's some satisfaction in getting things done through others. But mostly the aspirants had no idea what they were getting into.

First, let's make this clear – software managers don't write code. If part of your job is to write code, that's OK, but then you have two jobs that you need to time-multiplex across your week. While you're writing code, you're not managing. If your management job is under control, then you might have time to write a little code, but remember that your management job comes first.

Second, directing your subordinates is only a small part of your job. You will probably spend more time with people outside your organization. If you've done a good job, then your team is working on the right stuff. If you're busy directing them, then they're not working. On the other hand, the people outside your organization are probably not working on the right stuff – as you would define it. You need to help them correct the error of their ways.

Maybe you're a new manager. Maybe you've had some great bosses and you want to be just like them. But, because of the second caveat above, you've only seen a small percentage of what they do on a day-to-day, week-to-week, month-to-month basis. It's hard to emulate an iceberg.

So you ask yourself, "What do managers do?" Entire libraries have been written in response to that question. As a manager, you are generally familiar with the answer (or you should be reading a different book). In this chapter, I will hit a few highlights in answer to the slightly more specific question: "What do software managers do?"

I remember four words from my first management class when I worked at HP nearly forty years ago. Those four words describe the primary facets of management. Why they have stuck with me, I have no idea. But, when I started working on this chapter, they popped up: Leadership, Organization, Planning, and Control. Let's see how they apply to managing software.

Leadership

Leadership is one of the pillars of the Geodesic Philosophy. Software teams, like any group, need leaders to guide them along their path. A team may try to analyze the situation. They may come up with strategies for solving problems. But they look to their leaders to validate their ideas.

In software development, there may be many leaders in a team: a manager, an architect, a quality leader, a leader for the Nutrient Extraction module. To be a leader you just need a domain, and someone to follow you.

Before people can follow you, they need to know where you're going. That implies three things:

1. *You* know where you're going. That's your *vision*.
2. You've successfully communicated your vision to your followers.
3. You've convinced them that they want to share your vision and help make it real.

Once you're identified as a leader, a whole slew of responsibilities fall on your shoulders. You're responsible for the welfare of your followers, both as individuals and together. You are the face of your domain to the rest of the world. People will expect you to lead them to places you've never been; and you need to do that exuding confidence and panache.

In the Leadership section of this chapter, I start by expanding on Sun Tzu's terse definition of leadership, then discuss vision and decision making.

Organization

Organization covers the part of the management job that decides who is on your team, and what roles each member will assume. Great managers construct teams whose achievements surpass the abilities of the individuals. Hiring the right people is important. Making sure that each person can contribute at the highest level is more important. But the best people have to be working on the right tasks, and each person needs to support the work of all the other team members to achieve that synergy. The Organization section discusses some of the challenges of managing software developers.

Planning

Software planning answers the ubiquitous questions: When will it be done? What will it do? And, what do I do next? Planning has the tenuous goal of predicting the future. Good planning not only predicts, but also sets up the underpinnings to make sure that the predictions are accurate. The Planning section goes into more detail about creating and maintaining plans for software development.

Control

When my son was two years old, I knew that someday he would be a manager because he knew exactly what he wanted, and he didn't want to do it himself. Getting things done through other people is the essence of management. Even if you want, you can't do everything yourself. So, you delegate activities to the members of your team.

When you delegate, you are still accountable for the outcome. If you ask Jack to create the Packet Queue, you need to know that the Packet Queue does what it's supposed to, and that its interfaces work with the rest of the system, and that it's been thoroughly tested. You could sit with Jack and go through every line of code, and check every interface, and review every test. But that level of micromanagement would limit your team to a few frustrated people.

To delegate responsibility for a task while maintaining your personal accountability for that task, you implement controls. A control could be as simple as, "Meet with me on Tuesday to update me on the status of your task." Or you could use the controls that are built into a common process – the module creation process – for Jack's task.

To understand delegation, I recommend reading *Managing Management Time* (William Oncken, Jr., 1987). After reading this book early in my career, I immediately became a better manager.

The Control section introduces some concepts from control theory at a high level and applies them to managing software development.

3.1   *Non-Sequitur* – Three Stupid Questions

| Please sir, I want some more. |
Oliver Twist, Charles Dickens, 1839

One of your goals as a software manager is to manage people who are smarter than you, who know more than you and who do their jobs better than you could. In your first management job, you probably don't get the cream of the crop. But eventually you'll have a star or two in your group and you need to help those stars shine as brightly as the moon.

How do I manage something I don't know how to do? If you didn't ask that question at least once in your career, you should have. As with most activities, there are a lot more ways to do it wrong than there are to do it right. Let's look at some of the possibilities:

- Try to learn what they do – a noble goal that's doomed to failure. The only effective way to learn is to do it, and if you do it, you will be in the way.
- Ignore them (I'm sure they'll be fine) – that works until they're not fine.
- Give them aggressive goals – setting impossible goals is the hallmark of the pointy-haired manager.

Maybe before we decide on management techniques for your star performers, we should understand what you want from them. Primarily, you want:

- Creativity

- Productivity
- Leadership
- Furthering the organization's goals

For this they need freedom from constraints that stifle creativity, freedom from distractions and overhead that sap productivity, mentoring and feedback that enhance their leadership skills and opportunities, and knowledge of and commitment to the organization's goals. For the first two, you need to get out of the way. For the second two, you need to nudge them along the right path.

As you nudge, your first instincts will be to tell them what to do. But we already established that you're incompetent to do what they do. When your instincts are to tell, ask questions instead. In particular, ask the three stupid questions.

The three stupid questions are the questions that they should have asked already. They're "stupid" questions because they're the ones you ask over and over. They're "three" because too many questions will just confuse people. They might be two stupid questions or five stupid questions, but no more. The inspiration for the stupid questions can come from lots of places, like the principles of the Geodesic Manifesto, or the Lean principles, or the Architecture Design Principles (sorry for the forward references). They're different in every situation, or I would list them. With a little practice, you will know what they are for each of your stars and for each topic. Here are some generic examples:

- How does this fit into the requirements?
- How do we measure this?
- Can we do this within the current architecture framework?
- When do we need to make this decision?

Many times, the stupid questions I asked have triggered re-evaluation of a proposed solution, initiated discussions that resulted in group synergy and inspired creativity. Asking questions moves the responsibility for the solution from you to the ones who answer the questions. That's the core of building a synergistic team.

Asking the same stupid questions over and over helps build the decision-making ethos for your group. When your team starts to ask the stupid questions for themselves, you can move on to a new set of stupid questions.

You'll never get more without asking.

3.2 Leadership

You will have no problem finding books on leadership: from *The Art of War* (Sun Tzu, 5th century BC), to *The Prince* (Niccolo Machiavelli, c. 1513), to *Leadership Secrets of Attila the Hun* (Wess Roberts, 1990), and *The 21 Irrefutable Laws of Leadership* (John C. Maxwell,

1998) (Jehovah gave Moses ten irrefutable laws, but leaders need twenty one?). All of them try to assess why people follow great leaders, and to recommend how you, too, can be a great leader.

3.2.1   Leadership in *The Art of War*

Sun Tzu and ancient commentator Jia Lin (c. 9th century AD) boiled leadership down to five traits:

> Leadership is a matter of intelligence, trustworthiness, humaneness, courage, and sternness.
> – Sun Tzu
>
> Reliance on intelligence alone results in rebelliousness. Exercise of humaneness alone results in weakness. Fixation on trust results in folly. Dependence on the strength of courage results in violence. Excessive sternness of command results in cruelty. When one has all five virtues together, then one can be a military leader.
> – Jia Lin

The Art of War, translated by Thomas Cleary, 1988

Intelligence
When managing a software team, the trait of intelligence means knowledge and competence in the practice of writing software. If you have not written software recently, then you will need to make up for that through some other technical competence, or in a deep understanding of your customers. Software developers expect their leaders to have the big picture about the project and where it's going. They need your help in resolving technical conflict. They need to trust you to evaluate their own technical competence. If they don't respect your technical chops, you will have a much tougher road to follow.

Trustworthiness
Because of the complexity of software, there are so many things you cannot know that you have no choice but to trust in your team. Likewise, the constraints of management often prevent you from fully explaining the rationale behind your actions; your team needs to trust that you are doing the best possible for them and for the larger organization.

You need to establish a trust pact with your team. Your team needs to trust that you will do what you promise, or explain why you can't, and that you will act in their best interest. In turn, you need to trust that your team will do what is needed when you ask for it, and even when you don't.

The fabric of trust quickly unravels if even a single strand is broken. Remember the famous Reagan-era phrase, "Trust, but verify." Verification is part of trust, not an intrusion. If you quickly address any transgressions with objective feedback, then trust will grow.

As a manager you have two loyalties: to your team and to your boss. When there is a conflict, loyalty to your boss takes precedence. Some day you will be backed into a corner and will need to do something that violates the trust pact with your team. If, before that happens, you have filled up a reservoir of trust, you will be ok after the storm passes. If your reservoir is nearly empty, you may never recover.

Humaneness
Life is not always about programming.

Some days I can write a thousand lines of new code; some days, I churn on the same twenty lines all day. Some days I can plow through fixing a dozen bugs; some days even the thought of fixing a bug turns my stomach. Some days I can write code that operates flawlessly; some days I introduce multiple catastrophic bugs.

Maybe my wife is sick. Maybe I had an argument with my son. Maybe I had an argument with my boss. Maybe I have a big golf tournament tomorrow. Maybe I just got back from vacation and I have a hundred emails that need my attention. Maybe my proposal was rejected in favor of one that I believe is inferior.

I care about my title. I care about my salary. I care about having a window cube. I care about my invention and I want it to be used. I care about my friends and want them to succeed. I care about the integrity of the code. I care about a thousand things. I can't list them, but I know them when I see them.

The performance of your team members can vary from day to day, and they will seldom give you the reason because they will seldom know the reason.

On their good days, offer appreciation, admiration and respect.

On their bad days, remember their good days. Offer encouragement before rebuke. Be slow to judge, but when censure is needed, lay aside your anger. Deliver the message with respect and help them maintain their dignity. Even if you must fire them or lay them off, treat them with sympathy and kindness.

Before they were software developers, they were people.

Courage
Managerial courage comes in two forms.

The first is making tough decisions within your own territory, like resolving technical conflict or dealing with low performing team members. Recognize the difference between bravery and foolhardiness. Bravery means doing something that is likely to succeed. When you have a tough decision to make, do your best to understand all sides of the issue. Understand the costs and benefits. Make sure you can explain your rationale, even if you will never give the explanation out loud. Then be steadfast in your decision. Most of the time making the decision is more important than the decision itself. But when you are wrong, have the courage to change.

The second form of courage is representing and fighting for the interests of your team outside your organization. Your team needs to believe that you will protect them from the seemingly arbitrary decisions that come from on high. They don't expect that you will always win the corporate battles, but they need to know you fought the good fight, and that when you lose, you will do your best to communicate the true rationale for the decision.

Sternness

Negative feedback, or sternness, is the key to improving your organization. Things go wrong every day, and if they're not fixed today, the same things will go wrong tomorrow.

Unfortunately, the responsibility for most of the delivery of negative feedback falls on the manager. It's the most distasteful part of the job, and is the hardest management trait to master because it requires mastery of all the other traits: intelligence to understand the problem, trustworthiness to gain the acceptance of the feedback, humaneness to maintain respect and dignity of all involved, and courage to face the issue and the people who need to change.

Sternness needs to be proportional to the extent of the problem. You can't react at the same level to someone checking in code without a review as you do to a dysfunctional relationship between the GUI team and the algorithm team.

In most cases, people will self-correct if you merely point out the problem. If that doesn't work, help them come up with their own solution. An occasional burst of passion may be necessary to induce self-improvement.

As a last resort, dictate a solution. A management edict is sure to incite anger and resentment, but it will resolve the issue. Make sure the benefit is worth the cost.

3.2.2 Vision

Vision is the story you tell to guide and motivate your team on their path to a better future. Although Sun Tsu does not mention vision as one of the five leadership traits, The Art of War is full of discussions of leaders' vision disguised in other terms, such as strategy. A software team needs vision more than an army. Software developers make many decisions every day that Sun Tsu would expect to be in the domain of the commanders of the army – a decision to rewrite a key architecture component is as critical to a software team as the decision to move the flanking force from the east to the west for an attacking army. A vision helps form a framework for making those decisions without managers needing to micromanage the developers.

The importance of vision is one of the pillars of the Geodesic Philosophy that separates it from Agile. The software manager is responsible for making sure that there is a vision, and that the team understands it and contributes to its evolution.

3.2.2.1   Legend

Young Arthur rode into the woods on his pony Galahad. On the day that Merlin presented the pony to him, Arthur had settled on the name "Princess" until Merlin pointed out the obvious error in those days before gender ambiguity. Arthur didn't feel that "Prince", "Duke" or "Earl" were quite right for this dappled gray pony. "We will call him Galahad," Merlin declared with a twinkle in his eyes, leaving no room for further discussion or creativity. "Galahad? What kind of name is that?" asked Arthur. "It will all make sense in a few years," said Merlin.

That "in a few years" stuff was getting old. Today's lesson was functional programming with Haskell. "When am I ever going to use this?" Arthur asked. "You will use it in a few years," Merlin replied. "Even if you never use it, there are lessons in functional programming that will improve your code forever."

So today Arthur was playing hooky. He had heard the other boys talking about a lake in these woods with fish a long as your leg, and you could dive from an outcropping as tall as the turrets on the lord's castle. Others had said the woods were enchanted, and that sometimes people went in and never came out. That story felt more real, with the path narrowing and the tree branches so low that he had to dismount and lead Galahad along the path.

Up ahead, he saw a break in the woods, with streaks of sunlight darting like arrows through the leaves. The path opened onto a lake with deep blue water that rippled in the sun, reflecting jewels of brilliance. A fish jumped to his left. He saw the outcropping to his right with a path that led from the water to the top.

He was trying to decide whether to fish or swim when the lake started to roil with the turbulence of a hundred fish. A point of steel appeared, gleaming against the blue of the lake. The point grew into the shaft of a sword. The hilt appeared, grasped by a hand in a green glove. Not a glove, he saw as the arm rose from the lake – not a glove, but seaweed. Next, he saw the head of a woman with green hair, and her shoulders covered in a green robe, and the woman stood on a pedestal of polished green marble. Water flowed off her robes and the turbulence subsided.

"Arthur," she boomed, "I am the Lady of the Lake."

Arthur couldn't think of what to say. She already knew his name, and telling her that he was "The Boy Who Played Hooky" was likely to get him in more trouble. So he waited for her to continue.

"England is in turmoil. There is no king. The houses fight against each other. Brigands rule the highways."

That sounded bad, but what could he do? Arthur still didn't speak.

"You will unite England. You will pull the sword from the stone and will assume your rightful place as King. I will give you an enchanted sword named Excalibur. You will use it to unite the houses. You will build a castle and you will call it Camelot. There you will have great round table, and knights from all of Europe will come to serve at your table where all are equal. They will clear the brigands from the roads and England will have a time of great peace."

"Cool," Arthur said.

"During the time of great peace, your knights will search for the proof that NP=P."

"That's the Holy Grail of software!" Arthur said.

"But although they will see shadows of it in the distance, they will never find it.

"Amid the great peace lie the seeds of the treachery that will destroy it. Your greatest knight and your only love will betray you. You son will gather armies against you, and as you die, chaos will return to the land."

"Why do you tell me this?" Arthur asked.

"It will all make sense in a few years," the lady said and slowly submerged into the lake.

Arthur shrugged and pulled off his tunic. "Swim now. Fish later." He jumped into the lake and swam for the outcropping.

3.2.2.2   Elements of Vision

At its core, the legend of King Arthur tells a tale of leadership – its successes and its failings. Arthur earned the right to lead England by pulling the sword from the stone. Most software managers earned the right to lead by first leading without the title, and then getting a promotion. The fall and death of Arthur show how a mistake made long ago can return to extinguish the brightest flame. Bad software architecture decisions can lead to the inability to change the software, which can lead to death.

Mostly, the legend of Arthur tells a tale of vision. Without Excalibur, Camelot and the Round Table, there would be no story.

Most of us will not have the Lady of the Lake to give us our vision, but we can look at what she says to understand the three elements of a vision:

- **Problem Statement** – First, the vision story describes a problem that needs to be solved. In Arthur's case, that's the turmoil in England. In software, it might be, "Our competitor's product has improved and they're gaining market share." It needs to be clear to everyone involved that the threat posed by the problem is serious, that proceeding as you have so far will lead to dire consequences, and that solving the problem will require changes – changes to the software, changes to the architecture or changes to development processes, or all of the above. Remember that change is the fuel that feeds the Geodesic Philosophy.

- **Picture of the Future** – Second, the vision story paints an appealing picture of the future – Camelot and the Round Table, and the great peace they bring. In software, it might be "a new product that changes the way users think about data analysis." The future must avoid the dire consequences that the current problem leads to. It's okay to hear objections about the future being unattainable, but not about its being undesirable.

- **Talisman** – Third, the vision offers a talisman that appears to make it possible to get from the present to the future – Arthur's enchanted sword Excalibur. In software, it's often a new technology that has recently been developed or acquired or improved, or a technology that needs to be invented. The talisman provides hope that the future is attainable It answers the question, "What's different this time?" It plants the seed for how to get from the present to the future. Team members can start imagining steps that move in the right direction. Once enough steps are imagined, they can imagine a full path. When the future is attained, you might look back and see that the talisman was only a small part of the solution, but without it, you could never have started.

Once the elements are in place, give it a name – Camelot. The name provides a buoy to hang onto in a sea of infinite possibilities. The name gives it legitimacy. The name symbolizes the future and the path to get there. The name enables two people to share the goal that the vision implies.

3.2.2.3   Communicating the Vision
Your vision story needs to go viral.

Start by trying the story on a trusted partner or two. Include leaders in your team, or peers, or maybe your boss. Find which parts of the story resonate, and which parts fall flat. Don't move past that group until all of you believe that the story works.

Then expand your audience and talk about it at every opportunity. Have group meetings where you present the story. Talk about it one on one with members of the team. Talk with customers and users and sales and marketing. Get their feedback. Improve the story if you can. Give them permission to make it their story.

And listen. Listen to the story as it comes back to you, and try to hear how it has changed. Listen to objections and try to hear if they are roadblocks or constructive criticism. Listen to the roar of enthusiasm, or the silence of apathy. Adapt the story and tell it again, until you hear wheels turning.

Once the team starts moving toward the goal, they will be hard to stop. But you can't stop telling the story, because the story will need to change. The problem you're solving might expand to include related problems. There will be new details in that painting of the future. There will be additional talismans. You will add details about the path to the future.

The team needs a shared ethos that guides them in discerning right from wrong. Listen to how the team uses the story to make decisions. Listen to how the story has shaped their values. They will need your help with the gray areas. They will need your help with priorities and proportion. Make that part of the story.

3.2.2.4   When Your Vision is Part of a Greater Vision

Most software managers do not own the major, overarching vision. That vision comes from somewhere above them. But they still need to help their team come to a common minor vision for their part of the major vision, and they need to help their team connect to the major vision.

The minor vision must still include the three elements of vision, but each element must tie into the major vision.

- The problem statement should include any aspect of the problem that's specific to the charter of your team, and it may be extended to include other problems that are unique to your team, such as architectural issues or quality issues.
- The picture of the future needs to address how your team's accomplishments will contribute to the success of the major vision.
- For the talisman, you can leverage the major vision's talisman, or you can use one that is unique to your team.

When communicating the minor vision, always discuss how it relates to the major vision. Make sure that the owner of the major vision knows the role that your team plays. When your team members listen to communication of the major vision, they will listen for mention of that role. Even a brief mention will help validate their work; the lack of a mention will lead them to question their worth.

The minor vision will change as you and your team learn more about it. The major vision will also change. Adapt the minor vision as the major vision transforms. And help the major vision change based on feedback from your team. Hearing your team's feedback incorporated into the major vision helps connect your team to the major vision.

3.2.2.5   The Seeds of Destruction

> There will be time, there will be time
> To prepare a face to meet the faces that you meet;
> There will be time to murder and create,
> And time for all the works and days of hands

> That lift and drop a question on your plate;
> Time for you and time for me,
> And time yet for a hundred indecisions,
> And for a hundred visions and revisions,
> Before the taking of a toast and tea.

The Love Song of J. Alfred Prufrock, T.S. Eliot, 1915

Lurking behind your vision story is another story that holds the seeds of its destruction.

One of those seeds is feature creep. As your team moves along the vision's path, you will need to expand the vision, but you will also need to contain it. As you keep telling the story, make it clear what you won't do. You can't afford for your team to be chasing the Holy Grail. For the vision to live, the team needs success, and they need *frequent* success. A long slog along a path that fails will sap the energy from your team. You also can't afford complexity. If too many pieces need to come together all at once, the team will hit the wall when they need to integrate all those pieces.

Sometimes the vision contains the seeds of its own destruction – a goal too lofty, or a schedule too aggressive, or a talisman not yet ready for the burden of supporting the vision. Don't let your enthusiasm for the beauty of the vision blind you to reality's dull glow.

The seeds of destruction can grow within the team. In the Arthur legend, Guinevere and Lancelot put their personal happiness ahead of the vision. A single team member, who has a different idea of what's important or of how to proceed, can cause the vision to collapse. In society, dissenting voices are healthy, reminding us that there are many different goals and many ways to achieve the goals we share. But a software team needs a shared goal and a shared path to attain that goal. The goal and path are dynamic and changing, but they remain shared. The united team moves like a school of fish, with each member turning to adjust to the turning of all the others.

Dissension within the team can have one of three effects:

- The team can split into factions.
- The team can dissolve into individuals, with each person having a different goal and direction.
- The team can remain whole, but with a new goal and direction, as if the school of fish were suddenly transported to a different sea.

The first two effects are always bad; a unified team will create better software than a divided team. Once factions are formed, they are difficult to re-unite. However, you can re-unite the individuals under the banner of a new vision.

The third effect could be good or bad, but regardless, you will not be able to move the team back to the original vision. The new vision might be better than the original. It might fix fatal flaws. It might be easier to attain. If so, you should adopt the new vision and move on, helping the team attain their goals. If you can't adopt the new vision, you need to consider your options because you have lost the authority to manage the team.

Most often, the seeds of destruction lie outside the team – Arthur's son Mordred gathering an army to conquer Camelot. Competitors can change the way your customers think about the software. New government regulations can force major changes to the vision and path. Internal competition can obviate the need for the project. Executives can withdraw the funding for the project. You can try to treat these events as changes and try to adapt the vision to the new environment, but often these changes are so severe and so sudden that you will need to make a complete reexamination of the vision.

3.2.3   *Non-Sequitur* – A Skinny Overview of Lean

> Jack Sprat could eat no fat;
> His wife could eat no lean.
> And so betwixt the two of them,
> They licked the platter clean.

Traditional English Nursery Rhyme

The image of the tall thin Jack Sprat and his robust wife come to mind as I consider how to tell the story of Lean Thinking. Can we eliminate the fat from our methodology, or are we doomed to carry around extra weight for eternity?

Lean is a way of thinking that attempts to maximize efficiency by eliminating waste. In this section, I provide a brief overview of Lean as background for the decision-making discussion that follows, and for the discussion of methodology frameworks that comes later.

Lean came out of the Japanese auto industry's (initially Toyota's) manufacturing processes. To compete with Detroit, they developed a way to be much more efficient building cars by using just-in-time supply chains and relentless elimination of waste and inefficiencies. Lean thinking made its way into product development where keeping options open and making decisions as late as possible improved their time to market. Lean came to software development with the book:

> *Lean Software Development – An Agile Toolkit*
> Mary and Tom Poppendieck, 2003

The Poppendiecks took the principals from Lean product development and applied them to software development, providing thinking tools you can use to analyze and improve software methodologies.

The most important concept in Lean software development is the expanded definition of the word 'waste'. Waste is anything that does not create value for the customer. The Poppendiecks list seven kinds of waste for software development:

- **Partially done work** – the time spent on it was wasted and it gets in the way of other things since it often needs to be maintained as the system changes around it. Either finish it or delete it, but don't leave it hanging around.
- **Unnecessary processes** – processes are often put in place to avoid an abomination that happened in the past. If the process does not apply to the current situation, then following that process is waste.
- **Extra features** – in the Tree of Life parable, no one asked for the plums, but they created problems that needed to be addressed. That happens a lot. You will also see teams creating "micro-features" that are specific to the needs of a single user, when a more general solution would be much better.
- **Task switching** – multitasking is sometimes necessary, but it has a cost. See the discussion in Limits to Agility.
- **Waiting** – if you are waiting for something to happen, then you are not doing the most important thing. Conversely, if someone is waiting for you to finish something, you are creating waste.
- **Motion** – Both physical motion (going to the next building to discuss a problem with a fellow developer) and virtual motion (handing off responsibility for a document) cause inefficiency.
- **Bugs** – Bugs cause you to revisit things that you thought were done. Finding and fixing bugs early is the best way to avoid bug-waste.

Lean thinking is based on seven principles that guide decision making.

- **Eliminate waste** – minimize all seven kinds of waste to improve efficiency.
- **Amplify learning** – use measurement of controlled experiments with short feedback loops to improve both the software and the methodology. Measurement plays an important part in the Geodesic Philosophy.
- **Decide as late as possible** – keep your options open and build in as many options as practical, then decide based on a common ethos. Deciding too early can lock you into a bad decision.
- **Deliver as fast as possible** – Getting something that works as soon as possible gives you something to measure. To meet this goal, understand your limits to agility and eliminate waste from the latency and frequency of every critical process.
- **Empower the team** – the best decisions are made by the people with the best information. Usually, that's the development team, not the managers.
- **Build integrity in** – Integrity comprises both the user's view of quality – functionality and reliability, and the developer's view – architecture and testing. To build integrity into the software requires good coding practices within a vision of how the system is likely to evolve, and the goal of finding and fixing bugs as early as possible.

- **See the whole** – When writing code, consider how each change affects the architecture and quality. When evaluating a methodology, look at the whole environment and try to anticipate how each change will affect the system.

Applying these seven principles to the software problem is not easy. First the organization's leadership needs to embrace the Lean mindset. It's not enough for a manager to embrace the principles. The entire team needs to embrace them. They need to be part of the culture of the organization. You need Lean thinking to be part of your decision-making ethos.

Which leads us to...

3.2.4　Decision Making

One of the pillars of the Geodesic Manifesto is "a decision-making ethos to guide us as we change the vision, plan, architecture and methodology." I chose the word 'ethos' rather than 'mindset' or 'values' because of its relation to ethics – knowledge of right and wrong – and the notion that an ethos defines the spirit of a culture. When the members of a team share an ethos, they all can distinguish good decisions from bad. They all know when to question decisions. They all participate in the evolution of the ethos.

You can start with a framework, like Lean Thinking, as the basis of your ethos, but the ethos must expand to include notions of right and wrong that are specific to your culture. For example, I often reviewed product presentations that were intended for customers. I helped the authors craft their presentations into clear and compelling stories. Soon I saw those authors helping others, and the quality of presentations improved without my further intervention.

3.2.4.1　Shades of Gray

Try this. Walk into a new car dealer and tell the sales representative that you want to test drive two different vehicles – a sedan and an SUV, for example. Almost always, the sales rep will ask a few questions, will decide which of those two vehicles you are more likely to buy that day, and will only show you one of them. If you really want to see the other car, you will have to go to a different dealer or come back another day.

Car sales reps have learned that their best chance of a sale comes when the customer has only one choice – buy *this* car, or don't buy a car. Most customers don't deal well with ambiguity. The third option (buy *that* car), can put the customer into a long analysis loop that will seldom result in a sale. So, the first thing that sales reps do is to eliminate options. Sales reps prefer black-and-white choices.

Now try this. Ask a group of software developers how to solve a complex software problem. The first thing they will do is to propose a few potential solutions. Then they will drill down into one or two of them, and then propose variations on the chosen solution, and maybe come back to one of the rejected solutions. They will discuss for a long time before finally choosing a path, but even then, they will keep some of the rejected solutions in mind in case they're needed. Software developers deal in shades of gray because they have learned that they cannot fully understand a problem until they have solved it.

Both the black-and-white and shades-of-gray modes are valid in the right circumstances. Most of us have a tendency toward one mode or the other. I am a shades-of-gray person – no decision is so good that it can't be changed. My younger son is a black-and-white person – he was five years old when he changed his mind for the first time (and he was very proud of that first change).

When you need a decision, determine if you need a black-and-white decision – choose one alternative and never look back – or a shades-of-gray decision – choose, but keep your options open.

3.2.4.2   Decision Authority

Most decisions in a software project are made by developers. Some are trivial – what to name a variable; some are moderate – how to modify an existing module to implement new functionality; and some are complex – how to architect a new module. Most of the time, having software developers make decisions is the best practice, as long as a reasonable peer review process is in place.

Some decisions need to be made by the software manager. Those decisions may be complex, may have implications outside the development team, or may need information that only the manager has.

Other decisions fall somewhere between those extremes. From the manager's view, there are four levels of decision making.

1. I don't need to know about the decision; just follow the peer review process.
2. Inform me of the decision after you commit. I won't challenge the decision, but I need to know what happened.
3. I need to validate the decision before you commit. I may challenge the decision.
4. I need to make the decision. The consequences of the decision are too far-reaching, and I need to take responsibility.

You need to train your staff how to determine the level of a decision. The criteria may be different for each member of your team, depending on the amount of trust that member has earned. That means that you need to train each member independently.

3.2.4.3   Making the Decision

In the few cases when you need to make the decision, your highest priority is to understand the problem, the options and the consequences. Consult with everyone that you can. After some analysis, you can probably eliminate most of the options, and you will be left with one or two that resolve the problem, or you will find that none of the options resolves the problem, but one or two are the best of a bad lot.

If more than one viable option is left, then choose one. Most of the time, further analysis will leave the choices fuzzy because the analysis is trying to predict the future, a particularly risky endeavor. Most of the time, having a decision is more important than the second-order differences between the options. Use your judgment to decide when "most of the time" does not apply and you need to take a long time to decide. If you find that most of the time "most of the time" does not apply, then you're doing something wrong.

A team looks to its leaders for clarity, so, once you've decided, the decision should be black and white. The short-term path forward should be clear to everyone involved. If your decision needs to deal with uncertainty, the way that uncertainty will be resolved needs to be black and white – something like, "We will revisit 'this aspect' of the decision in two weeks when we have 'this information'."

Then communicate the decision to everyone who needs to know. This is one of the few times that telling is more important than listening. All your listening should have happened earlier. Write it down; written words last – spoken words fade away.

Finally, validate that your team has accepted the decision. A decision is only as good as the execution that follows.

3.2.4.4   Timing of Decisions

The world is divided into expediters and procrastinators. The expediters make decisions as early as possible. They don't want any loose ends hanging around. The procrastinators make decisions as late as possible. Why decide today when tomorrow will do?

In most situations, the expediters win, but not in decision making. Early decisions often suffer from lack of information, and tie you into a course that may be suboptimal. As long as a decision is made before the last practical moment, procrastinators make better decisions because they know all those things they learned while the expediters were prematurely executing.

Making decisions at the last practical moment is one of the principals of Lean Thinking, and is a key tenet of Agile methodologies. In Geodesic Philosophy, the definitive decision is made at the last practical moment, but well before that, the team's leaders set up the ethos that frames the decision and gives clues to other decision makers about the likely outcome.

In other words, expedite the ethos, but procrastinate the decision.

3.2.4.5 Building the Decision-Making Ethos

The decision-making ethos is part of your team's culture. It is already there, even if you haven't done anything. The current ethos could be as simple as "Always ask Bob," or "Have a meeting and wait for consensus or acquiescence." There could be more than one ethos. Victoria might be empirical, and Albert consultative.

If something is important to the success of your team, it's always better to define it explicitly rather than to let it be defined only in folklore. That's true for architecture and methodology. It's also true for your decision-making ethos.

Making cultural change is a slow process that requires vigilance and consistency on the part of the leaders. Start with the Lean principles. Do some training to get your team familiar with them. Then, at every opportunity, force team members to think by asking questions about how a decision relates to the principles. Eventually other people will start asking those questions, and the cultural change has started.

Then start adding additional questions that need to be answered for certain classes of decisions. Maybe these relate to architecture and methodology, or to testing and measurements. Again, you'll know the change has occurred when you see it in other people.

An important part of the ethos concerns when to seek help. Some of the most destructive things in software happen when a single developer makes a bad decision without telling anyone. Peer review is one way to combat that – every decision needs someone else to validate it. But coaching developers to know when a decision is beyond their skill level is one of your jobs as a manager.

3.3 Organization

As a software manager, the only way you get things done is through your team. They are the feet that move you, and the eyes and ears that feed you information. Building the right team and making that team productive is the most important thing you can do to make your software projects successful.

In this section, I will briefly discuss a few aspects of software team management. Beware that in these few pages I cannot hope to be thorough. I will touch on the following topics:

- understanding the capabilities and limitations of your team
- common misconceptions about software developers
- building the team

3.3.1 Software Developer Capabilities and Complexity Limits

> People who develop software have a wide range of ability, motivation and temperament.

A truth from The Geodesic Manifesto

True or false? – software developers are like other people.

At the risk of sounding like a Buddhist master, the answer is, "Both true and false." Like other people, developers eat and breathe. They have friends and spouses and children. Like everyone, they suffer and exalt in the human condition. But unlike others, they write software. They have pride in the software worlds they create where the laws of physics don't apply. In their world, they fix things and break things, add features and create bugs. Some can make complex problems seem simple and others can make simple problems seem complex. Many of them are addicted to writing software, with a constant craving for the rush they get when things work as expected.

As a software manager, you need to understand the software side of each member of your team. Each developer has capabilities and limits. To get the most from your team, you need to push each member to work close to the limits, and you need to help them understand their limits, for that's the only way they can extend their limits. But beware that developers working past their limits can poison the whole system you're trying to develop.

The most important limit to understand for each developer is the complexity limit.

Some developers can hold the entire system in their heads. When discussing a problem or an enhancement with them, they immediately know the best place to make changes and the general structure of the changes. They battle complexity with simplification. They have high complexity limits.

Other developers have deep understanding of parts of the system, or of particular algorithms and can develop new features with architectural help from others. They have medium complexity limits.

Still other developers get lost in the details and address every problem as if they were swimming in a school of sardines with a goldfish net and a plastic bag. They battle complexity with complexity and they usually lose. They have low complexity limits.

Every team has developers with a range of complexity limits. More than anything else, high quality software requires that all the developers work within their limits. One developer trying to work beyond the limit for a couple weeks can create problems that might take years to rectify.

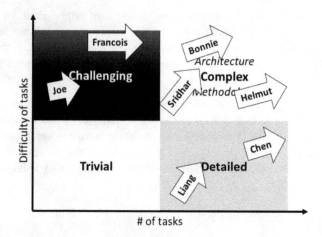

The Complexity Model can serve as a platform for understanding your team's capabilities. On the model diagram I have placed a few arrows. Each arrow represents a fictional team member with their current capability and a trend. I have always kept a similar mental model of my team. It helps when assigning tasks and when planning how to help developers grow their limits.

You also need some commentary for each team member. Francois is an expert in discrete optimization problems and has developed new optimization techniques for very difficult problems. Liang is learning quickly; she writes solid code, but takes longer than average to finish. These sound bites help you understand the current capabilities of your team members, but don't let the words create a box that the team member can't get out of.

It's important that you and your team member agree on your assessment. High-skill developers, like Francois and Bonnie, usually have a good understanding of their capabilities and their limitations. Low-skill developers often have an inflated view of their capability. Helping them to understand their limitations is the best way to help them improve.

3.3.2   The Myth of Fungibility

The word 'fungible' means capable of being used in place of another. It's often used with commodities: salt is fungible – one teaspoon is quite like another, notwithstanding the availability and marketing of gourmet sea salt. And the concept is used, if not the word, to apply to resources: for example, disk space, or Commander Denniston's notion of the uniformity of soldiers (see Lessons from "The Imitation Game").

Many managers who are not familiar with software developers have the mistaken notion that developers are fungible. This is especially true of high-level managers and accountants who manage developers by headcount rather than by name. By headcount, if you have 100 developers, and one leaves, then it follows logically that your projects should be delayed by at most 1%. But if the one who left is the expert for a key algorithm, then the delay could be large, and the quality of the resulting product could be seriously compromised.

Developers are not fungible. Each one is unique, with unique skill sets and with unique understanding of the system. If Francois leaves, you may ask Joe to complete his tasks, but Joe does not magically become Francois. Joe has to learn new skills and develop his own understanding of parts of the system that are new to him. Maybe Joe can succeed, but maybe the new tasks are beyond his complexity limit and they will never get done with acceptable quality.

3.3.3 Negative Productivity

Another headcounter misconception is the hope that moving developers from project to project can accelerate development. If you move five developers from a low priority project to a high priority project that currently has five developers, the high priority project should happen twice as fast. Right?

There are two problems with this thinking. The first is the parallelization myth. Some tasks cannot be split up and done in parallel. If you need to get from Chicago to Los Angeles, it takes 30 hours to drive one car; it also takes 30 hours to drive two cars. One woman can have a baby in nine months; three women cannot have a baby in three months.

The second problem is that productivity is not additive.

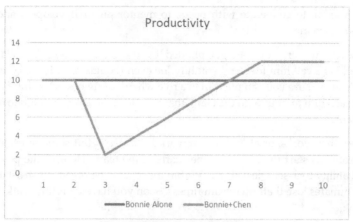

Bonnie & Chen's Productivity

Let's define productivity as the amount of working code per week, measured in the fictional units, WCs. Suppose Bonnie's productivity is 10 WCs. Chen is working on another project and also has productivity of 10 WCs. If we add Chen to Bonnie's project, his productivity starts at 0 WCs because he knows nothing about this project. Over the course of six weeks Chen's productivity only gets to 5 WCs, because this project does not match his skill set as well as the previous one. Meanwhile Bonnie's productivity initially drops to 2 WCs because she's spending so much time helping Chen, and her productivity gradually stabilizes at 7 WCs. She can't return to 10 WCs because she's still helping Chen and dealing with the mistakes that Chen is making because of the skill set mismatch.

To summarize, without Chen, total productivity was 10 WCs. With Chen it starts at 2 WCs and reaches a steady state of 12 WCs. After about four months, the total output with Chen finally exceeds the total output of Bonnie alone. Until then, putting Chen on the project added negative productivity. It's even worse if we consider that Chen could have been working at 10 WCs all this time if we had left him on his previous project.

This was a good result because, eventually, total productivity increased with both Chen and Bonnie on the project. Sometimes it doesn't. Some developers can never increase the team's productivity – they suck more WCs out of the productive people than they add. As a manager, you need to identify these developers and make them harmless by removing them from the team or, if that's not possible, minimizing their impact on highly productive team members.

3.3.4   Organizational Poison

Discussions about hiring of software engineers often refer to a parameter called "team fit" that has equal or greater weight compared to technical competence. The ability to work in a team, to cooperate with peers, to mentor junior developers and to lead projects are extremely important.

Sometimes, however, you can get blinded by the sheer technical brilliance of a developer. Let's call him Joe. And you hire Joe even though you are concerned about team fit. You are sure you can put him in a role where teamwork is less important; that you can teach him to fit in with the team; that your team is strong enough to overcome his problems.

Sometimes that works, or at least it can work for a while. But sometimes, Joe's team fitness problems start to spread to other parts of the team. He uses the power of his technical ability to assemble a clique. Within that clique, he breeds mistrust and a few of his teammates lose their own team fitness. Soon you have a mutiny walking up the gangplank.

Joe is organizational poison. Often you can see it in his resume, at least in retrospect. He has lots of short duration positions with gaps between them. You often can't get the whole truth from references. Sometimes Joe's reputation is big enough that you will have heard about him.

Once you identify the problem, you need to get him out of your team as fast as possible. You will not be able to mentor him through this. And the technical brilliance can't make up for the organization problems. You need to find the managerial courage to do the right thing.

3.3.5   Myth of Indispensability

No one is indispensable. If a developer disappears, the team will fill the gap, maybe not immediately, and probably with some cost to schedules or quality. I've seen it happen time after time. The developer disappears and is soon forgotten – so forgotten that developers laugh when they see unfamiliar initials in a comment. "Who is RJE?" they chuckle.

But it's easy to believe in indispensability. Managers and team members have leaned on a key developer for so long – to fix bugs, to implement new features, to improve processes – that it's hard to imagine how the gap will be filled if the developer leaves. That in itself is not bad. But managers and developers make three kinds of mistakes based on the myth of indispensability.

- Managers make bad decisions based on the threat, real or perceived, that a developer will leave if the developer disagrees with the decision.
- Managers keep people who are bad for the team, either because they are negative productivity generators, or because they are organizational poison.
- Developers limit their opportunities by letting others perceive them to be indispensable.

Taking the best path often requires a great deal of managerial courage.

3.3.6   Managerial Courage

Software managers make tradeoffs. Day after day, week after week, decisions that are good for one parameter are bad for others. Software managers trade off features versus schedule, completeness versus ease of use, satisfying customers versus satisfying employees, long-term benefits versus short-term gains. These decisions are hard, but great software managers have the wisdom and the courage to make decisions that optimize the Greater Good of the organization. They need to be the Scarecrow, using wisdom to understand the consequences of the decision and to plan how to mitigate the risk of those consequences. And they need to be the Lion, with the courage to make the right decision despite the consequences.

But sometimes managers are so afraid of the bad side effects of their decisions that they don't have the courage to make the decision that gets the primary effect they need. In my experience, when managerial courage fails, it's usually the Tin Man's failure, lack of heart. Some managers live in constant fear over how the members of their team will react. It's easy to make courageous decisions about the technology, because technical decisions can be reversed at some cost – at worst, you can throw away some code and start over. But technology decisions are easy because the code won't frown at you in the lunch room. Decisions that affect people can't be reversed. Once you've lost the trust of an employee, you will never get it back completely. The two of you will circle each other suspiciously, tiptoeing cautiously lest you open old wounds.

Which brings me back to the Myth of Indispensability.

Hiring good people is hard. First you have to get a personnel requisition, a unicorn that is difficult to find and can disappear at any time. Then you need to find candidates and out of those find the right candidate. Then, since good candidates have many options, you need to convince that candidate to join your team. Then you need to invest in bringing your new employee up to speed, and only then do you begin to see a gain in productivity for your team. So, it is understandable that managers live in constant fear of losing people.

You can't let that fear obstruct your ability to optimize the Greater Good.

If Wally is contributing negative productivity, he cannot possibly contribute to the Greater Good. You need to remove him from the team even if it means losing the trust of his friend Ashok. If Wally's cynical attitude is causing morale problems in the rest of the team, then he is organizational poison and it's even more important to remove him.

A software team I knew had a lot of redundant projects. I wondered why, and finally found that the management of this team had constructed a complex, Rube-Goldberg-like theory in which any attempt to remove a redundant project would result in the departure of a key developer. So, rather than expose themselves to this risk, they continued to maintain and enhance the redundant projects. But not once had they talked to the key developer about their problem. Maybe he also wondered why there were so many redundant projects.

It's easier to find the courage to make difficult heart decisions if you use wisdom first. Map out the consequences. Bring in the affected people and explain the decision. Even if they don't agree (and they won't) at least they will understand that you thought hard about it and that you cared enough about them to get their input.

3.3.7   The Legend of the 10x Developer

Legend[1]
Jack, a junior developer, needed to cross a field. He boldly strode into the field and was knocked back to the start. "I see what I did wrong," he said, and stepped back into the field and was knocked back to the start after two steps. Over and over he stepped and was knocked back until finally he made it across the field, battered and bleeding, and sat down to breakfast – blueberry bagels with strawberry schmear and a caramel macchiato.

Soon after, Jill, a senior developer, arrived at the field. She saw all the potholes left by Jack and got down on hands and knees with a stick in her hand. She crawled forward, detonating land mines with the stick. Always moving forward, she slowly made her way across the field wearing holes in her pants and driving dirt into her palms. When she arrived, she sat down to lunch – pizza with artichokes and capers, and a craft IPA.

Jack cooed, "Wow! that was impressive!"

Jill replied, "Someday you'll learn how to get by the landmines without hurting yourself too much."

Then, Victoria, a 10x developer, arrived at the field. She paused, evaluating the landscape. Then she confidently walked across the field and sat down to dinner – sushi and salmon teriyaki with a buttery chardonnay.

"Wow!" said Jack.

"How did you do that?" asked Jill. "The field is full of landmines."

---

[1] I read this somewhere, but now I can't find the original. If this is yours or if you know where it came from, please let me know so I can properly cite the source.

Victoria cocked her head as if in thought. "I didn't plant any landmines," she said, and took a sip of her wine.

Reality

The 10x developer is real. I've encountered enough of them in my day to know that I'm not one of them. They really can pump out code 10x faster than an average developer, and the code just works – no bugs, no performance problems, no usability problems, no maintainability problems. Sometimes they can complete a project that average developers can't. How many 'x' is that? A 10x developer makes everyone on the team better by building simple, easy to use infrastructure, by designing a clean architecture, by fixing problems introduced by others in ways that those problems can never appear again.

What makes them so good?

- They see the whole picture at once. That means that they know the consequences of every decision they make. They know the five special cases they need to cover and can build those cases into their architecture in such a way that they don't look like special cases. And the whole picture they see morphs into a new picture as they learn more about the problem.
- They continually validate what they write. They validate with traditional testing, but also with thought experiments. They ask, "What if?" at every turn, running the code in their heads looking for potential faults.
- They fix problems immediately. They know that no matter how disruptive it will be to fix a problem, fixing it now will be less disruptive than fixing it later.
- They spend time learning and building tools for analysis and debug. Every hour spent improving productivity will pay back with many hours later on.

What makes them so annoying?

- They're always right, or at least they think they are. So, you often have to spend a lot of energy convincing them to see your point of view.
- The rapid rate of change makes it hard for others to keep up.
- Often, they are poor communicators – in many cases because they forget to communicate, not because they can't.
- Often, they have low tolerance for mediocrity, a trait that makes them seem intimidating to the average developer.

Mature 10x programmers understand that they have these tendencies and will work to accommodate them. Less mature 10x programmers need a manager or mentor's help – first to recognize their problems and then to address them.

How do you become a 10x developer? Start by becoming 2x better than you are. If you do that three times, you're almost there. That may sound facetious, but incremental change is the only way you can change. Look at the list of good points above and try to see how you could employ some of them in your work. If you can't keep the whole picture in your head, maybe you can draw the picture or write it down so you don't need to. Practice finding problems in your code without testing; after a while this will become second nature. Build a tool that automates a task you find yourself doing over and over. And maybe most important, find someone who's better than you and try to learn from them, whether as a mentor or just by observing how they work.

3.3.8 Building A Team

I interviewed over a thousand people in my career. Hiring was often the most important part of my job. My boss, the CEO, made that clear by stopping by my office every day and asking about it, and by increasing the compensation for almost every offer I was about to make. There were times when we had so many openings that if we found a good people, we would find jobs that fit their skills. More often, we were looking for specific skills and had to talk to many people before we found a fit.

In this section, I will provide a few highlights that I have found essential for successful hiring. I make no attempt to be complete, and recommend that you consult one of the many books on hiring for a more complete picture.

3.3.8.1 Capability vs. Bandwidth

The first step in hiring is to know what you are looking for. The most fundamental question is whether you are hiring to increase capability or to increase bandwidth. You increase capability when you need to hire someone with skills that are missing from your team. Maybe you need someone with experience solving a specific class of challenging problem. You increase bandwidth when your team already has all the skills you need, but you need more people to handle the load. Maybe your validation team can't keep up with the development team, or you need to free up one or two of your developers to work on a new project that they can't start until they have replacements to train.

In the boom times when you have more openings than you can possibly fill, you can hire for bandwidth, but most of the time, when getting funding for an opening is difficult, you need to hire for capability. When funding was tight, I almost never approved hiring for bandwidth. There are always alternatives to increasing bandwidth, but a missing skill can't be patched over.

3.3.8.2 The Job Description

Writing a job description has two purposes. First, it describes the position and the candidate evaluation criteria. It provides a guide for the interview team to craft their interview questions. It helps your recruiters find candidates who will be a good fit for the position.

Second, it is an advertisement. It's the first thing a potential candidate will see. It needs to be compelling and to paint a picture that will appeal to the type of candidate you are trying to attract. Sometimes your position could be filled by candidates with different profiles – maybe someone with five years of experience, or someone with a fresh PhD. In that case, I often posted two job descriptions for the same job opening that each appealed to a different candidate profile. A side benefit of having more jobs posted is that it makes it look like the group is thriving – I know that's a lie, but advertising is only partly about truth.

3.3.8.3   The Interview Team

Identify the core interview team for the position. This is the group that will be included in every candidate interview. It's hard to compare three candidates unless most of the interviewers are common.

Before any candidates are brought in, get together with the team. Make sure everyone understands the job, and decide on interview roles and questions for each member of the interview team. Avoiding redundancy during the interview is good for getting the best information, but also, redundancy looks bad to the candidate who wants to work with a high performing team.

The interview team, like the job description, has two purposes. Its primary purpose is to make a recommendation about whether or not to hire a candidate. Its secondary purpose is to represent the organization to the candidate in a positive light. Whether or not you decide to make an offer, the candidate should walk away impressed by the quality of your people and the professionalism of the organization.

3.3.8.4   The Candidate

All candidates, from the ones browsing your group's job openings on the web, to the ones who don't get past the phone screen, to the ones you hire, are potential members of your team. From the beginning, treat them as if you had already hired them. All candidates are ambassadors, because every candidate will talk to their friends and word travels fast. If a candidate feels treated poorly or insulted, then you will have trouble getting other candidates to apply.

The most common mistake I have seen is timing. A candidate's time scale is different from yours. You are considering five people for the position and expecting to complete the process in a month. The candidate is interviewing for one position and expecting to complete the process in a week. For you, if you respond to the candidate's email in three days, that's fast; for the candidate, that's an eternity. Always respond immediately to a candidate, even if the response is, "I'll be able to answer on Tuesday." Every delay gives the candidate opportunity to consider alternatives.

3.3.8.5   Screening

Designate one member of the interview team to do screening, an initial discussion with the candidate to assess the probability of a fit. If the candidate is local, try to do the screening face-to-face. But if you must do it via phone, then come up with some good questions that don't require writing or drawing.

Bringing a candidate in for an interview that finds a poor fit wastes the time of the candidate and of the interview team. If that happens, in the spirit of Lean's "eliminate waste" principle, try to figure out why the screening failed.

3.3.8.6   The Interview

Once again, the interview has two purposes: gather information to evaluate the candidate's fit for the job, and represent the group and the position to the candidate in a positive manner so that if an offer is made, there is a good chance of acceptance.

Most interviews should be done in one pass – either in one day, or within a couple days if you need to accommodate the candidate's schedule constraints, for example, by interviewing in the evening. Provide a schedule to the candidate that lists the interviewers and the times.

For some senior candidates, you may want a two-pass interview, where the composition of the second pass responds to information gained during the first pass.

Each interviewer should focus on his or her assigned technical area, but should leave time for the candidate to ask questions or to have a general discussion.

3.3.8.7   The Decision

After the interview, get the interview team together to assess the candidate's fit for the position. You're trying to make a multi-year commitment based on a few hours of discussion. Sometimes it's clear that the candidate is a great fit, or that the candidate is not qualified. Those decisions are easy.

The hard ones are when it's not clear. My rule of thumb is that most of the team should be positive and no one negative to make an offer. The risk of making a bad hire is high compared to the benefit of making an OK hire. It's better to keep looking if there's no enthusiasm for the candidate.

Never take more than a week to decide. If you do, the candidate loses interest. If you can't decide in a week, then the enthusiasm isn't there and the above rule applies.

3.3.8.8   The Close

If you have decided not to make an offer, tell the candidate immediately. There is no excuse for leaving the candidate hanging. If you used a recruiter to find the candidate, let the recruiter pass on the decision. Otherwise, the hiring manager should inform the candidate over the phone, not by email or text. In most cases, a simple, "We decided not to make an offer," will suffice. If the candidate presses for reasons, it's best to decline, "I prefer not to elaborate on our internal decision-making process." There's no upside in trying to give the candidate constructive feedback unless you think you may hire him or her for a different position.

If you have decided to make an offer, there are many ways of going through the offer negotiation that will depend on your style, and the constraints and culture of your organization. I will just make this observation: I have never regretted paying too much for a great developer, but I have often regretted losing a great developer because the offer was too low.

3.4 *Non-Sequitur* – Devoid of Meeting

As a young manager, I used to judge my worth by the fullness of my calendar – more meetings meant more worth. I went to staff meetings, status meetings, review meetings, one-on-ones, design meetings and lunch meetings – those were the best. Who knows when I had time to prepare for all of them, or when I had time to perform the action items that inevitably went to the most junior attendee. I proudly declared, "I'll see if I can squeeze you in," to my many supplicants. Those were the days before laptops and smart phones, when multi-tasking meant doodling in my notebook while listening to someone from corporate drone on about a regulation I would never follow. Those doodles made people nervous because they always thought I was drawing unflattering pictures of them.

Eventually I learned that meetings were not the goal, but a necessary evil placed in the path between here and there. Meetings, like business trips, lost their luster. Near the end of my career, I proudly displayed my nearly empty calendar, dotted with the occasional dentist appointment and all-hands meeting – which I would attend by phone after stopping by to grab a snack on the way to my desk.

If you must have a meeting, then meeting behavior is important.

- Start on time.
- Have an agenda.
- Make sure the right people are there.
- Assign a scribe to note action items.
- Avoid rat-holes.
- Follow up on the action items.
- Finish on time, but after you've completed the goal of the meeting.

Just type "meeting best practices" into your favorite search engine and read all about it.

But most likely, you won't find the most important meeting behaviors:

- Don't have a meeting if you don't need one.
- If you must have a meeting, minimize the time wasted by the attendees.

When Jack and Jill Coder are in a meeting, they're not writing code. They're not testing code. They're not reviewing other people's code. Maybe Jill brought her laptop to the meeting and she's multi-tasking, not really looking at test results while not really paying attention to the drone of the presentation. She's not really getting any benefit out of this hour. Maybe Jack is actively engaged in a discussion with the presenter about the flaws in the reasoning behind the decision that has already been made and ninety-two percent of which has been implemented. Someone should have talked to Jack last week.

Meetings are a little harder to avoid in these days of the open office plan, where the only way to have a discussion with the door closed is to schedule one of the overbooked conference rooms, because conference rooms own all the doors. Let's discount those informal meetings and concentrate on the monsters with lots of attendees, especially the recurring meetings that waste time on a weekly basis.

Here are some questions you should ask before you schedule a meeting, or before you accept the invitation, noting that you probably need to accept invitations from your boss even if it's against your better judgment.

Who benefits from this meeting?
Often, only the person who called the meeting gets anything out of it. Staff meetings and review meetings are notoriously for the benefit of the manager who called them. If only one person benefits from a ten-person meeting that means the meeting is ten percent efficient. There are times when that's OK, but you should pause to justify it before you schedule it. It's easy to tell who benefits by counting the noses that are pointed toward the discussion compared with the noses pointing toward personal device screens.

If this is a recurring meeting, do we need to have today's instance of the meeting?
I've attended many staff meetings, including my own, in which no one got any benefit. I scheduled staff meetings because they were expected, and because it was good to reserve the time for when we needed to work through something as a group. I routinely cancelled my staff meeting if there was no crucial topic, and everyone got an unencumbered hour.

Is there another way to attain the goal?
Often you can meet the goal with a few short face-to-face meetings, or with email or with a document. Use judgment to decide if the alternative is more efficient.

On the other hand, the twenty-person, thirty-reply email chain is not an effective way to resolve an issue. Call a meeting and get a decision.

If we need the meeting, can we get it done in half the time?

Work expands so as to fill the time available for its completion.

Parkinson's Law, Cyril Northcote Parkinson, The Economist, 1955
(https://www.economist.com/news/1955/11/19/parkinsons-law)

The meeting starts with what I call, "The Mandatory Fifteen-minute Equipment Delay." As technology evolved from Polycom phones to video projectors to web-based teleconferencing, the delay didn't change, but the cause of the delay did. The meeting room full of tech-savvy nerds can't figure out how to get the screen to display what's on the laptop, and to make it show up in Germany, too. How many engineers does it take to make a Skype call?

Then, there are the compulsory introductions – never mind that you've been working with these people for ten years. And a restatement of the objectives, which would be a lot easier if you'd written them down any one of the last five times you put them on the white board, which doesn't have either a marker or an eraser that works.

By the time you're done, the hour meeting conducted twenty minutes of business and felt rushed, so the next meeting is scheduled for an hour and a half.

Instead, next time move back a generation of technology, skip the preliminaries and schedule it for a half hour.

Are all these people necessary?
There are always people, like the early me, who measure their worth by the meetings they attend. Maybe it's prestige, or fear of missing something, or just that they prefer sitting in a conference room with donuts and coffee to doing actual work at their desk. They sit in the meeting without saying a useful word, pulling oxygen from the already depleted atmosphere, and eating the chocolate-covered donut you had your eyes on.

Get rid of them. Make it clear that their careers are better served by doing something rather than by hearing something. Give them donuts if that helps.

Cancel a few meetings. The time you save will be your own. Use it to do a little leadership, or organization, or planning, or control. You won't miss them.

3.5   Planning

When will it be done?

Ever since this project was conceived, people have been asking that question – managers, marketing, sales representatives and customers. As a dutiful manager who wants to keep your job, you know that you must answer and you must be optimistic or they will find someone who is. You know that trying to predict the future is doomed, and that if you really could predict the future, there are more profitable ways to leverage that talent than managing this project. So, you answer with a guess that has no basis other than the churning of your bowels. You answer and try to voice caveats and disclaimers, but your questioners only hear the date. Now you must deliver.

This section talks about planning in the world of software where everything is changing around you. The Agile Manifesto devalues planning with its value statement: "Responding to change over following a plan." But we can't avoid planning, because while you are lamenting about needing to predict the future, everyone else – marketing, sales, management and customers – are also trying to predict. And they need your plan to build their own plans. What we need to avoid are plans that can't adapt to the changes roiling around them. Instead of devaluing planning, let's, "Plan for change and change the plan when necessary."

3.5.1   The Planning Metaphor

> It winds from Chicago to LA
> More than two thousand miles all the way
> Get your kicks on Route sixty-six
> Now you go through Saint Looey
> Joplin, Missouri
> And Oklahoma City is mighty pretty
> You see Amarillo
> Gallup, New Mexico
> Flagstaff, Arizona
> Don't forget Winona
> Kingman, Barstow, San Bernardino

Route 66, Bobby Troup, 1946

I remember those pre-GPS days when we would go to the AAA (Automobile Association of America) office, where a helpful agent would grab a handful of beautiful paper maps, folded in a flat rectangular origami I could never reproduce, and mark our route in blue highlighter, circling points of interest along the way. While my Dad drove, I would find each city we passed and mentally measure our creeping progress.

The planning metaphor is a traveler who is at a starting point, Chicago, and who wants to get to a destination, Los Angeles. The traveler chooses a route, marked with milestones to measure progress, and makes an estimate of an arrival time (ETA). The traveler trudges along the way, checking off the milestones, and updating the ETA. If detours or unexpected traffic cause delays, the traveler might change the estimate, or drive faster, risking the highway patrol, or drive longer each day until the lost time is made up. Clearly, adding more cars doesn't help.

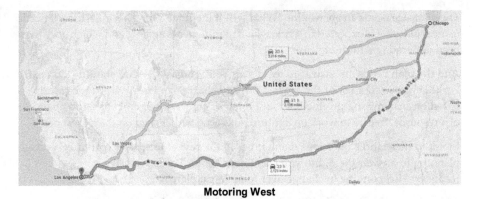

Motoring West

https://www.google.com/maps

The blue-highlighted route above roughly follows the path of the old Route 66. But there are other routes with different properties. Maybe I chose the southern route because I wanted to visit my aunt in Amarillo.

A real plan will be more complicated. Cousin Jack starts in Iowa, and Jill starts in Kansas City. They need to meet in Denver where they will pick up Joe and Jane and caravan the rest of the way. That makes Denver an integration point that no one can pass until they all get there.

And the real plan is changing. Maybe we discover that we need another integration point in Las Vegas, so I need to detour from the southern route to meet the rest of the group. And the destination is no longer Los Angeles, but instead we need to go to Guadalajara, and I didn't bring my passport. With all the changes, the ETA is getting later and later. The project is slipping. "Slipping" is outside the map metaphor, but instead evokes the image of an inexorable slide down the icy side of a mountain into a canyon full of wolves.

3.5.2   What is a plan?

A plan is a set of dependent tasks that converge toward a set of milestones. Each task is assigned to a set of resources (human or otherwise), has a duration, and its start time may depend on the completion of some other tasks. Each milestone targets some subset of the requirements that constitute a deliverable. The final milestone is the release of the system.

At any point, the plan needs an answer for "**When will it be done?**" The rest of the organization is depending on successful completion of your project. They are putting plans in place that may be expensive and irreversible. An accurate assessment of the schedule should include both the estimated date and the uncertainty. The rest of the organization doesn't like uncertainty, but they deserve to know.

The plan also needs an answer for "**What will it include?**" For each milestone, it needs to describe what is expected to work, which requirements are met and which ones have been deferred to a future release.

And the plan needs an answer to team members who ask, "**What should I do next?**" For this you need a list of the highest priority short term tasks, where the priority is based on maximizing productivity and minimizing risk. Remember that the best use of a resource may be to work on a future milestone, rather than on the closest one.

I refer to these three questions many times in the rest of this book. You need enough planning to answer them, but you don't need more. That's what the Agile Manifesto means by "Responding to change over following a plan."

There are two kinds of plans: roadmaps that show a high-level view of the future of the software, and detail plans that show specific software development tasks assigned to specific people.

All software plans are dynamic. They change based on external factors – new requirements and commitments, and competition. They change based on internal factors – architectural and algorithmic problems, changes in the makeup of the team, etc. Keeping roadmaps up to date is important to do periodically. Keeping detail plans up to date is impossible. In the section How to Create the Initial Plan for a Release below, I show a way to do almost-detail planning that allows the development team to self-organize for specific tasks, and that can provide answers to the three planning questions posed above.

3.5.3 Maximize Productivity

At the beginning of any project, only a few people are able to work productively. Most software developers need the basic architectural infrastructure in place before they can do anything. And the infrastructure needs the complete attention of a few developers. Maybe some of the product validation team can start working on developing tests, but they won't be productive until they can run the software on their tests.

The early milestones of your plan need to focus on providing the critical mass of infrastructure and functionality that allows the entire team to work productively. Identify what's needed to complete some useful subset of the functionality. It won't be complete. It may not conform to the requirements. It may be slow and difficult to use. But having something that works means that a lot of non-development tasks can get started – software validation, measurement systems, training and documentation. In most projects, these tasks end up on the critical path to the initial release.

3.5.4 Minimize Risk

Most software schedule delays are caused one of these two reasons:

- Resource Risk: a critical resource is not available when needed.
- Invention Risk: a feature took longer than expected to implement or to reach its quality goals.

Except for adding redundancy (and I've never been in an organization that tolerated redundant resources), there's little you can do about resource risk. If developers leave the group or become ill, you will need to scramble to find a way to complete their tasks. If promised developers are tied up on other projects, or if hiring is slower than projected, you will need to find a way to complete their tasks with existing developers.

You can, however, reduce invention risk by scheduling high-risk tasks early in the development timeline.

First, identify the highest risk software development tasks. Typically, these are the tasks that the team has never done before, or where there are many possible approaches, or where meeting critical parameters will be difficult, or where interfacing to other systems is required. Most of these tasks are in the Challenging quadrant of The Complexity Model.

Second, make sure that these tasks are assigned to appropriate resources. The most common cause of Invention Risk delay is that the task is beyond the complexity threshold (see Software Developer Capabilities and Complexity Limits) of the assigned developer.

Third, make sure that software validation (testing beyond the developer's unit tests) of high invention-risk tasks is done immediately after development completion. As a developer, one of my pet peeves was needing to fix critical problems late in the schedule because software validation didn't happen until months after the development was completed.

3.5.5   Managing Change

Change and the opportunities it presents are central to the Geodesic Philosophy. To successfully manage change, you need to understand the types of change; you need to manage change along two axes.

The first axis is the source of the change. *External* changes are induced by better understanding of the requirements. *Internal* changes are induced by better understanding of the implementation. External changes affect the value of the solution. Internal changes affect the cost of the implementation by influencing the productivity of the development team and the quality of the solution.

The second axis is impact. *Additive* changes can be made by writing new code without modifying the existing architecture and infrastructure. *Structural* changes need significant modification to the architecture and infrastructure. Additive changes typically do not add a lot of entropy because they are isolated and don't affect existing functionality. Structural changes can add a lot of entropy because they will require changes to existing code. If a lot of new requirements need structural changes, then the architecture is failing to meet its goals of flexibility and sufficiency.

	Internal	External
Structural	Cost/Cost Tradeoff	Cost/Benefit Tradeoff
Additive	Silent	No-Brainer

Source/Impact Quadrants

In the figure above, I show four change quadrants.

- Internal/Additive – I labeled this 'silent', because these changes will mostly happen without your hearing about them.
- External/Additive – These changes are low risk and the decision to make the change is based totally on the value of the change.
- Internal/Structural – There is a cost to making the change, and once the change is complete, it will reduce the cost of developing and maintaining the system. But it's never as simple as that. Borrowing a term from finance, you need to compare the cost of the implementation to the Present Value of all those future savings. The value of future productivity improvements gets discounted heavily by management compared to the future value of the system. Given the choice between internal and external changes, management will almost always choose external. Management's reluctance to do major internal changes is perhaps the greatest cause for poor software quality. If you want to make an internal-structural change, you need to work harder to sell the concept to your management.
- External/Structural – Since the implementation cost of this change is high, the value to customers must also be high. The decision of whether, and when, to implement this change will require comparing this change to all the other changes in the requirements backlog.

3.5.6   Roadmaps

The vision is the story of the future solution to the problems of the present with no detail between. The vision depends on the talisman to magically get us from here to there.

The roadmap is the story of how to get there. It shows how the product will evolve over time. It doesn't need to show much detail, but most of the magic should be gone. It has milestones that coincide with product deliverables to customers. Each milestone includes changes in the product.

The roadmap comes in three views, depending on the audience.

1.   The Commitment View only shows committed product changes. This view is suitable for showing to customers and users. Once made, commitments have high priority because if you miss a commitment, you have betrayed a trust and you must accept responsibility and apologize. Then you must listen to the wounded, angry tirade that follows.

2.   The Executive View shows all the product changes that are expected within a planning horizon. This view is suitable for showing to management and other internal players. Many of the changes are not committed, but have a reasonable chance of making it. The Executive View should also show the staffing assumptions that are needed for the plan to succeed.

3.   The Project View contains everything in the Management view plus architecture and other infrastructure changes that are not visible to users. This view provides a guide for the development team to self-organize. It's important to have a roadmap for infrastructure, so that the development team knows the big picture of what's important. It's also important to keep it separate from the Executive View, because if executives see what needs to be done one of several not-so-pleasant things might happen:

   o   Management will decide to remove funding from infrastructure projects because they don't see a direct relation to customers. See the discussion in Managing Change.

   o   Management will dive deep into the changes and try to "help" which is likely to be non-productive and distracting to the intended purpose of the changes.

   o   Management will see the amount of infrastructure work and lose faith that the development team has things under control.

3.5.7   The Software Uncertainty Principle

In 1927, Werner Heisenberg proposed his famous Uncertainty Principle, one of the founding pillars of quantum mechanics. Stated mathematically:

$$\Delta_x \times \Delta_m \geq \frac{h}{4\pi}$$

Or in words, the uncertainty of position (Δ_x) times the uncertainty of momentum (Δ_m) must be larger than Planck's constant over 4π. The more accurately we know the position of an object, the less accurately we can know its momentum. Or the common, not-quite-right interpretation: we can know where it is, or where it's going, but not both. Since Planck's constant is very small, the uncertainty principle doesn't apply to real life. I can pretty accurately know both the location and momentum of my golf ball when it hits that window.

The Software Uncertainty Principle has three components: schedule, content and quality:

$$\Delta_S \times \Delta_C \times \Delta_Q \geq \frac{b}{4\pi}$$

Where b is Bob's constant, which isn't really a constant, or even a number, but it looks good in the formula.

For any project, you can lock down two of those components, and the third will vary. For example, if you demand that the project deliver ten features in three months, then the quality of the deliverable will be low. If you demand that the ten features be delivered with high quality, then the schedule will slip. If you demand that the project complete in three months with high quality, then only some of the features will be delivered.

It doesn't take long for a software team to figure out that delivering low quality software is not a good idea, so the Software Uncertainty Principle simplifies to the schedule-content tradeoff. The early releases of a product tend to be content-driven, because the product is only useful if you deliver a critical mass of features with good quality. So, the delivery date remains uncertain up to, and sometimes including, the day of the release. As the software matures, releases tend to be schedule-driven because of commitments to customers, and some of the lower priority features will be deferred to later releases. Often features are removed in the last days of the release when it becomes clear that you can't deliver them with the required quality.

3.5.8   Planning Horizons

Successful software lasts forever. If you think that's an exaggeration, think about Microsoft Excel™, which has been around for over thirty years. I expect it will be around for at least another thirty years. Sixty years round to forever in the world of software.

Excel went through many phases in its life.

- Invention – The initial development phase with the goal of building a spreadsheet that was better than VisiCalc, the first personal-computer-based spreadsheet.

- Competition – Improve the product to win market share from competitors such as Lotus 1-2-3.
- Industry Standard – Continue to improve the product to establish and maintain its position as the most used spreadsheet.
- Commodity – Maintain the product's value in the presence of equivalent free products like Google Sheets and Apple's Numbers.
- Paradigm Shift – The spreadsheet becomes obsolete because another way to solve the problem of data analysis and presentation becomes the norm. This hasn't happened to Excel, and maybe it never will, but when a dominant product dies, a paradigm shift is the most likely reason.

Imagine that you are the first software manager overseeing the invention of Excel. Now imagine presenting to your boss the thirty-year plan for Excel. Now imagine derisive laughter and the boot that follows. Your planning horizon needs to match the life-cycle phase of the product.

You can only see as far as you can see. I'm sorry if that sounds trivially obvious, but when you are planning, no one hands you a highlighted AAA map. You invent the map as you invent the software. You can see the mountain ahead of you. Maybe you know about a few mountains you must traverse. But there are other mountains ahead, and rivers and deserts, that you can't know about until you get closer.

During the invention phase, you can only see a few months into the future. The requirements are changing and causing changes to your plans. But most of the changes come from the implementation itself, as you discover architectural and algorithmic problems that you did not anticipate. Sometimes tasks that you thought were important are left behind when you discover alternative routes that no longer need them. More often, new tasks pop up that are critical to delivering the product you need to compete in the market. You need one detail, feature-driven plan that's focused on making that product as soon as possible with the highest possible quality.

Now imagine that you are the software manager of Excel during the Competition stage. The product has a few years' track record. You have customers actively using the product and giving you input about how to improve it. You have committed specific changes, with specific dates, to some of those customers. You have several competitors who are improving their products, sometimes in surprising and compelling ways. You have bug reports filling up in your inbox. You have a bigger software developer team, funded by the growing product revenue. You have an established software architecture that was designed to support a much simpler product than the one you see ahead of you. You need multiple related plans. You need a roadmap, and you need detail plans for the projects you will deliver. Some of the detail plans will be feature-driven, and some will be schedule-driven.

3.5.9 Detail Plans

Before we talk about detail plans for software projects, let's look at a simple project where a detail plan works – painting our bedroom. First, we create the project dependency graph.

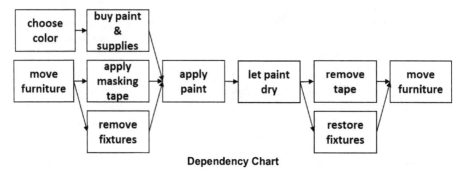

Dependency Chart

Here we see that we can't apply paint until we have bought the paint and all the prep work is completed. My wife and I are doing this project together, so we need to assign tasks to each of us. We can estimate how long each task takes, look at what tasks can be done in parallel, and put together a Gantt chart.

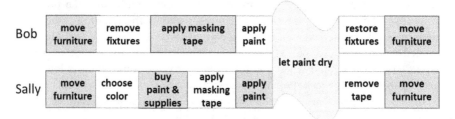

Gantt Chart

Now we can answer the three planning questions:

- When will it be done? – Our estimate says that if we start at 9:00AM on Saturday, we'll be done by noon on Sunday. What could go wrong? Sally might need to go to two paint stores to find the color she wants. We might need to do some touchup on Sunday after the paint dries. One of the switch plates might crack and need to be replaced. The upper bound is probably about 5:00 PM on Sunday.
- What will it include? – New paint with the old fixtures and with furniture in the same locations.
- What do I do next? – Everything we do is in the Gantt chart, except lunch and dinner. The smell of paint interferes with the appreciation of wine, so we will eat out.

The plan is simple. There's only one decision – choose color. We use a standard methodology for how to apply paint (rollers and brushes). We have a standard architecture for electrical fixtures. If something goes wrong, the schedule might slip, but the structure of the plan won't change.

Software schedules are a lot harder. Every task is full of decisions. Some of those decisions affect other tasks. You can't even write down all the tasks because most of the tasks haven't been invented yet. Sometimes a later task will make changes that require you to go back to an earlier task and start over. The requirements that you started with have been augmented and contracted, and all the priorities are different.

My father thought it was a good idea that I spend a couple summers doing manual labor so I would know that I didn't want to do that again. I think every software manager should put together at least one detail plan like the painting plan so that they will know that they never want to do that again.

You need to have a plan, but you can't do detail planning the traditional way, like the painting plan. In the next section, I present one way to do semi-detail planning that meets the need to answer the planning questions, but doesn't lock you into a lot of low-level decisions that are better left to the developers.

3.5.10   How to Create the Initial Plan for a Release

Remember that our goal is to create a release plan that can respond to change, and can answer the three planning questions: When will it be done? What will it include? What do I do next? You also need to maximize productivity and minimize risk.

Some vocabulary:

- A **release** is a version of the software that you will distribute to customers. You will give it a name or a number. That release will be used by customers for a while. You may ship updates to the release, but those will not make major changes to the product.

If your paradigm is continuous release, or releases so frequent that none of them is an event, then think of this as some bigger chunk of development.

- Releases have **features**. A feature is an aspect of the software that is visible to a user. You can define these features straight out of the requirements, or with the user stories that are common in Agile methodologies, or with a specification. For the sake of this planning discussion, I will use 'feature' for everything that goes into the release, whether it is a new capability, an enhancement to an existing feature, an architectural change that's invisible to users, or a significant bug fix.

- Features are implemented with **tasks**. Simple features could be completed with one task while others may require several tasks. A task can be completed by one developer.

The first step is to create an initial plan – your first best guess at answering the questions before much coding has been done. (You'll never be able to plan faster than some of your developers write code!)

What follows is one way to create that initial plan that I've used many times. It works for me, but I've never seen anyone I mentored do it the same way that I do. So, I offer this as a prototype for your education. Feel free to make it your own.

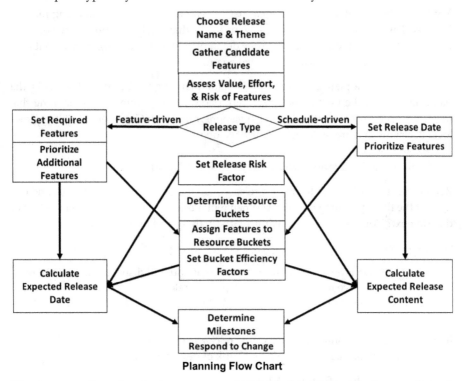

Planning Flow Chart

Here you see a flow chart for how to create the initial plan. I know it looks complicated, but bear with me. Once you've done this a few times, it's like cooking your favorite meal. You no longer need to look at the recipe.

In the discussion that follows, I will often say that *you* need to do something. If you try to do it alone, you will fail. You will become the epitome of the clueless pointy-haired boss. You need to do these things with your team. Get their input in one-on-ones and small groups; resist the managerial temptation to have a big meeting. Synthesize the inputs and give it back to them. Listen to their feedback. If you build the plan together, everyone will feel that it's their own plan.

Choose Release Name & Theme

I have always felt it essential that a release have a name and a theme.

The name gives it substance, something to hold onto, a way to distinguish it from other releases past and future. A number is a fine name. Five-dot-three is short, easy to remember and gives enough information. Numbers also have the benefit of relating multiple releases in time; five-dot-two probably comes before five-dot-three. Which came first, Windows Vista or Windows XP?

The theme of a release is a short phrase, or two, but no more than three, that describes the primary changes in the release. Returning to the example of Excel, a release theme might be pivot tables, or calculation speedup. The theme gives us a way to talk about the release without presenting a five-page spreadsheet. The themes will include many features and tasks, but they will not be the only content in the release.

Gather Candidate Features

The next few steps regarding features are presented as sequential, but they are really part of an iterative process. You will gather candidate features and sometime later will return, add new ones and remove others. It's like the instruction in my grandmother's bread recipe – add flour and knead until it feels like dough.

The candidate features are ones you might include in the release. They might be features that fit with the theme, or features that you must include because you have committed them to customers, or because they are critical in some other way. There will also be a bunch of candidates that are pets of team members and associates. You will not be able to do everything, and each candidate will take effort to review and prioritize, so you need to be a bit ruthless in cutting chaff from the list.

Assess Value, Effort & Risk of Features

Each feature has three parameters.

Value is an assessment of how important the feature is to the product. I usually determine if value is high, medium or low. But the low ones probably didn't make it to the candidate list.

Effort is the estimated work time needed to implement the feature, usually in developer days.

Risk assesses the uncertainty in the estimates. A feature in the challenging quadrant of the Complexity Model will have higher risk than a feature in the detail quadrant. This is a qualitative rather than a quantitative assessment. It's more important to know why the feature is risky than to give it a risk level of six.

Set Release Date & Prioritize Features

If this is a schedule-driven release, set the release date. Then your goal will be, given the specified timeframe, to maximize the value of the features that are in this release. To that end, you need to prioritize the features in roughly the order you want them to be worked on. Use the value, effort and risk assessment to sort the list of candidates. Every release and every developer team are different, so I can't give you a formula to use for the sorting. Sort until it feels like dough.

This prioritized list is similar to the product backlog used in the Scrum methodology.

Set Required Features & Prioritize Additional Features

The goal for a feature-driven release is to complete the required features as early as possible, and to include as much additional value as possible without delaying the required features.

A feature-driven release will have a set of required features. When that set is done, the release can go out. It will also have a set of optional features, because some parts of the team will not be fully consumed implementing the required features. Prioritize those features as described above.

Determine Resource Buckets & Assign Features

A resource bucket is a group of team members who have similar skill sets. You might have three developer buckets, two validation buckets and a documentation bucket.

Next you assign feature effort to each bucket for each feature. If a feature has an effort of 100, you might assign 60 to a developer bucket, 30 to a validation bucket and 10 to the documentation bucket.

The idea is that on average all the people in the bucket will be busy, so you can use the buckets to estimate when all the tasks in the release will be completed. This assumption means we don't have to worry too much about dependencies at this level of planning. The team members will work it out.

Set Release Risk Factor & Bucket Efficiency Factors

To make this work, you need a couple fudge factors.

The Release Risk Factor (RRF) accounts for the fact that requirements will change before the release is out. An RRF of 60% means that we expect that we know 60% of the release content now and that 40% we will find out later.

Each bucket will have a Bucket Efficiency Factor (BEF) that accounts for two things. First, team members have other responsibilities that take up some percentage of their time – things like meetings, bug fixes, vacations, etc. Second, effort estimates are always optimistic. Team members give estimates using a more liberal definition of done. They estimate only the work they can see, but all the rework and hidden work is not included.

When you have worked with your team long enough, you will get a feeling for how much to scale the effort estimate to match reality. I often needed to use a factor of three or more – if the estimate was one week, the completion could be expected in three weeks. A high BEF is not an insult. It usually means that the team member is working on the hardest problems.

Calculate Expected Release Date or Release Content

Now you have all the information you need to calculate the result – the content for a schedule-driven release, or the date for a feature-driven release. I have done the calculation using a complex spreadsheet. I will leave that as an exercise for the reader.

Most likely, the first time through this process, you won't like the answer, so you will go back a few steps, make changes and iterate until you get a reasonable answer.

Determine Milestones

Now you can start defining intermediate milestones to help measure progress toward the release. A milestone acts as a point of focus for the team. It should have clear deliverables and offer a significant level of improvement over the previous milestone.

The milestones depict the high-level dependencies in the release. They are one way you can make sure that high risk tasks are done early, and that infrastructure is completed in time for it to be used effectively. Knowing the sequence of milestones helps the developers make tradeoffs. If the team has the option to take shortcuts to reach milestone A earlier, it's better if they know whether those shortcuts need to be eliminated for milestone B or for Milestone E.

Each resource bucket might be moving toward a different milestone. For example, the pivot table bucket might be moving toward a "Simple Pivot Table" milestone, while the calculation speedup bucket might be moving toward a "Re-architect Function Calculation" milestone.

Milestones are different from the Scrum methodology's sprint, or XP's interval. The sprint is moving toward one or more milestones, but it may require several sprints to reach a milestone.

Early in the release cycle, you may not know enough to define all the milestones. You should always define at least the next two milestones for each bucket. That gives the team enough context to do the current one and to mentally prepare for the next.

Responding to Change

Periodically, you need to review the plan to update the estimates of remaining features, and to evaluate the current estimate of release date or content. You should do this at least at each milestone, and probably more often, like weekly or bi-weekly. You will also need to add and remove features based on changing requirements and new commitments. Once the initial plan is in place, and the spreadsheet that calculates the result, it's easy to make changes.

3.5.11 Specifications

What is a Specification?

A specification is a contract between the implementer and the consumers of that implementation. A specification documents the externally visible features of the software. It does not discuss how to implement the features, although inevitably some implementation decisions will influence the specifications.

Specifications have a few consumers:

- The software developers who are going to implement the capability
- The testing team who are going to validate that the requirements have been met
- The product documentation team who are going to explain to end-users how to use the capabilities.
- The customers or customer advocates who are going to validate the requirements with customers

Specifications Are Not Inherently Evil

Software developers hate to write specs and the consumers hate to read them. They are sometimes necessary, and sometimes create more problems than they solve. Using the Lean principle, "Decide as late as possible," will help you avoid writing problematic specs.

The writing of specifications is the first step on the path that removes degrees of freedom from the development team. This can be good – the move from all possible variations of a requirement like, "simple text format," to one specific text format removes a lot of confusion and makes it possible to implement something quickly and to begin test development. But it can also be bad – a "user control to choose solution heuristics" may lead you to delineate all the known heuristics and keep you from finding a new and better one later.

All of the externally visible features will need to be specified, but you can choose to write the specs in the order that makes the most sense for the project, and you can choose to write loose specs first and to tighten them up later. You can determine the order and the firmness based on the answers to three questions:

- When does someone need this spec in order to do their job?
- How likely is this spec to change as we learn more about the requirements or the implementation? If it's changeable, write a loose spec or wait until the requirement is more solid.
- What is the distance between the developer and the customer of this spec? If the customer sits across the aisle from the developer, the spec can be loose or maybe it's not necessary at all because the two of them can negotiate

changes daily. If the customer is in another building or another country or another company, then the spec needs to be tight.

Characteristics of a Good Spec

Writing tight specifications requires the same mindset as programming – you need to be complete, precise, and cover all the ways that things could go wrong. But you need to do it in a language that looks more like Legalese than C++ or Python. The specification is your contract with the consumer of the spec. When something goes wrong later, the consumer can point to the spec and say, "That's a bug!" Or you can point to the spec and say, "That's how it's supposed to work!" which feels satisfying until the user says, "That's not how I want it to work. Change the spec."

Sample Specification Process

The process I have used for specifications includes the following steps:

- Generate a list of necessary specifications based on the requirements. Since the requirements are likely to change, this list is likely to change. Keep the list small. A specification is only necessary if it's required for someone to do their job.
- Designate an author for each spec and decide on a target timeline for the steps that follow. Deadlines are necessary or the natural process of procrastination will delay specs until they are no longer useful.
- Write the spec.
- Decide who will review the spec. At least one member from every category of stakeholder should be included.
- Send the spec out for review. Some reviewers are good at reading specs and simulating the implications of the spec in their minds to find errors, omissions and loopholes. Most reviewers are not. For critical specs, I strongly recommend holding a spec review meeting. A review meeting makes all reviewers better because it focuses the review into a short time period, and new ideas will arise based on the conversation.
- Incorporate feedback and re-review until convergence has occurred. Convergence is best achieved by consensus, but sometimes convergence by mandate is necessary.

3.5.12   The Definition of 'Done'

When a customer asks the question, "When will it be done?" it implies a definition of the word 'done' that means that software is ready for the customer to use productively, free of bugs and with at least the minimum set of capabilities available.

A software developer's answer to "When will it be done?" is likely to use a very different definition of 'done'. Maybe it means he wrote the code, but hasn't tested it yet, or hasn't integrated it into the system, or he hasn't yet fixed the bugs found by software validation.

When I was a software manager, I insisted that developers use a strict definition of 'done'. But later, when I became a developer again, I quickly found myself reverting to a loose definition, realizing my mistake, and after a quick self-slap across the cheek, fixing my definition. Developers so want 'done' to be easy that they forget about the tedious parts until they see the many flights of stairs ahead.

When planning, it is important to establish a definition of 'done' for each task so that when anyone asks the question, the answers will be consistent with the intention of the questioner. The definition should include:

- completeness goals – establish the subset of the requirements assigned to this task
- quality goals – code coverage, testing coverage, conformance to coding standards and coding process, etc.
- metric goals – if the requirements addressed by the task are parametric, then establish a threshold that must be met

For most tasks you can establish a common standard of done-ness. For coding tasks, maybe it's: coding complete with unit tests that cover at least 85% of the new code and peer review complete. You can also establish common standards for software validation tasks and other tasks.

Some tasks will need a custom standard of done-ness, especially if metrics are involved.

3.5.13 Communicating the Plan

So, you've created your initial plan and your spreadsheet tells you the release date and the content of the release. Whoopee! You know there's uncertainty in those results. When the release is done, it's likely that either the date or the content or both will be different from your initial prediction.

Talking about the plan has three challenges.

- Talking about uncertainty to people who expect absolutes, the black-and-white decision makers
- Avoiding the inevitable second-guessing when people don't like the date or the content
- Communicating changes in the plan

Uncertainty

Your plan has uncertainty. The challenge of uncertainty is that you don't know what it is. What you know is that there is risk, and you've assessed the risk of every feature, but you don't know how that risk affects everything else.

You could hide the uncertainty and surprise everyone later with unpleasant changes to the plan, but that doesn't sound like fun. Or you can communicate the uncertainty when you communicate the plan. Report a probability for each feature that might be included in the release instead of a Boolean in/out. Communicate the schedule with your probable date and a "possibly slipping to ...". Your black-and-white listeners won't like it, but if you're consistent they'll get used to it.

The first reaction to uncertainty from your black-and-white listeners is that you could remove the uncertainty if you worked harder on the plan. No, uncertainty is in the nature of software as curiosity is in the nature of cats.

To quantify the uncertainty, you could enhance your spreadsheet to do all its calculations with statistical distributions instead of numbers, but that's a lot more work than it's worth, and the distributions would be a guess. You could do a simple Monte-Carlo simulation to find the distributions – less work, but probably still not worth it. Instead do a few what-if calculations where you vary the effort of a few of the riskiest features. Then make some guesses.

Please Pull in the Schedule
Part of the game that sales people play while negotiating their target sales for the year is to hide some of the deals that they know about to keep their targets low. It's called sandbagging – building a temporary dam with a reservoir of deals that they can tap into when they need them. The target setters know this is happening, and they try to find the dams and break them down while the sales people try to build them up. As I said, it's a game.

Some of the people you communicate with will assume you are playing the same game, sandbagging to make sure you can meet your plan. So they will try to find the sandbags and remove them.

Sometimes you made errors in your assumptions or calculations, and you can fix it.

More often, I have seen people go through the exercise of tweaking the plan to fit a twelve-week development into an eight-week schedule. Doing so adds new risks and inefficiencies to the plan. Sixteen weeks later, the team is still struggling to finish.

Additional development resources are the thing most likely to help a schedule. But some tasks can't be sped up with more developers – three women can't have a baby in three months. And also, those promised extra developers were also promised to four other late projects and when you need them, they're not available.

Typically, projects have committed developers that are currently working on the project, and promised developers that aren't yet working on the project. When your boss asks, "When will it be done?" you need to give two answers: the answer he wants to hear that includes the promised developers, and the answer he doesn't want to hear that assumes they will never show up. There is plenty of uncertainty in the schedule of a fully staffed project. But there is 100% certainty that the tasks assigned to promised developers don't get done until they show up.

Communicating Changes to the Plan

You've planned for change, just as you're supposed to; and change happened, just as you expected. Now you need to change the plan and communicate the bad news.

What to communicate is clear – the new date and content compared to the old date and content.

When to communicate is a little harder. Minor changes can wait a little. It's easier for the organization if you make several adjustments at once, rather than throw out a new change every couple days.

Big changes need to be communicated as soon as you have confidence in the revised plan. Some people, like your boss, need to know that you're revising the plan even before you have confidence. When you communicate, it's important to be honest about the causes for the change, about the remaining uncertainty, and about what you're doing to reduce risk.

Constant Time to Completion

For those who ask, "When will it be done?" the most frustrating answer is what I call "constant time to completion". When I ask on January 1, you reply February 1. When I ask on February 1, you reply March 1. If I ask again on March 1 and you reply April 1, then it's apparent that an April Fool is running the project. Before I ask the third time, you need to reassess the plan and have an answer that's more than just a date. What's causing the delay? Is there an invention problem? A staffing problem? Changing requirements? What are you doing about it? And what's the real date?

3.6   Control

There's a disaster waiting around every corner. Your job is to prevent disasters, not to recover from them, although you will do plenty of that. So far in this chapter, I have discussed three of the four words that describe a manager's job: Leadership, Organization, and Planning. Now we move on to Control. Control is the way you make sure that all the things that you started with those other aspects of the job get done the way you want, and it's the way you make sure that disasters stay around the corner.

In this section, I discuss

- The four components of a control system.
- The types of control
- Applying the control model to delegation
- Applying the control model to the Software Plan

Two other aspects of control are presented in later chapters, after the prerequisite information has been discussed: Managing the Architecture and Managing the Methodology.

3.6.1   Teenagers Out of Control

When I was in high school, four friends and I dragged a toboggan to the top of the abandoned ski run north of town. Lookout Mountain had closed a couple years earlier and the runs were covered with light brush that was barely covered with snow. Four of us took our places in the toboggan at the top of the steepest run. We tried to plan our route, but only one of us could see. Larry pushed us off, intending to jump into the fifth spot at the back, but he didn't make it. Mark fell out about fifty yards down the hill. The rest of us made it another three hundred yards before we were tossed into the brush. The toboggan plummeted another half mile down the hill and across the abandoned parking lot, until it crashed into woods. A cross-country skier, clearly an expert, slalomed down the hill doing Telemark turns, stopping first to check on Mark, and then the rest of us. When she saw that we were all OK, we accepted her blunt assessment, "That was stupid!" She sped down the hill and we never saw her again. We dusted the snow from our jackets and caps and trudged down the hill to collect the toboggan. Not one of us asked, "Again?"

Let's look at the aspects of control illustrated by this story.

- **The Plan** – To exhibit control, you first need a plan. We tried to make a plan; that was good. Unfortunately, the plan was infeasible.
- **Deviation Measurement** – You need to measure deviations from the plan. Julie, who was in front, could see that we were heading off course, but the rest of us were blind.
- **Feedback Analysis** – You need an analyzer that can transform the measurements into corrective forces that get your closer to the plan. The skier had years of practice in making those transformations. The rest of us should have started a few feet up the bunny hill.
- **Corrective Forces** – You need the ability to apply forces to correct the course. We had never been in a toboggan before, and we had no idea how to steer. Whoops! Even if we knew how to change direction, we had no way to slow down. Double Whoops! The skier, on the other hand, could change both velocity and direction using Telemark turns.

In the rest of this section, we will apply these four components of control – a plan, deviation measurement, feedback analysis, and corrective forces – to some of the software problems you will face.

3.6.2   Types of Control Systems

The control system used by the cross-country skier is a *closed loop* system. She has a plan – ski down the hill to Mark without going too fast. She uses her eyes to measure deviations from her plan. She uses turns to change direction and velocity. Her instincts close the loop by responding to her current position and velocity with turns that change her course.

The toboggan ride was on a *ballistic* trajectory. 'Ballistic' means that you are relying on the laws of physics without active control. Ballistic missiles work because you can calculate a trajectory, knowing that variations in the environment, such as changes in wind direction, will have only a minor effect on the trajectory. Ballistic trajectories seldom work in management.

Another term that you will sometimes hear is *'open loop control'*, where feedback analysis is missing or is too primitive to make the correct transformations; it's 'open loop' because there is no feedback loop.

Let's consider the cruise control in a car, which is a *closed loop* system. The plan is to travel at 65mph. The deviation is the current speed minus 65mph. The throttle is the force that changes speed. The analyzer changes the throttle in response to changes in speed; that's the feedback loop. It's negative feedback because if the deviation is positive, - the current speed is greater than 65mph, it reduces the throttle, a negative change.

You can imagine a simple, open loop cruise control that sets the throttle, but doesn't change it in response to increased speed caused by going downhill. Your actual speed may range from 45mph to 85mph, depending on the steepness of the hill. You can imagine a mediocre engineer trying to fix the problem by measuring the angle of ascent/descent and changing the throttle in response to that measurement. After a lot of tuning to find the right correlation between angle and speed, the angle response factor, it might work better, but it's still an open loop system because it's not measuring the deviation from the plan. (If the mediocre engineer was a software developer, he would probably give the driver the option of changing the angle response factor, which would require three incomprehensible pages in the manual that no driver would ever read.)

A system like the mediocre cruise control is often called a kludge – a system that solves problem X by creating problem Y. Kludges tend to foster more kludges. After finding that angle measurement does not get good enough control, the mediocre engineer will try measuring wind velocity. Unfortunately, kludges are sometimes necessary because either you can't practically measure the deviation from the plan, or you can't directly apply forces that correct the course. When that happens, by all means, implement the kludge, but remember that the solution is a kludge, and continue to search for real solutions.

One of the banes of closed-loop control systems is *control lag*. The skier needs to react immediately to changes in snow conditions, or to bushes or rocks in her path. If her reaction time were five seconds, she could not make it down the mountain. Minimizing control lag is one of the most important things in control systems.

3.6.3 Delegation

Most of what happens in your organization gets done by other people. If you could do it all yourself, your promotion to manager would never have happened. Delegation is the way you get things done through the people in your organization. All those things that your organization does are your responsibility. Ideally, they all get done exactly as you would do them, or better.

> Jack and Jill
> Went up the hill
> To fetch a pail of water.
> Jack fell down
> And broke his crown
> And Jill came tumbling after.

Traditional English nursery rhyme.

You need a large barrel full of water.

When you delegate the project to Jill, you remain responsible for the achieving the goal of that project, but you relinquish responsibility for how the goal is achieved. You own the goal. Jill owns the path to get there. If you try to own both the goal and the path, then Jill is going to feel micromanaged. If Jill owns both the goal and the path, then you have abdicated your responsibility.

One way to delegate is to use ballistic control. That works if you trust Jill as you trust the laws of physics. You can have a short discussion about the project with Jill, and send her on her trajectory. Sometime later the project will be done, and you will have your water.

The open-loop ballistic control sounds optimistic because even Jill can't be trusted completely. A closed-loop control system will work better, so, let's look at the problem of delegation using the four components of control.

3.6.3.1 Plan

First you need to sit down with Jill and make sure that she understands the goal – you need a barrel full of water. Then Jill develops a plan. She can get as much help from you as she needs, but she owns the plan. You need to review the plan and to offer feedback and advice because you need to be confident that the plan will achieve the goal. Jill's plan is to get a big pail and enlist Jack to help carry the water from the spring at the top of the hill to the barrel in your office.

The plan is dynamic. Both the goals and the details of the plan could change as the task proceeds.

3.6.3.2   Measure Deviation from the Plan

The plan should include a way to measure progress. That can be done using milestones with proposed progress and dates, or with periodic reviews.

Once you and Jill have agreed on the plan, schedule the first review, and at each review make sure that the next review is scheduled.

Critical projects need more frequent reviews to minimize control lag in the system. If you review a critical project every month, then it could be a month before you react to a problem.

Jill assures you that the barrel will be full a week from today, so you schedule the first review for tomorrow, when the barrel should be 20% full.

3.6.3.3   Analysis of Deviations

At each review, Jill should report deviations and propose corrective actions. Jack's fall and the ensuing crown-breaking has put her behind. She plans to power on without him and work on the weekend to catch up.

Some of the best corrective actions may be out of her control; for example, she needs Jack's help, but he can no longer fetch water. Your job is to raise concerns and remove barriers. You don't think Jill can fill the barrel in a week by herself. You can suggest that Joe is perfectly fetching. You can suggest that using pails to fetch water is antiquated and that Jill should install a pipeline.

Part of the correction may be a change to the goal, either to ease restrictions implied by the original, or to incorporate new requirements.

In this case, Jill goes off to find Joe and resume fetching. She will report back to you the following day.

3.6.3.4   Corrective Forces

Once you have agreed on corrective actions, Jill needs to incorporate them into her plan and report on their progress at the next review.

All of this should be done with a level of formality that matches the scope of the project. For simple projects, an occasional review at the water cooler is adequate. For big projects, you may want a formal review meeting with presentations and an appropriate amount of quivering.

It turns out that Joe is a great fetcher and also has an extra pail. At the next review, the project is back on track and Jill manages to fill the barrel in plenty of time and spends the weekend nursing Jack, who is much better, thank you.

3.6.4   Managing the Software Plan

In the Planning section of this chapter, I discussed how to build a plan for your software release. At the macro level, managing the plan is the same as managing any other delegation, with periodic reviews and milestone reviews. Deviations from the plan are usually tasks and features that are taking longer to complete than expected, or features that aren't adequately meeting the requirements, or changes in the requirements that require additional work.

The hardest part is to come up with the corrective forces when something goes wrong. There just aren't that many good options. Here are a few of them:

- Add staff or re-assign staff within the project to get the right people working on the right problems
- Drop features from the release, or simplify planned features
- Slip the schedule
- Rearchitect, refactor or rewrite sections of the code

Periodic project reviews work on the macro level, but you can't control a complex software project at the micro level with only periodic reviews. There is so much going on that you can't review everything. Instead, you need to set up an environment where coding can't fail – or at least has a low probability of failure. Think of it as setting up laws of physics so that coding can happen as a sequence of ballistic coding tasks. Here are some of the things you can do to ensure high quality code changes, and to minimize control lag between a coding change and feedback to the developer.

- Coding standards – especially if the standards are checked for all coding changes
- Code reviews or pair programming – at least two pairs of eyes look at all coding changes
- Unit test coverage requirements – all code needs to be tested by developers
- Continuous integration and testing – all code changes need to integrate with the complete product and to be validated against a high coverage test suite
- Architecture parameter validation – automated and manual validation that the integrity of the architecture is being maintained

All of the above are discussed in the Common Processes chapter. Review your methodology periodically to make sure it's meeting the needs of the team. Add new requirements and processes if they will help, but avoid the temptation to change the methodology to address every abomination that ever happened. If the methodology becomes too unwieldy, developers will find a way to avoid it.

3.7   *Non-Sequitur* – Managing Remote Sites

Software teams used to sit together in a corner of one floor of a building. That all changed when the internet came of age around 2000. Cheap global communications started to spread teams, first across town, then across the country and finally around the world. I know of Silicon Valley-based companies with remote development teams in Canada, France, Germany, Russia, Romania, Armenia, Egypt, India, Chile and China and Australia. Most of us will never again work in a co-located group.

3.7.1   Setting Up My First Remote Site

In 1999, I was VP of engineering, and hiring was so difficult in Silicon Valley (as it is today) that we decided to expand into India. We had no idea how to get started. We had no idea what we'd find when we got there. But we had to start. The mistakes we made can provide lessons for managing remote sites.

We talked to a few people who offered to set up our India office. They all seemed like charlatans – full of talk, devoid of technical competence, but tuned in to the unsavory workings of the Indian culture and government. We tried to find senior Indian technologists in our field, but they were already employed by our competitors. Then Jim, a single American employee, living on a boat moored in the San Francisco Bay and looking for adventure, volunteered to go to India and set up our site.

Jim moved to Bangalore and began the process of establishing our Indian subsidiary and finding office space. It soon became clear why we needed the charlatans. The Indian government officials placed hoops for us to jump through, then pulled them away and replaced them with closed doors. Eventually Jim, dutifully complying with the Foreign Corrupt Practices Act – a big disappointment to the needy officials, got through all the hoops and doors and had an Indian corporation and an office.

Now he needed to hire a team. No one with any standing wanted to work for an American startup with an American managing director. HP, IBM and Cisco had status. We had none. He could hire fresh graduates, but not from the most prestigious schools. He hired who we could and started to train them to support and test the product.

After about a year, Jim was going nuts. The process of starting the office had strained his psyche and he was ready to go home. I went to India on my first trip to interview candidates for the managing director, who would succeed Jim and carry on the group. We narrowed it down to two candidates: a dynamic, ambitious woman, and a senior manager from India's traditional technology industry. I leaned toward the woman, but was persuaded that the senior manager would offer more stability and respect for the organization. In retrospect, it was probably the right decision because the woman, who is now the managing director for the Indian subsidiary of a major American company, would have soon felt limited by the prospects of this position. The director we hired stayed in the position for over ten years.

The new director continued to have trouble hiring. Training the staff was slow and tedious. The team made some contributions, but it was not the flood of resources we had hoped for. We didn't make much progress until a few years later, when an Indian employee in the States decided to return home to work in India, and joined the team. With a technology leader in the group, we were able to hire and train more technologists. Finally, about ten years after its inception, the Indian team was contributing to product development.

3.7.2 Keys for Success

Since that time, I have worked with several other remote sites that worked a lot better than the early days of the first site. Here are the things that I believe are critical for a successful remote site.

Note that this section is written from a USA-centric viewpoint. Please feel free to translate to your own X-centric view.

Local Knowledge
You can't drop an ugly American (sorry, Jim) into foreign territory and expect him to behave like James Bond. Maybe an American who has had a few years' experience with the culture could succeed, but the best chance of success is to have a native on your side. An American has too much to learn and has to deal with the natural xenophobia of potential partners and employees.

Charter
It may not be evident from the story, but a big problem was that we didn't know what we wanted to achieve in India. A remote site needs a clear charter with clear boundaries. The charter gives them a purpose, making it easier to decide who to hire and to convince them to join. The boundaries help to minimize the need for communication, which is the biggest challenge in keeping the remote site productive.

Technical Leadership
You can't hire or train people without technical leadership. You can rotate American experts through the site until the staff at the hotel knows them by name, but until the site has local technical leadership, you won't make progress. Finding that leader is hard, but hiring anyone else without the leader is pointless.

Local Management
As the remote organization evolved, sometimes we would have Indian employees report directly to a manager in the States. That can work for senior employees, but never for junior employees. They need someone local that can watch over them and help them along. Even the senior employees need a local manager who understands

the local policies like vacations and holidays, and who can represent them in local political battles like office space.

Communication

Communication is by far the biggest challenge to making a remote site successful. You need to overcome the barriers of language, time zones and data bandwidth.

Americans forget that most of the world does not speak English. Many of the problems I've seen occur after someone at the remote site misinterpreted instructions given in English. It's important to verify not only the receipt of the message, but also the understanding of the message.

Often the time difference between sites is eight hours or more. That leaves a small window of times when interactive communication can happen. If you have three sites, there's often no good time for a meeting. That means that most communication will be through email and written documents. Both sides of an email exchange need to be very careful that the messages are clear and complete. If a clarification is needed, that means a delay of at least a full day.

Data bandwidth is much less of a problem than it was twenty years ago, but it still creates a barrier. You can't depend on copying large amounts of data instantaneously, like you can with the person sitting across the aisle from you. You will need to put processes in place to transfer key data periodically, and you may have to duplicate large portions of your infrastructure to make the remote site productive. For example, we made sure that software builds happened simultaneously in India and the States, with much of the testing framework also duplicated.

Control

Closed loop control systems that operate between remote sites will be unstable because of control lag. The full-day delay of an email/reply exchange is too long for most things you want to control. If you can get the remote team to the point that you can trust them like the laws of physics, then you can use ballistic control for most tasks, and only close the loop periodically.

Achieving that level of trust will take time, and you will see a lot of launches that miss the target. Bringing up a remote site requires a lot of trips from the States to the remote site. Those trips should include people from all the roles in your organization. Use those trips to plan and to coordinate activities. But mostly use those trips to train them on how you do software development.

By the time you've established the required trust level, you will have developed processes for how to launch ballistic projects. These processes need explicit documentation because they are the way that the organization will survive beyond the current group of employees.

3.8 Key Concepts

3.8.1 Leadership

The Five Traits of Leadership
- Intelligence – competence in writing software, or some related discipline
- Trustworthiness – establish trust with your team. Broken trust is difficult to repair.
- Humaneness – remember that your team members are people first, and coding resources second
- Courage – show courage by making tough decisions when they are needed and by sticking up for your team when they need you
- Sternness – Do not let bad behavior continue.

Vision
- A vision has three components – a problem statement, a picture of the future, and a talisman to provide hope.
- Communicate the vision until it permeates your team.
- Tie your vision to the greater vision of the whole organization.
- Recognize when the seeds of destruction of your vision have taken root, and adapt the vision to keep it healthy.

Lean Thinking
- Lean thinking is a way of avoiding and eliminating waste.
- Waste is anything that doesn't provide value to the customer, including partially done work, unnecessary processes, extra features, task switching, waiting, motion and bugs.
- Lean thinking depends on seven principles: eliminate waste, amplify learning, decide as late as possible, deliver as fast as possible, empower the team, build integrity in, and see the whole.

Decision Making
- Determine if you need a black-and-white decision, or a shades-of-gray decision.
- Establish the decision authority for each member of your team for each type of decision.
- In the spirit of Lean, decide as late as practical.
- Build a decision-making ethos into the culture of your team.

3.8.2 Organization

Understanding Your Team
- Understand the complexity limit and trend of each of your team members.
- Software developers are not fungible. Each developer has unique skills and habits.

- Adding more staff to a project can often decrease overall productivity. If a developer always decreases productivity on every assigned project, then that developer is a negative productivity generator.
- Some people are organizational poison. They hurt the productivity and morale of the organization. Identify these people early and remove them.
- No one is indispensable.
- 10x developers do exist.

Managerial Courage
- Managers make tradeoffs.
- Sometimes short-term suffering inhibits managers from making tough decisions.
- Always make decisions for the Greater Good of the organization, looking at the long-term benefits, not the short-term costs.

Building a Team
- Classify job openings by bandwidth or capability. Most of the time, capability is more important than bandwidth.
- The job description is a guide for interviewers, and an advertisement for candidates.
- A common interview team can compare candidates.
- Always treat candidates with respect, and recognize that a candidates time scale is usually tighter than yours.
- Do a good job of screening candidates to avoid wasting time on failed interviews.
- The interview is to get information about the candidate, and to present a positive impression to the candidate.
- Make timely hiring decisions. If in doubt, say no.

3.8.3   Planning

What is a Plan?
- A plan is a set of dependent tasks that converge toward a set of milestones.
- A plan needs to answer three questions:
  - When will it be done?
  - What will it contain?
  - What do I do next?
- A plan needs to maximize productivity while minimizing risk.
- If a difficult change has only internal benefit, you will need to work hard to get commitment from your management.
- The software uncertainty principle explains the tradeoff among quality, content and schedule. Since quality is a requirement, the principle reduces to a content vs. schedule tradeoff, leading to content-driven releases and schedule-driven releases.

- Establish a common definition of done for all development tasks, and augment it with additional criteria for some tasks.

Types of Plans
- A roadmap is a high-level story of how the system will evolve.
- Tailor the roadmap to the audience. Only show committed features to customers; funded features to management; and everything to the project team.
- Planning horizons need to match the life-cycle phase of the project. Early development has a very short horizon. As the product matures, the horizon gets longer.
- Detail plans lay out the tasks, task assignments and task dependencies; they are impractical for software development because so much is unknown and changing.
- You need a semi-detail plan to answer the planning questions.

Specifications
- A specification is a contract between the implementer and the consumers of that implementation.
- Write only specifications that are necessary, and, in the spirit of Lean, write it as late as practical or keep it loose.

3.8.4   Control

Types of Control Systems
- Closed-loop systems have these four components:
  o The plan
  o Deviation measurement
  o Feedback analysis
  o Corrective forces
- Ballistic control depends on predictability like the laws of physics.
- Open-loop control systems are sometimes necessary when one or more of the closed-loop components is not practical.
- Control lag can make closed-loop control systems unstable.

Delegation
- Delegation is necessary, but you retain responsibility for the outcome.
- Ensure a positive outcome by monitoring measurement, analysis and the plan.

Managing the Software Plan
- Manage the software plan as a series of ballistic tasks.
- Use closed-loop components on a macro level.
- Ensure integrity of ballistic tasks with common processes.

3.8.5   Managing Remote Sites

Keys for Success

- Knowledge of the local culture is essential.
- A remote site needs a clear charter.
- Seed the remote site team with technical leadership.
- Most remote team members need local management.
- Effective communication is the biggest factor for success. Confirm both the receipt and the understanding of messages.

4 THE ROLE OF THE SOFTWARE DEVELOPER

By the time that you landed your first software developer job, you thought that you had a pretty good idea what that job would entail. You would write code. You would create interesting architectures. You would solve challenging problems in ways that no one dreamed of. Striving for technical excellence and developing high-quality software were the primary attractions of software development as your chosen career.

It didn't take long, however, before you found that you were wrong. You fix other people's bugs. You struggle to fit your new code into the complex framework of an architecture that has evolved through generations of developers. You spend almost no time on challenging problems, but instead work mostly on plumbing – moving stuff from one place to another while contorting to fit into a space expressly designed to be inaccessible.

You found that the job of a software developer is only partly about writing code. You need to deal with people. Your boss demands more than you can deliver. Customers insist on new features that they can't possibly use. Your peers change your code in ways that make it unrecognizable. You argue with them for hours about how to do a ten-minute task. Being a productive member of a team is an important part of the role of a software developer.

The very existence of your job depends on the continued success of your employer. It's in your best interest to do things that assure that success. Your interactions with customers are essential to success, and improving your understanding of customers can have a big impact.

In this chapter, I will try to explain how the Geodesic Philosophy shapes the role of the software developer.

4.1 *Non-Sequitur* – Zen in the Art of Programming

I am a supplicant in the cult of software that has millions of proselytes who worship at the keyboard. Some are members of the congregation, happy to leave it at the office at the end of the day. Others are priests, delivering sermons full of shoulds and should-nots, leading the congregation to better software in their own dogmatic way. Still others are the monks, whose lives are dedicated to finding the true path to software enlightenment.

The cult lacks a great prophet like Buddha or Jesus or Muhammad. No single prophet can hope to explain the art of programming. We learn from the collective wisdom of

121

the cult. Great ideas become part of the credo and then fall aside when better ideas come along, leaving a few priests still ranting about the old ideas.

The cult of software is most like Eastern religions of Taoism and Zen Buddhism, with a focus on awareness of the whole as more than its parts, with intense periods of meditation, and with constant resolution of paradox. In the following, I present a few thoughts inspired by Eastern religion.

The Whole is Greater Than Its Parts

While each module of the architecture can stand on its own, the system needs each module to perform its function, and without the function, the system is not.

Every team member contributes to the system, but the system is bigger than the team. No team member can know the whole, but the whole comes from the efforts of the team. Complexity, vulnerability, opacity, rigidity and chaos mean nothing to the system. The system just is. The team seeks to understand the system, to overcome the Yin, and to achieve the Yang: simplicity, reliability, clarity, flexibility and predictability.

Software is Both a Verb and a Noun

Software does and software is. We think of software as a noun, but we use software as a verb. Even the legal underpinnings of software grant a license to use the software, not to own it.

The dichotomy between verb and noun trickles down to the implementation. The duality between functional programming and object-oriented programming focuses on whether the function or the data should be the organizing principle. In practice, neither focus works without the other, software is both function and data, just like an electron is both particle and wave, and a human is both spirit and body.

Everything is Connected

All the modules in the system affect all the other modules. Everything that happens during software execution can affect everything that happens later. This is why it is so difficult to make software work perfectly. A small error can lurk in the background and raise its head in an unrelated place. A complex software system defies comprehension.

When the Student is Ready, the Master Will Appear

Great programmers learn from great programmers; great managers learn from great managers. But you can't learn until you are ready. I can't push knowledge into your head; you must pull. When you are ready to learn a lesson, you will find the master to teach you. The master might be a senior co-worker, or an intern who has a new perspective, or a bad programmer whose mistakes are so egregious that you learn a new way to fix problems. Be open to learning and you will find a master.

Programming is Meditation

When programming, I spend hours staring at a screen, pondering the problem of the day. I search for serenity and insight and with them come solutions. Solutions appear from nowhere at exactly the moment I need them. I fall so deeply into concentration that I leave the office behind and I no longer hear the buzz of my co-workers. When interrupted, I reluctantly return to the office world, stashing at my meditative state in a corner of my mind, hoping I can find it again because although programming is not nirvana, it's close.

Divergent Paths Lead to the Same Place

> Yes, there are two paths you can go by
> But in the long run
> There's still time to change the road you're on

Led Zeppelin – Stairway to Heaven

Although *Stairway to Heaven* was probably inspired more by Celtic mysticism than by Eastern philosophy, the theme of divergent paths that lead to the same place is everywhere in software and in Eastern philosophy. When programming, each decision leads to more decisions that eventually lead to something that does the right thing. But a completely different decision path could lead to the same place. Sometimes those decisions lead into a cave with no exit, requiring a change in road and a restart. There is no decision so good you can't change it.

I am the Program and the Program is Me

I write software because I love both the act of writing software, and the art. The software must do *Something* specific, but *How* it does it is completely up to me. I get satisfaction from the *Something*, and satisfaction from the *How*. In the aesthetics of software development, form begets function. From the integration of form and function, I feel a mystical oneness between software and self. I am the program, and the program is me. I will die, but the program will carry on, one slender thread in the fabric of the universe.

4.2   Technical Excellence

> Developers strive for the highest level of technical excellence and assume responsibility for quality.

A Principle of the Geodesic Manifesto

The Geodesic Philosophy depends on developers who have pride in the software they create. At the end of the day, they look back at what they created and believe they could not have done better. But the next day, they can look at it again and find ways to break it, and then find ways to improve it. Great software development requires constant vigilance, constant searching for problems, and immediate fixes.

In the <u>Quality</u> chapter, I make it clear that software developers are responsible for quality because no one else can change it. You need to actively seek bugs and fix them. You need to fix the root causes that lead to bugs. You need to improve the functionality of the system so that users will say, "It just works!"

Great developers achieve technical excellence by using an aesthetic sense to guide them as they code, but most can explain only small parts of that aesthetic. If you ask, they will start to recite from the coding standards – "Functions should be no longer than thirty lines" – "Variable names should be expressive, but short enough to type quickly." I agree that those are important, but the substance of what you write is more important than its form.

Try to deepen your understanding of your aesthetics. When you come across some code that needs to improve, try to understand why. Here are a few ways to look at the problem that can help you.

The five traits of the <u>Yin-Yang Model</u> provide a good basis to evaluate what you have written. You must fight **complexity** by finding simpler ways to solve problems, by eliminating code that's no longer useful, and by maintaining a robust architecture. You must fight **rigidity** by creating code that's easy to extend, fight **opacity** with extensive diagnostics, fight **chaos** by using predictable algorithms, fight **vulnerability** by early and deep testing.

But those five traits are not enough; the suitability of what you write also drives your aesthetics. If execution time is critical for your application, then never allow what you write to be a performance problem. If you write user interfaces, keep them intuitive and consistent. Whatever is important for the software you create, do it well.

Another dimension to your aesthetics can come from the <u>Lean</u> principles. I have filled in some ideas for each principle based on my own aesthetics, but you should add your own.

- **Eliminate waste** – Remove dead code. Be frugal with memory usage and execution time. Review code thoroughly to avoid bugs.
- **Amplify learning** – Measure everything that's important. Add diagnostics to gather better information. Build quick prototypes to help you understand the problem.
- **Decide as late as possible** – Parameterize code so you can commit the parameters after you have measured. Build flexibility into your architecture.
- **Deliver as fast as possible** – Build quick prototypes. Spend time anticipating the trend of future requirements, but not the details. Keep incremental tasks small to improve agility.

- **Build integrity in** – Test. Test. Test. Review code for bugs as well as suitability. Keep architectures modular with clean dependencies to avoid unexpected interactions.
- **See the whole** – Develop software in the context of an architect and a high-level plan. Use exploratory testing to understand the system.
- **Empower the team** – Be a good team member. Which leads us to…

4.3   Teamwork

> - We build synergistic teams that improve the performance of every individual.
> - We encourage frequent and open communication among team members.

Principles of the Geodesic Manifesto

The Geodesic Philosophy depends on development teams that work nearly independently with little direction from management. A vision to get things started, and an occasional course correction should be all that's needed.

In the section Managing the Software Plan, I say to managers, "There is so much going on that you can't review everything. Instead, you need to set up an environment where coding can't fail – or at least has a low probability of failure. Think of it as setting up laws of physics so that coding can happen as a sequence of ballistic coding tasks." Before there's a self-organizing team, your manager needs to trust you like the laws of physics. You need to earn that trust and then maintain it through the inevitable ups and downs of development.

4.3.1   Achieving Synergy

While trust is necessary for the formation of a self-organizing team, it's not enough to achieve the synergy we need to become a super-team that "improves the performance of every individual." Synergy means that the whole is greater than the sum of the parts. Achieving synergy requires the right behavior from all the members of the team.

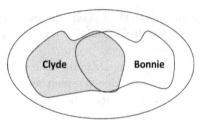

Initial Capabilities of Bonnie and Clyde

Let's take a quick (and simplified) look at how synergy happens by using a Venn diagram. At the start of the project, both Bonnie and Clyde have skills with some overlap, but not the complete set of skills (the large oval) that are needed to complete the project. Eventually, the union of the skills of Bonnie and Clyde need to grow to contain the green oval. The overlap between Bonnie and Clyde's skillset is good, because it means that for some tasks, either Bonnie or Clyde can do them without needing to learn anything new. But that's not synergy.

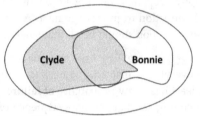

After Bonnie Teaches Clyde

Suppose that Bonnie teaches Clyde one of her skills. The overlap is bigger, and that's good, but it's still not synergy.

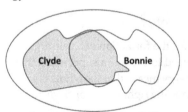

Bonnie Learns a New Skill

Now suppose that Bonnie learns a new skill needed for the project. Again, that's good, but it's not synergy.

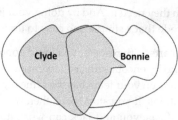

Bonnie and Clyde Achieve Synergy

Now Bonnie encounters a new problem and she's stumped. She gets together with Clyde and they discuss the problem. Initially, Clyde is also stumped. Then he comes up with half an idea and sketches it on the white board. Bonnie changes part of it and adds to it. They go on like this for a few minutes – proposing, rejecting, improving – until they are certain that the white board sketch will work in the code. Bonnie implements it and it works. That's synergy. Together they found a solution that neither could have found alone.

4.3.2   Synergistic-Team Values

Methodology frameworks like Scrum and XP try to achieve synergy with processes that encourage synergy. Scrum's daily meeting gives team members the opportunity to identify tasks where synergy might be achieved. XP's mandate of pair programming encourages the kind of problem-solving that Bonnie and Clyde used.

But the processes alone are not enough. Achieving synergy every day in big teams requires everyone on that team to share a common set of values. Both Scrum and XP advocate a set of values to guide team members on how to be a productive member of a team. The Geodesic Philosophy has its own set of values to make teams successful.

- Mutual Success
- Mutual Ownership
- Common Understanding
- Continuous Improvement

Mutual Success

Everyone on the team contributes to the success of everyone else on the team. Saying that no one succeeds unless everyone succeeds sounds like a Soviet value. To make this an American value, let's say that your success will be greater if everyone else also succeeds. Software development is not a zero-sum game. If the product of your efforts is better, then there will be more recognition for the whole team, bigger raise budgets, and new opportunities.

Your goal then is to help make everyone on the team successful, from the 10x developer to the architect to the new college hire who is struggling to find the cafeteria. You do

127

that by helping them when they need it. And by doing your job in ways that make their jobs easier – like writing code that's simple and easy to understand.

Making others successful starts with respect. You build good working relationships by fostering mutual respect and by encouraging collaboration. Mutual respect begins with the assumption that everyone on your team has the same high-level goals and that they are acting with good intentions. If you start there, then when you have a conflict with Jack, and there *will* be conflicts, you and Jack can work it out and come to the right conclusion.

Strive to resolve conflicts with patience and kindness and open, constructive feedback. Listen to Jack and work to understand his views. Adopt the good points of his ideas and modify yours. Eventually, you will both come to a shared conclusion that's better than where either of you started.

Mutual success implies that you need to help your co-workers improve. That doesn't mean that you need to point out every error they ever make. You help them improve through your leadership and by your example.

If you are a senior developer, then review the Leadership section above. All the points there apply to senior developers as well as managers. It's harder for developers because you don't have the scepter of authority to affirm your leadership. You assert your leadership by being right more often than others, by knowing more than others, by insisting on high standards for everything done by you and the others around you, by listening to everyone and acknowledging their contributions.

One of the most important leadership roles for a senior developer is mentorship. Pick one or two promising junior developers, and assume an informal mentorship role with them. Understand what problems they face, both technical and organizational, and help them work through those problems. Spend time with them at the keyboard, guiding them around the code base. Help them understand the nuances that are only documented through folklore. Teach them the ethos for how to make architectural decisions. When they come to you for help, put your work aside and make them first on your priority list. If you can't help them with a particular problem, then guide them to the people who can help and follow through to make sure that the help they need is delivered.

If everyone on the team shares the value of mutual success, then they want you to succeed as much as you want them to succeed. Don't be afraid to ask for help. Asking for help is not a sign of weakness. If you are stuck on a problem, or if you're considering two alternative approaches, find someone to talk with. Get their ideas. Maybe together you can find a third approach that's better.

Mutual Ownership

Mutual ownership is both a top-down and bottom-up concept. From the top, everyone on the team owns the success of the project, as exemplified by the Mutual Success value. From the bottom, everyone owns all the details that are necessary for that success.

No one owns a line of code – everyone owns all the lines. Once you have committed code to the repository, it's fair game for anyone to change, for better or for worse. The best way to ensure that those changes are for better is to write code that's easy to understand and fits well within the framework of the system architecture.

You own the fun parts of the project and the tedious parts. Take pride in whatever you do. If today's task is shoveling snow, do the best snow shoveling you can. When you are done, admire the ice-free concrete and the smooth white vertical walls of the snow banks. Then hope that spring brings you more projects with a better climate.

Common Understanding

Everyone on the team should have a shared understanding of the goals of the project, the plan for meeting those goals, and the status of the plan. The only way this happens is with frequent and open communication among the team members.

Frequent means that any time that anything changes, communication should start. Scrum's famous daily meeting is one way to ensure frequent communication, but it's not the only way. Less formal means are often more effective. Conversations in the break room or at lunch can bring clarity to complex issues. More formal means may sometimes be necessary. Writing a spec, or a status email or a page on your project's wiki can solidify concepts and make them part of the legacy of the project.

Open means that you communicate the bad as well as the good. If an experiment didn't work out the way you hoped, or if you're behind schedule, you need to let the team know. The Mutual Success value will get you the help you need. The team can only respond to adversity if they are fully informed.

Open also means that you listen to (or read) the communication of others in the same way you hope they listen to yours. One of my most common frustrations when I was a developer was writing a carefully crafted email delineating three points, and finding that all ten people on the distribution list stopped after the first point. There's a lot of stuff in your inbox. Make sure that the stuff from your team members has high priority.

Continuous Improvement

The Geodesic Philosophy is built around the continuous improvement loop – measure, analyze, improve. Everything is subject to improvement: the code, the processes, the plan, lunch.

If the thing you're trying to change has an objective metric, then it's clear what to do. Measure; analyze; implement; and measure again. If the new measurement isn't better, then try again.

If the thing you're trying to implement can only be evaluated subjectively, then it's harder to know if you improved. That's where the shared ethos, the final pillar of the Geodesic Manifesto, becomes important. The ethos attempts to standardize how the team evaluates subjective ideas. It helps you decompose abstract ideas into components that you can measure more objectively, just as "Being a Good Team Member" breaks down into the four values of Mutual Success, Mutual Ownership, Common Understanding and Continuous Improvement.

Continuously improve the ethos. Whether it's written down or shared through folklore, the way your team makes decisions will have a huge impact on the team's ability to succeed. The first step in improving the ethos is to understand it. Recognize that the ethos is multi-dimensional – how you make decisions about architecture is different from how you make decisions about the priorities of requirements. This book is full of lists, like this good-team-member values list, that can help frame the ethos discussion in your team. Use my lists or create your own, but make the whole team aware that there is an ethos that needs to evolve with the team.

4.3.3 *Non-Sequitur* – Becoming Dispensable

As a senior developer, your legacy is your enemy. You are the indispensable expert in your domain, but the constant bombardment of requests to improve what you've done keeps you from doing anything new. The team's perception of your indispensability keeps those requests coming. Your sense of duty keeps you making those improvements. On one hand you feel good about being an indispensable expert, but on the other hand your spirit is yearning to break free and to do new things. You have fallen into the Myth of Indispensability trap.

Some developers work hard to create the perception of indispensability because they equate it with job security. And then when their secure job becomes miserable, they jump ship because it's the only way they can imagine escaping it. A new job is not the only hope. You are not truly indispensable. You can become dispensable instead.

Your manager, Mandy, read the start of this section and laughed, knowing that none of her team members could work through the process of becoming dispensable. She was right; you need her help to do it. So, long before the misery of indispensability sets in, you need to enlist her help to set you free.

To become dispensable, you first need to convince yourself. Imagine if you left the team, how it would heal. All those unique things you do would be replaced by unique things that others do. All the knowledge you have would be spread around to the remaining team members. Maybe you can see that your legacy will live on and prosper with new eyes looking at it. Maybe you can see that your legacy will be better without you. Let's call this the "minus-you future".

Now that you're mentally free, start working to make the minus-you future happen. Find other developers and teach them your code. Some will be anxious to learn because your old stuff is new stuff to them. Encourage them to do those unique things you do. Start distributing the requests. Soon you will feel the burden of indispensability start to lift. The people who always came to you with their problems will start going to the others. You will still be the expert, but not the beast of burden.

Now you can start that new project. Becoming dispensable is the best thing you can do for yourself and for your team.

4.4   Customer Interaction

> • We have frequent interaction with customers and users.
> • Developers must learn to think like their customers.

Principles of the Geodesic Manifesto

Whereas you have obligations to customers, they don't have obligations to you. If they are successful in using your product, they will continue to use it. If the product does not deliver the success they expect, then at some point, they will reach a threshold of pain and annoyance that will cause them to switch to an alternative solution. You may know about the switch in time to react and fix the problems, but often the switch will happen silently and you will only know much later when an expected revenue event doesn't happen.

To avoid this, your team must continually interact with customers, getting their feedback and their desires for how to improve the product. As a developer, you will only rarely talk directly to a customer, and when you do, often it will because the customer is having a problem with your part of the software, and a discussion of potential new features would not be appropriate.

So how do you get customer feedback? The next best thing to getting it directly from customers is to get it from the people that talk with customers every day. I call them your Customer Advocates. They will have different titles in every organization, but you will know who they are. Part of their job is to synthesize what they hear from customers and be available to you to discuss ideas for how to improve the product.

4.4.1 Think Like a Customer

The Geodesic Manifesto includes this phrase: "Developers must learn to think like their customers." That phrase was inspired by the phrase, "Think like a fish," from a keynote address I heard a few years ago. Joe Costello, former CEO of Cadence Design Systems, Inc., told this story of learning to fish, which I paraphrase below. You can see the video of his 2006 Design Automation Conference keynote, "iPod or Iridium - Which One Are You Going to Be?" here:

https://youtu.be/eWpKL8fung0.

The fish story starts at about 26:30, but it's worthwhile to spend an hour to watch the whole video because he says a lot of what I'm trying to say much better, and with more enthusiasm, than I do.

> When Joe was a grad student at Berkeley, he went fishing with his lab partner Ned and Ned's brother Neil. They drove up north from Berkeley to a river that was crowded with fishermen who were catching nothing. Neil disappeared upstream and returned in twenty minutes with a stringer of ten fish.
>
> "How did you do that?" Joe asked. "No one is catching anything. Can you teach me?"
>
> "I'll show you," Neil said and took them upstream. After following Neil's instructions, within twenty minutes Joe and Ned also had a stringer full of fish.
>
> "So what is the secret?" Joe asked. "What lets you catch fish when no one else can?"
>
> "Joe," Neil said, "it's really simple. You gotta think like a fish."
>
> When Neil went to a stream, he studied fish. He tried to answer a lot of questions. What type of fish was he after? What kinds of things did they eat during this part of the year? Did they like fast water or slow water? Sunshine or shade? "Pretend you're a fish," Neil said. "You're in the water, looking up? What do you see? What food is falling in the creek?" Neil crawled around in the bushes and found bugs and grubs. "Joe," he said, holding up a bug, "your lure's gotta look like that!"

Paraphrased from Joe Costello, "iPod or Iridium - Which One Are You Going to Be?", DAC 2006

Neil had mastered the art of thinking like a fish. That was why he was catching fish when no one else could.

As a software developer, you make a lot of decisions every day. How you make those decisions can have far-reaching impacts on the product and the customers. You can't ask your boss about every decision, so you need a framework, or an ethos, for making them. You can try to go back to the requirements, but the requirements are never complete. You need to make good decisions with incomplete and ambiguous requirements. Just as Neil learned to think like a fish, your job is to think like a customer.

Create an imaginary customer and give your customer a name – Dawn. Ask a lot of questions of your customer representatives to understand Dawn. Why is Dawn using this software? What alternatives does she have? How does she learn to use it? Does she read the manual, or use online help, or just flail around until something works? What information does she expect from the software? How can you make her job easier? Once you understand Dawn, you can become Dawn while you code. You can ask yourself over and over, "What would Dawn want?"

Maybe you need another user – Ron – who has a different personality and different needs. You might need a whole cast of imaginary friends that you can ask about what you're doing.

The user stories common in Agile methodologies are an attempt to help you think like a customer. They help you translate requirements into code, and give you a way to evaluate that code. They are a great tool, but they can never be complete. If you can think like a customer, you can create your own user stories on the fly as you need them.

You also need to think like your competitors. If I were Lucifer, how would I get Dawn to come to the dark side? How do you make sure that Dawn has no reason to look at alternatives?

All those questions you asked as you were getting to know Dawn and Lucifer have answers that change over time. Dawn might have new alternatives. Lucifer might have new strategies. Dawn might learn in a different way now that the user interface is more intuitive. Thinking like a customer or competitor means changing how you think as you get new information.

4.4.2 *Non-Sequitur* – The Tyranny of the Customer

The customer is king. Bernie Aronson, my boss and CEO for most of my time at Synplicity, would stop me at this point. "No," he would say, "the customer is God." He taught us to do everything we can to get a new customer, and everything we can to keep an old customer. Customers pay the bills. Customers are the reason we get paid to do the things we love.

There is enough written about how important customers are for your business, and how to listen to them, and learn from them, and sell to them. I'm not going to add to that bibliography. In this short section, I ask you to temporarily suspend your preconceived notions about the omni-portance of the customer, so that I can explain why customers are evil.

Customers do not have your best interests at heart. They fill their hearts with their own best interests, which are often antithetical to yours. At the most obvious, they want lower prices while you want higher prices. But more subtly, they want more value for the money they pay. If you were selling door handles, this wouldn't be an issue. If customers want locks on their door handles, they need to buy the more expensive version. It's obvious that the lock-able door handle costs more to manufacture, so they expect to pay more. But in software, if a feature is missing, customers know that it's just a matter of programming to add it, and once the feature is available, it doesn't cost you more to provide it. The customer will argue that by selling a virtual door handle product, that you've already implied the existence of a virtual lock, and that they have already paid for it. Indeed, since they haven't had the benefit of that lock, they deserve a price reduction for their pain and suffering. And by the principle that the customer is God, you will give them both the lock and the price, and hope to make it up by selling your virtual door handle to a new group of customers who will only buy if you provide a lock.

As long as customers are driving you to improve your product in a way that benefits lots of other customers, your efforts to improve the product are good for them and good for you. But when customers drive you to improve your product in a way that only one customer can use, then they are beginning to destroy you by increasing the entropy in your system.

Here's how it happens. Your product has a limitation. Maybe it's a bug. Maybe it's a requirement that you didn't get right or haven't completed yet. That limitation affects customer A and customer B. You can fix the limitation in a generally useful way in six months, but neither A nor B can wait that long. Customer A proposes a workaround that needs you to implement hack X. Customer B's workaround needs hack Y. You try to get B to use hack X, but they won't do it. Nor will A use hack Y. So, you quickly implement both hacks, X and Y, with the intention that they are temporary hidden features that you will remove as soon as the general solution is available. Customers A and B proceed to integrate their respective hacks into their methodology and they stop complaining about the limitation.

Six months pass and you have fixed the limitation in the most general way. The solution is beautiful. It completely removes the need for hacks X and Y. It can do so much more and is so much easier to use that you go back to customers A and B to tell them they can stop using hacks X and Y and move to the new solution. Customer A says they can't stop using hack X. It's an integral part of their methodology now. They've written five thousand lines of Perl scripts to make it work and they can't risk changing. Customer B says they can't stop using hack Y. They're using it not just for the original limitation, but also for several other limitations that they didn't bother to tell you about because they have worked around them with hack Y.

So now, you have three different ways to avoid the original limitation. The temporary hacks have become permanent micro-features and you have to go back and make sure they're robust because it looks like they'll be in the product forever.

Multiply this by hundreds of limitations and your product soon becomes full of micro-features, each of which only one customer can use. Just the burden of remembering where they all came from can slow you down.

Customers don't want to destroy you. They need you to succeed because they depend on you. The river doesn't want to wash away the mountain; it wants to flow to the sea. But it can only get there if it takes part of the mountain with it.

Sometimes you need to say no. You can't let customers drive you into ruin. Sometimes the best thing for both of you is when customers don't get what they want, they get what they need.

Now, please return to your previously held belief that the customer is God.

4.5   Key Concepts

- Technical Excellence requires an aesthetic sense to guide technical decisions.
    - o   Use the five traits of the Yin-Yang Model, the Lean principles and key parameters of your application to build your aesthetics.
- Team synergy comes from developers getting together to solve problems in ways that none could do alone.
- Successful teams value these four things:
    - o   Mutual Success
    - o   Mutual Ownership
    - o   Common Understanding
    - o   Continuous Improvement
- Use customer advocates to understand customers when customers are not available.
- Think like a customer by creating customer personas.

Part 2:
CODING

Tree & Bricks, Royal Botanic Gardens, Richmond, UK

5 ARCHITECTURE

Architecture is one of the four pillars of the Geodesic Manifesto, forming the foundation for how software design proceeds as the system converges to its intended purpose.

Software architecture defines the structure of the software system. It comprises the components of the system and the interfaces between those components. Each of the components performs one or more functions and may interface to one or more other components.

Architecture is at the cusp between engineering and art. Great architecture is both beautiful and functional. Great building architects become famous for their work: Frank Lloyd Wright (Falling Water and the Guggenheim Museum), Christopher Wren (St. Paul's Cathedral), I.M. Pei (Rock and Roll Hall of Fame), and Buckminster Fuller (the Geodesic Dome). Great software architects are seldom well known and great software architectures are seldom the work of one person. Nonetheless, great software architecture has a beauty of its own, delivering powerful functionality with stunning simplicity that can endure the constant battering of software developers who are more interested in expediency than aesthetics.

Bad software architecture can look a lot like the Winchester Mystery House in San Jose. Sarah Winchester expanded the house haphazardly for years, and ended up with numerous useless doors that open onto walls, or dangerous doors that open outside on the third floor with a twenty-foot drop on the other side.

Every software system has an architecture, but some architectures are more comprehensible than others. Since software architectures are seldom written down, understanding a system's architecture may require some archaeology, a disciplined dig, carefully brushing away dust and sand to find the hard artifacts that tell the story of its purpose and history.

In this chapter, we will try to understand the concepts behind good software architecture. I present four principles for evaluating architecture:
- Modularity
- Flexibility
- Consistency
- Sufficiency

I discuss how to describe architecture. I discuss the role of information modeling in architecture development. I walk through a fictional example architecture. I discuss how to evolve an architecture to adapt to the ever-changing requirements, and finally how to manage the architecture.

137

5.1 *Non-Sequitur* – Ancient Architecture

Before we dive into the subject of software architecture, let's look at examples of architecture from the distant past, dig into their purpose and origins, and see what they can teach us about software.

Stonehenge

Stonehenge, near Salisbury, England, 3000-2000BC

Stonehenge, the iconic construction of the ancient Britons, is shrouded in mystery. Who built it? Why was it built? Was it a religious site or an astronomical observatory? How did the stones get here from their probable source in Wales, 150 miles away? How did the builders place the cross stones atop the vertical stones?

Mysterious shrouds obscure the origins and purpose of a lot of software. Who built it and why? How did it change over time? Is its apparent primary purpose its only purpose, or is it used in other ways that need to be considered as it changes? Like the builders of Stonehenge, the software creators are long gone and left no record of their means or intentions. Often, the only alternative is to treat it like an ancient relic – handle with care and change as little as possible.

The Tower of Babel

Tower of Babel, Pieter Bruegel the Elder, 1563, Kunsthistorisches Museum, Vienna, Austria

In the Biblical story of the Tower of Babel, the post-diluvian citizens of the earth spoke one language. When they decided to build a tower to reach into Heaven, God frustrated their efforts by forcing them to speak many languages. Unable to communicate, the citizens abandoned the tower and scattered across the face of the earth.

The story is a tale of the sin of pride – what made them think they could build a stairway to heaven? But pride is the only one of the Seven Deadly Sins[1] that is also a virtue. Pride makes us strive to achieve lofty goals. If you succeed, your pride is labeled self-confidence and competence. If you fail, it is labeled hubris and a haughty spirit. Pride goeth before the fall, but also before the flight.

Developing successful software requires a great deal of pride to set lofty, seemingly impossible goals. If you succeed, you are a genius. If not, you're just part of another failed startup.

The story of the Tower of Babel also highlights the importance of communication, and, in particular, the importance of a common language. I don't mean English; I've seen too many people engaged in English conversations where no communication happened. When two people share a common language in software development, they can use the same set of words to describe a concept, and they mean the same thing. That's why, in the upcoming discussion of software architecture, I emphasize the importance of names that provide a common vocabulary for the team's communication.

---

[1] Anger, envy, gluttony, greed, lust, pride and sloth

Colosseum

Colosseum, Rome, Italy, 80AD

The once-great Colosseum is now a shadow of its former self. The days of gladiators, lions and Christian martyrs are far behind us. Earthquakes and looters have gradually turned the Colosseum into ruins – a pockmarked reminder of Rome's cruel and majestic past.

When a software architecture has been around for a few years, it begins to look like this, crumbling walls, unsafe to walk on, full of holes that expose the fragile underpinnings of its former glory. You have to abandon any hope of restoring its former glory and just strive to keep it working while minimizing the dangers that lurk on every level.

Hagia Sofia

The Hagia Sophia, the Church of the Holy Wisdom, in Istanbul started as a Christian church, then later became a mosque, and is now a museum. It is one of the earliest examples of Byzantine architecture, with a central dome, supported by four massive columns, which are in turn buttressed by semi-domes, giving the building the fractal appearance of a cluster of mushrooms. The Hagia Sophia's dome architecture formed a design pattern that served as a model for many other buildings in Istanbul, including the Blue Mosque (directly behind me as I took the photo below) and the Süleymaniye Mosque that dominates the skyline in its part of the city.

Hagia Sophia, Istanbul, Turkey, 537AD

The use of design patterns, a general design idea that can be applied in multiple contexts, is central to software architecture. Software design patterns were popularized by the famous 1994 book *Design Patterns: Elements of Reusable Object-Oriented Software*, by the "Gang of Four": Gamma, Helm, Johnson and Vlissides. The book introduced the concept of patterns, and described the details of many patterns.

Design patterns are different from reuse. Patterns must be implemented anew for each use, whereas reuse attempts to use the same code in different contexts. The primary benefit of patterns is that the basic design is well understood and its name is part of the common language that facilitates communication about the software design. Design patterns contribute to the consistency principle of software architecture.

5.2   Resources for Architecture Design

This chapter provides a high-level overview of architecture design. I strongly suggest that you use additional resources to get more detailed information. In preparing this chapter, I read two books that I will review in this section. Both of them provide valuable insights into the architecture design and implementation problem.

5.2.1 Clean Architecture – A Craftsman's Guide to Software Structure and Design – Robert C. Martin, 2018

> The goal of software architecture is to minimize the human resources required to build and maintain the required system.

Clean Architecture - A Craftsman's Guide to Software Structure and Design, Robert C. Martin, 2018

In *Clean Architecture*, Bob Martin, a.k.a. Uncle Bob, presents sets of principles for software architecture design, and discusses how to use those principles to create systems that are easy to implement and maintain. Those principles will help you create a system with a cool software temperature where entropy increase is slow.

The first set of principles, the five SOLID principles, applies to classes in an object-oriented architecture.

S Single Responsibility Principle – A module should only change in response to changes in one other module. The example from the Clean Dependencies principle above of putting error checking methods in the AST node illustrates a violation of this principle because the AST node must be changed in response to both the parser and the analyzer.

O Open-Closed Principle – When new behavior is needed, you should be able to implement it by adding new code, without changing existing code. The module is open for addition, but closed to change. You make this happen by separating things that need to change for different reasons. This principle is important in developing an evolvable infrastructure.

L Liskov Substitution Principle – MIT Professor Barbara Liskov formulated this principle in the '90s. It defines the concept of a subtype and the equivalence of types. For example, in the Architecture Example later in this chapter we need a packet to represent nutrients. When we start designing, we don't know the best way to implement the packet, but we know the "shape" of a packet – the general information that's available. If we observe the substitution principle, we can start with one packet implementation and later replace it with a better implementation and everything will still work. This is extremely important in maintaining the flexibility of the architecture.

I Interface Segregation Principle – Use abstraction to isolate a module from irrelevant changes that occur in a dependent module. For example, the Architecture Example's view of the controller is that there are two controller interfaces, one for consumption and another for gem output. This isolates gem synthesis from changes in the consumption controller. This principle is important for creating an architecture with a cool temperature.

D Dependency Inversion Principle – Low-level modules should depend on high-level modules, not the other way around. The essence of this principle is that, wherever possible, modules should depend on abstract classes rather than concrete classes. Those abstractions are defined at the high level, and the low-level concrete classes derive from them. This principle helps with my Clean Dependencies principle.

The SOLID principles present guidelines for achieving modularity and flexibility (but not consistency or sufficiency). But they are not required. If a module does not use the Liskov Substitution Principle, for example, that doesn't mean it has a bad design. Maybe that principle didn't apply.

Martin then presents a set of principles that apply to components. Martin's use of the word 'component' is closer to the Unified Modeling Language (UML) definition, as opposed to my more general usage as an part of the system. His components are reusable collections of code that are released together. The component principles help you decide what code should be grouped together into components, manage the dependencies among components, and make tradeoffs between stability and abstraction. Some of the key concepts:

- Anticipating why code will need to change is important. Group together code that needs to change for similar reasons.
- Avoid dependency loops.
- Components that many other components depend on need to be stable, and stable components need abstract interfaces so they can change without breaking all the components that depend on them.

Martin then discusses how to apply these principles to software architecture design. Good software architecture improves the development, deployment and maintenance of systems. Good software architecture helps you to keep your options open for as long as possible, and to avoid committing to details until you absolutely must. Good architecture decouples the parts of the system so they don't interact except at the interfaces. Martin recommends ways to draw the boundaries of the system to minimize coupling and maximize flexibility.

Clean Architecture is a valuable resource for software architects. The prose is approachable and interesting. Its organization takes you through the problem one step at a time. Martin's extensive experience in creating architectures provides a broad background of examples and anecdotes that help illustrate the principles he presents.

5.2.2   Building Evolutionary Architectures – Support Constant Change
Neal Ford, Rebecca Parsons, Patrick Kua, 2017

> An evolutionary architecture supports guided, incremental change across multiple dimensions.
>
> *Building Evolutionary Architectures – Support Constant Change,*
> Neal Ford et al, 2017

Whereas Bob Martin sets forth principles for creating good architectures, Ford et al discuss how to control the changes in the system so that the architecture stays effective. Like my discussion of <u>evolvable infrastructure</u> below, the authors use the word "evolve" in the pre-Darwinian sense: to gradually transform and improve.

The key contribution of *Building Evolutionary Architectures* is the concept of the ***fitness function*** that validates a specific attribute of the architecture. If the architecture needs to deliver a transactions-per-second target, there should be a transactions-per-second fitness function. If the architecture should have no coupling between modules A and B, then there should be a fitness function that analyzes the source code to verify that lack of coupling. Fitness functions are separate from all the other tests of the system. They provide a way to validate that changes in the system maintain the integrity of the architecture.

The authors borrow the term *fitness function* from genetic optimization, which uses the fitness function to estimate the probability of survival of an individual. However, they emphasize that architecture evolution is a directed process rather than a series of random changes that may or may not survive.

The authors evaluate several kinds of architectures based on three criteria: ability to make incremental changes and to rapidly deploy those changes, ability to create and maintain fitness functions, and appropriate coupling. Unfortunately, these criteria are not orthogonal because bad coupling strongly affects the other two criteria.

The authors also present some practical advice on how to build evolutionary architectures and how to improve existing architectures to be more evolvable. They discuss how to overcome some of the organization's natural resistance to putting architecture at the forefront of development. While improved architecture has many benefits, it's hard to make a direct correlation to improvements in the product. The authors' approach to evolutionary architecture can quickly demonstrate meaningful benefits that can set the ball rolling toward more improvements.

I recommend *Building Evolutionary Architectures* as a worthwhile read for architects and software managers. It often seems rambling and disorganized, but there are many kernels of wisdom within that will reward a careful reading.

5.3   Architecture Design Principles

Pieta, Michelangelo

> Every block of stone has a statue inside it and it is the task of the sculptor to discover it.

Michelangelo

Michelangelo's description of his creative process is pretty unsatisfying, but I can cut him a little slack because the process of creation is difficult to describe, especially when you're Michelangelo and the rest of us aren't. The trouble with Michelangelo's block-of-stone metaphor is that there are an infinite number of statues inside that block, most of them bad. Michelangelo used his incredible aesthetic intuition to discover the best one.

The process of creating a software architecture likewise defies description. Like Michelangelo's *David* and the *Pieta*, the architecture is there waiting for you. In software, you don't have a stone to constrain you, just the requirements and your own aesthetic principles that help you cut away the cruft and find the simplest, most flexible, and most self-consistent structure for the problem at hand.

When I design an architecture, I continuously evaluate four aesthetic properties of a good architecture: modularity, flexibility, consistency and sufficiency. These properties form the basis of an ethos to guide architectural decision-making.

5.3.1   Modularity

Modularity is the ability of each component of the architecture to stand on its own. Modularity is the primary weapon in the fight against entropy[1]. Modular components

---

[1] It might be worthwhile to review section <u>Software Thermodynamic Model</u>.

have low temperature – a change in a modular component is unlikely to create a bug that manifests in a different component.

There are four attributes of a modular component:

- Single Clear Purpose
- No unexpected side effects
- Independently testable
- Clean dependencies

Single Clear Purpose

A modular component has a single, clear purpose for its existence. Components with multiple purposes tend to have higher temperatures than single-purpose components. A clear purpose makes it easier to understand and easier to test.

When users of the architecture need to add or modify a capability, it should be clear which module they should extend, or whether they should create a new module. I have seen a tendency among software developers to extend an existing module rather than to create a new one. For example, an existing module reads a file to create a data structure. If you need to do post-processing of the data structure, the easy path might be to extend the existing module instead of creating a post-processing module. Developers avoid the overhead cost of creating a new module, but pay for that cost many times later because of the added complexity and higher temperature of the module.

No Unexpected Side Effects

Modules should do their jobs without unexpected side effects. Unexpected side effects increase the temperature of the module. The users of the module will write code that anticipates the absence of those side effects and will spend hours debugging issues caused by the side effects.

For example, an analysis component should not modify the data structure it is analyzing. I remember a case of an analysis tool that worked with a graph data structure. When I shut down the analysis tool, it deleted one of the nodes in the graph because some other use of the analysis tool needed that. It took days to find a way to stop that deletion.

Independently Testable

A modular component can be tested on its own to verify that the component does what it's supposed to do. Module tests should be sufficient to guarantee correct operation of the module. Of course, it is likely that system-level tests will find additional problems with components, but it should be possible to extend the module tests to cover those problems.

Clean Dependencies

Managing the dependencies within the system is one of the key aspects of the architecture. Clean dependencies make it possible to have modularity and flexibility. Dependencies need to obey two rules:

1. High level modules should not depend on the implementation of low-level modules.
2. Low-level modules should know nothing about the high-level modules that use them.

Breaking the first rule removes a lot of flexibility in how you implement your low-level modules. It means you can't change the low-level module without changing the high-level module. As changes become more complicated and convoluted, you are more likely to increase entropy. For example, a C-compiler will need to parse the source code and create an Abstract Syntax Tree (AST). The parser only needs to know that each AST node's children are stored in an ordered collection of nodes. If the implementation of that collection leaks into the parser, for example, knowing that the collection is a linked list and accessing the link directly, then you will find it difficult to change the collection to use an array.

The essence of the second rule is that high-level modules use low-level modules to implement policies, and the low-level modules provide just enough capability to make that easy. Breaking the second rule makes it difficult to reuse low-level modules, and makes it difficult to have clear ownership of modules. As an example of how *not* to do it, if our AST node contains a method that checks for errors and warnings, then the developer of the parser needs to change the AST as the parser changes. The developer of the semantic analysis engine will also need to change the AST, sometimes in ways that are incompatible with the parser's needs. To work around that, the AST node will need a mode bit to know if it's being used by the parser or the analysis engine. With the addition of that bit, the AST node knows of the existence of the parser and the analysis engine. Sometime the parser developer will forget to set or clear the bit and there's a bug that could have been avoided by obeying the second rule.

In addition to the module dependencies of the implementation, you also need to consider the dependencies of how the code is organized for building and deploying your system. A package P (C++ library, Java jar file, etc.) can depend on other packages, but if any of those also depend on P, then you have a mess. Clean dependencies are required to test a package independently.

5.3.2 Flexibility

Flexibility is the ease of adapting the architecture to changes. We expect that the requirements as we understand them today are wrong or incomplete so it is important that the architecture can adapt to unanticipated changes. A good architecture should be able to accommodate a wide range of changes without compromising the integrity of the architecture.

In many cases, we know up front where changes are likely to occur. For example, if we are building a C-compiler, we know that we will need to add new optimizations, and will find reasons for new error and warning messages. Those should be easy to add.

The big test of flexibility is how well the architecture can adapt to unexpected changes. For example, our C-compiler needs to keep up with changes in the language standard. The C++ 11 standard added lambda functions – functions defined locally within the scope of a larger function. It's unlikely that our original architecture anticipated this change. How many components will need to change? Can we quickly modify existing components to accommodate this change? What new components must be developed? Well-designed architectures can adapt to unexpected changes with only minor impact to the existing code.

5.3.3   Consistency

Consistency considers whether conceptually similar modules of the architecture are also concretely similar. I look at consistency in three areas:

Names – a consistent naming convention makes it much easier for developers to use and modify the architecture. For example, if "WidgetManager" is the name of the module that creates and destroys widgets, then it's pretty clear that the "GadgetManager" creates and destroys gadgets. If instead, we name it "GadgetBuilder", then it's not clear how related they are.

Interfaces – similar components should have similar interfaces. If WidgetManager has methods for create, destroy and find, then you should expect that GadgetManager will also have them. You can enforce this with abstract interface classes, but using a convention is often good enough.

Structure – the component structure for data should be similar. If the widget subsystem has WidgetManager, WidgetReader and WidgetWriter components, then you would not expect that the GadgetManager does reading and writing for gadgets.

5.3.4   Sufficiency

Sufficiency is the ability of the architecture to address all the system requirements including customer requirements – like performance, and internal requirements – like testability. Since architecture design is full of tradeoffs, the architecture doesn't need to exceed the requirements, although it's nice to have some margin.

As you are designing the architecture, scan through the requirements, asking if each requirement can easily be met with the current state of the architecture. Modify the architecture and scan again until all the requirements can be met. Use the same process if you are updating an existing architecture, or when major new requirements are discovered.

During the design process, sufficiency is a matter of speculation. You can't know if the architecture will support your performance needs until an initial implementation is complete. And then, you can only know if you have tests available to measure performance. While you design, you need to consider how you will prove that your design is sufficient. You also should know which requirements are most likely to be problems and make sure that you can measure them early in the implementation process.

5.4   Describing Architectures

Software architectures are best described with a combination of diagrams and supporting text descriptions. Although some architects use the Unified Modeling Language (UML) diagrams, other ways of describing the architecture also work well. You should use the best way to get across the meaning to your audience, hiding details for most of the system, and exposing details to illustrate specific features. You may need to show multiple views of the architecture, each highlighting a different aspect of the architecture.

Let's look at some examples of architecture diagrams for open source systems (without trying to understand the architectures), pointing out the techniques used to convey the information.

5.4.1   GNU C Compiler (gcc)

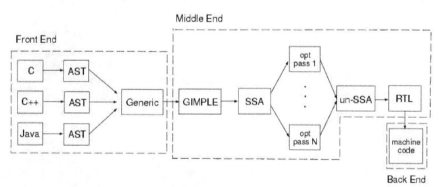

GCC Flow Diagram

By AlexeySmirnov at English Wikibooks - Transferred from en.wikibooks to Commons., GFDL, https://commons.wikimedia.org/w/index.php?curid=61787689, from

https://en.wikibooks.org/wiki/GNU_C_Compiler_Internals/GNU_C_Compiler_Archite
cture

This diagram shows a directed graph describing how the compiler transforms the text description of the input program through the compilation process to create the machine executable version of that program. Each box represents a different way of representing the program. Each edge is a processing step in the flow.

The "opt pass" boxes are a little misleading in the diagram because they actually modify the SSA, and the un-SSA is really an optimized version of the GIMPLE representation. The diagram is probably good enough because the text description that accompanies the diagram makes that clear. I would, however, have drawn that differently:

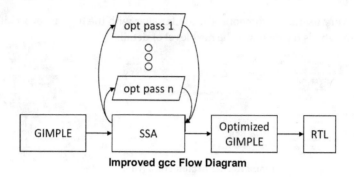

Improved gcc Flow Diagram

5.4.2   Linux Kernel

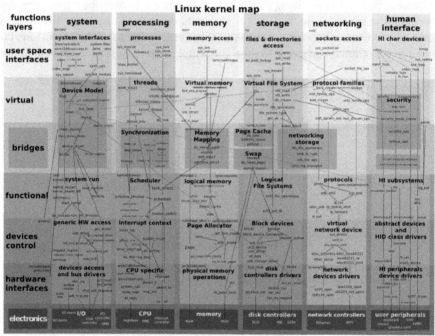

Linux Kernel Architecture (Flat)

As you would expect, the architecture of the Linux Kernel is quite complex. This diagram does a good job of showing a lot of information on one page. The matrix organization helps with understanding how the pieces fit together. This diagram would be very useful for someone already familiar with the high-level architecture of the system, who is trying to get the next level of detail.

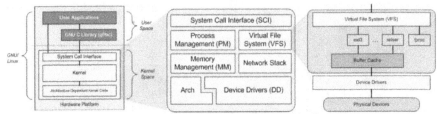

Linux Kernel Architecture (Hierarchical)

M. Tim Jones, https://www.ibm.com/developerworks/library/l-linux-kernel

Another approach to describing a complex architecture is to describe it hierarchically. The diagrams above show the highest-level architecture and then successively more detailed information. This approach makes it easier to understand the big picture, but the matrix diagram is better able to show the complex interactions among the modules.

5.4.3   TensorFlow™

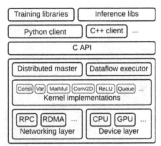

TensorFlow Architecture

Reproduced from work created and shared by Google and used according to terms described in the Creative Commons 3.0 Attribution License. From https://www.tensorflow.org/extend/architecture

TensorFlow is a software library for building machine learning applications with a C-language interface (API). This diagram shows the modules of TensorFlow, organized hierarchically. It has no arrows because the modules are nearly independent and the interactions are determined by the control flow developed by the client. The architecture of a machine learning system is determined by the user of TensorFlow, not dictated by the library.

5.5   Information-Centric Design

The great conservation principles – energy, momentum, angular momentum (or spin in quantum mechanics) and electric charge – got me through my undergraduate degree program in physics. When I approached a difficult homework problem, my first thoughts went to these conservation principles. Asking the right questions about conservation often led me to the solution. How are energy and momentum transferred between two objects in a collision? When an atom decays from one quantum state to another, how is momentum conserved? The conservation principles acted as inspiration for solutions to problems, and as validation that the answers were correct.

There are no conservation principles in software architecture design. However, I get similar inspiration and validation from following the information as it flows through a program. As I design an architecture, I am always asking myself where the information comes from and where it's going? Can I use more of this information or use it better? Can I dispose of it? How do I store it? How do I represent it for this algorithm? How do I present it to the user? What facilities do I need to transform this data?

Even though it's not strictly true[1], treating information as conserved is a helpful way to look at software architecture. Information can be treated like energy in classical thermodynamics, where the first law states that energy cannot be created or destroyed. The subset of information that is lost because it is discarded or ignored is similar to thermodynamic entropy[2], the energy that is lost to heat and cannot be recovered.

The decisions for how to represent information are an important foundation to any architecture. The representation of information should be compact, flexible and complete.

Compact representations don't use two bits of information when one will do. (On the other hand, I've seen developers try to cram two bits of information into a single bit with frustrating results.) Avoid redundancy in the representation. Redundancy will make it difficult to modify the information while maintaining consistency.

Just as requirements change over time, the information that's needed by the software will change in ways that are difficult to anticipate. Flexible representations make it easy to add additional attributes to the information that you keep around. You will have data, like the information from a database record, and meta-data, like a bit that marks that this record has been modified.

---

[1] Some forms of artificial intelligence or optimization algorithms create information by synthesizing it from hints in unrelated data.

[2] Not to be confused with information theory's entropy, which is a measure of how much information is available rather than what's lost.

I would say that the completeness attribute is obvious, but that's seldom true. Often, when completeness is lacking, the information you need is available, but there's no way to get it from where you are. In the gcc architecture diagram above, you see that the source code is transformed into multiple representations of the program. It's not shown, but each representation links back to the previous representation so that an error found in the right-most representation can report the line number of the source code problem.

Many Agile methodologies (notably Extreme Programming) proscribe development of features and capabilities that are not needed today. I strongly disagree. The flexibility and completeness of information representation are too important to delay development until you need them. In the spirit of keeping your options open, you need enough flexibility and completeness that the cost of developing a capability that might not be used should be discounted heavily for the future savings it will bring.

5.6   An Architecture Example

To explore the concepts of architecture, I need an example. Ideally, I would discuss the architecture of one or more open source systems. But if I choose, for example, the Linux Kernel architecture, then the discussion would quickly become about the Linux Kernel rather than about the concepts of architecture design.

The example needs to be:

- From a domain that almost everyone will understand
- Rich enough that we can explore alternatives
- Simple enough that we're not spending a lot of time on details

For the example, I've chosen the architecture of a simplified version of the human digestive system, the SHDS. I know this isn't a software architecture, but it's similar to lots of real software architectures. Think of food as input data; each stage of the system makes transformations to that data. There are inputs and outputs and an interface to a controller and a security system. We can explore alternatives to the existing architecture and try to understand why the existing architecture is so good. We can explore enhancements to the architecture that might be feasible in a software implementation, but not in a human. All in all, I think we can learn a lot from this example. I'll rename the components so that we don't have to be continually reminded of all the icky stuff that goes on in a real HDS.

5.6.1 Black Box Model

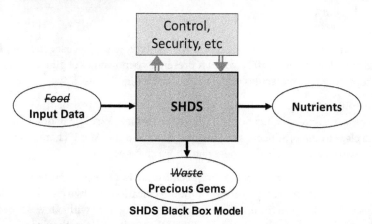

SHDS Black Box Model

The SHDS takes in input data (i.e., food). It processes that data to separate the good stuff from the bad. It further processes the good stuff to make it useful to the rest of the body in the form of nutrients. And it prepares the waste products for discharge at a time that is socially acceptable. Despite Juliet's protestation ("A rose by any other name would smell as sweet."), I hope we can further remove ourselves from the icky by changing the name from 'waste' to 'precious gems'. The SHDS interfaces to a controller that controls the hunger urge, thus initiating food intake, or precious gem output. And it interfaces to a security system that rejects some potential intake and purges the system if bad food gets past the initial screening.

The above diagram is the Black Box Model of the system. It's the view that other modules in the system (i.e., the simplified human) will see when they interface to the SHDS. It's also the view that will be used for black box testing. It shows the primary inputs and outputs in blue, and the control interfaces in gray. I've often seen designers forget about the control interface when they design an architecture. They think that they can just hack in the controls when they need them. This is a big mistake. The control interface is just as important as the data and is one of the keys to making the module usable in many situations.

In many cases, the form of the input and output data is predefined, and you must conform to that definition. In other cases, the form needs to be defined and negotiated with the users of the data.

In our case, since we are not actually going to process food, let's use a text stream of English sentences (like the text of this chapter) as the input to SHDS. The nutrient and gem outputs will each be a stream of four-character strings. The first of those four characters defines the output type:

- 'a' – amino acid

- 's' – sugar
- 'l' – lipid
- 'g' – gem

The following three characters represent the subtype (e.g., glucose, sucrose, lactose, etc.) and the intensity. So "sg02" would represent two molecules of glucose, and "av05" would represent five molecules of the amino acid valine.

Since the output streams are an important interface to the rest of the system, there should be a formal specification for the data format. Writing it down makes the interface clear to the producers and consumers of the data. And if changes are needed, it gives a baseline from which to negotiate those changes.

In general, the need for formality in specification is inversely proportional to the conceptual distance between the users of the specification. So, two developers with the same boss who sit across the aisle from each other can get by with a few scribbles on a white board. But if one is in San Jose and the other in Bangalore, they need a spec. Or even if the physical distance is close, if the two developers are in different organizations, they need a spec. If there are three or more users, regardless of distance, they need a spec.

In this case, since it's just me and you, I'm not going to write a spec. I hope you'll forgive me.

We will also need to specify the API for the control and security interfaces. You will see that develop in the next few sections.

5.6.2 Data Flow Model

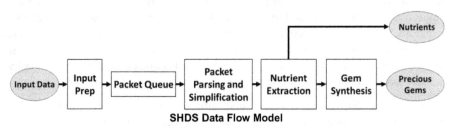

SHDS Data Flow Model

At the next level of detail, we can see the components and data interfaces of the SHDS.

- Input Prep (aka mouth) takes in large chunks of input data and breaks it into smaller chunks called 'packets.'
- Packet Queue (the esophagus and the storage function of the stomach) stores the packets until the next stage is ready to process them.

- Packet Parsing and Simplification (the processing function of the stomach) further breaks down the packets into fragments (i.e., proteins, starches, fats, etc.).
- Nutrient Extraction modifies the fragments into nutrients that can be absorbed by the blood stream (i.e, amino acids, sugars, lipids, etc.)
- Gem Prep transforms what's left into rubies, emeralds and sapphires.

This architecture represents a pipeline, which is an important architecture design pattern. Each module takes its input from one place and feeds its output to one place. Pipelines are easily parallelized – the process of packet parsing and simplification can go on at the same time as input prep is chewing on its input and at the same time as nutrient extraction.

Names are important. The names should give a person familiar with the domain some clue about what the module is doing. For example, "Input Prep" is better than the metaphorical name "Mouth", because the human mouth does many things in addition to input preparation and it implies a specific implementation with lips, teeth and a tongue. Avoid adding a redundant noun like 'Module' to all the names. The name "Input Prep Module" conveys no more information than "Input Prep", and the two additional syllables are enough to trigger use of a TLA (three-letter acronym), like IPM, that will completely obfuscate the function of the module and will continually cause confusion with the thousands of other things that IPM might stand for. (Lest you call me a hypocrite, note that the name SHDS was chosen intentionally because it obfuscates the function of the system. A quick internet search found eight other things that SHDS could mean.) In the above example, "Packet Parsing and Simplification" is doomed to become PPS because if a typical software developer says those ten syllables one hundred times per day, it will more than double his average verbal output.

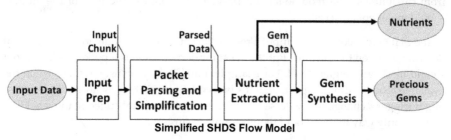

Simplified SHDS Flow Model

When we start to implement this, we will find that there is a packet queue inside of Nutrient Extraction and in Gem Synthesis. So, for consistency, we will subsume the explicit Packet Queue into Packet Parsing and Simplification. The above diagram also specifies the type of data that is passed between modules.

Adding the Control Interface

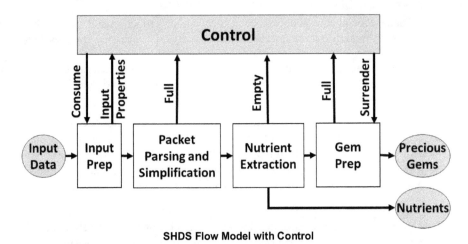

SHDS Flow Model with Control

Now let's look at the control interface. This interface controls when to consume input data and when to surrender the gems.

Consider the consumption control. Packet Parsing and Simplification delivers a signal that describes how full it is. Nutrient Extraction delivers a signal that describes how empty it is. Input prep also delivers a signal (input properties) that describes the input data it is prepping. Control considers these inputs and delivers a signal to Input Prep telling it whether to consume.

Naïve or lazy architects tend to embed the control within the modules of the architecture, but that would transgress the Clear Purpose attribute of modularity, and would limit the flexibility of the architecture. It's important to separate policy decisions from capabilities. The module should provide capabilities. The user of the module should make policy decisions.

In the SHDS, we could have Input Prep or Packet Queue include an algorithm that determines when to consume. But the consumption decision is a policy decision, so it should made at a higher level. For example, I am likely to consume more when the available food is pumpkin pie than if it's broccoli. But a visit to my doctor or my tailor might trigger a change to my dessert policy. If control was embedded in the real HDS, then the only way to diet would require stomach surgery.

The API to the control interface will be fairly simple. The controller will poll the modules to get the status and will call module methods to cause the appropriate response. We will need to define the data structure that defines the input properties.

5.6.3   Adding the Security Interface

The security interface tries to avoid, or recover from, input data that could harm the system.

- Input Prep sends properties of its data to the security system to ask if it's ok to swallow. (Don't swallow peach pits or moldy cheese.) If the input is not OK, then Input Prep removes the data to the Rejected Input container.
- Packet Parsing and Simplification may detect bad data that got past the Input Prep screening. That data is sent back through Packet Queue and Input Prep to the Rejected Input container.
- If bad data is detected in Nutrient Extraction or Gem Prep, it is expedited forward to the Rejected Output container.

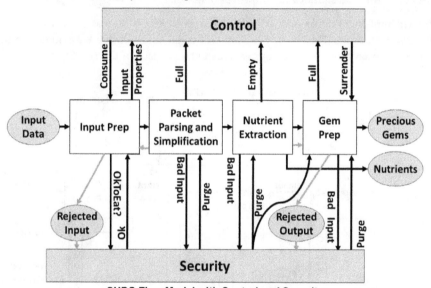

SHDS Flow Model with Control and Security

Adding the control interface hardly changed the architecture of the SHDS, however, adding the security interface had a major impact on the system. There are additional system outputs, and the simple pipeline now needs to have sections that move data in the reverse direction or that bypass processing steps.

In the software implementation, we can fix this complexity, but first, let's try to understand the design criteria that led to this architecture.

In complex living organisms, body openings are dangerous places. They expose the body to infection and infestation. So digestive systems have one or two openings (the Venus fly trap has one opening; I couldn't find an animal with one opening.) And, while security is an important consideration, it is better to accommodate the security needs within the two-opening system than to add additional openings just for security that are likely to cause more security problems than they solve.

But in the software implementation, virtual body openings are not risky and are cheap. Let's also assume that we need to diagnose the causes of the bad data so that we can improve the entire system (i.e., the entire simplified human). It will be easier to diagnose if we have separate rejected-data containers for each module where the problem is detected. Since software developers spend much more time debugging code than writing it, anything we do to improve debug will also improve productivity.

The figure above shows the final version of the SHDS architecture. Although this does not look simpler than the previous version, the revised architecture removes the back-flow problems and significantly improves diagnosis.

We will implement the security API with two security modules that get registered with the SHDS modules. The security system will create and manage these modules and will provide a reference to the appropriate module in each of the SHDS modules.

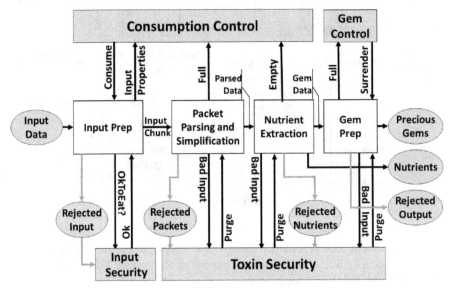

Final SHDS Flow Model

To meet the Single Clear Purpose attribute of Modularity, we have also split the control interface into two pieces: one for consumption and another for gem output. At least from the SHDS viewpoint, these are separate decisions, and from the flexibility principle, they should be made separately.

5.7   Hierarchical Architectures

When I was a young engineer, I wanted to work on "systems". But when I told people my desire, I became very confused because everyone had a different idea about the definition of 'system'. I came to understand that engineers defined 'system' as the level above where they were working. A chip designer considered the printed circuit board full of chips to be a system, while the board designer considered the computer to be a system, etc. Thus, systems are hierarchical, and the same can be said for architecture.

Going down in the hierarchy, each module in the SHDS has an architecture for its implementation, whose modules have architectures, etc., until we reach the atomic components that cannot be broken down further. In the real HDS, these are enzymes, hormones, DNA, and other complex molecules.

Going up the hierarchy, the SHDS is a module in the Simplified Human. And the Simplified Human may be a member of a Simplified Family or an employee in a Simplified Corporation. Each of these uses may add additional requirements for the capabilities of the SHDS. For example, being a Simplified Boy Scout may require the SHDS to increase tolerance for wood chips and sand.

It's hard to generalize about how to handle the upper levels of the architecture. In my experience, software teams are pretty good about trying to understand what their subsystem needs to do, because the methodology of trying to understand requirements has been expounded so pervasively. And users of the system are often very clear in pointing out the deficiencies of the system.

To understand the lower levels of the architecture, let's start by looking at the architecture of the Nutrient Extraction module from the SHDS.

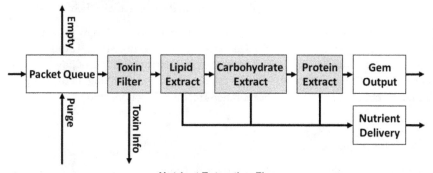

Nutrient Extraction Flow

- Packet Queue stores the incoming packets from Packet Parsing and Simplification. It lets the Control System know if it's empty, and purges its data if the Security System determines that the input is dangerous.

- Toxin Filter looks at the incoming packets and determines if they are potentially harmful. If so, it removes them from the stream and sends info to the Security System.
- The three extraction modules remove nutrients from the stream and send them to the Nutrient Delivery module.
- The Nutrient Delivery module sends nutrients to the output stream.
- The Gem Output module sends the remaining stream contents, after nutrients have been extracted, to the Gem Synthesis module.

We use the same Packet Queue as in the other SHDS modules. They are the same, but they each store a different kind of data. Re-usable modules are essential to good architecture design. Adding some options to a module so it can be re-used is almost always better than re-implementing the module from scratch (as long as the options don't compromise the module's modularity):

- It's easier to understand – since you already know what a Packet Queue is, I don't have to explain it again; I only need to tell you that it's storing the parsed packets instead of the mixed packets.
- It's easier to maintain – if, for example, we need to change the format of the packet, we only need to update one queue module.

The three extraction modules of the module are the instances of the same class, but are each configured to extract different nutrients. These three, together with Toxin Filter and Gem Output are all instances of an abstract Extraction Stage module that form a five-member linked list. This architecture is very flexible and modular. If we need to add a different type of extraction or analysis, it can easily fit into this structure.

Decisions about module re-use are an important part of good architecture design. Fewer modules mean less to develop and to maintain, and will lead to better overall quality. So, if you see two modules that are almost the same, make them the same.

On the other hand, it's important to follow the architecture design principles. The human mouth, for example, is used as part of the digestive, respiratory and communication subsystems. This violates the modularity principle of having a single clear purpose. Chewing interferes with both breathing and speaking. In the Simplified Human software system, I would separate these three functions into three modules.

5.8   Converging to an Architecture

It's common to think that the high-level data and control flow diagrams shown above are the architecture. Understanding the system at that level is essential to creating an architecture, but the architecture needs to contemplate the implementation and deployment of all those modules to be useful. The architecture needs to include decisions about which interfaces can be shared and which should be independent, how the code should be organized, how to manage interactions between the modules' development teams, and much more.

The flow diagram shown above looks simple, but it went through many iterations before achieving this simplicity. Some of those iterations were just in drawing and re-drawing the diagrams. But the most effective changes came from implementing a prototype of the system. Writing code, even if all the functions are stubbed, forces you to consider a lot of details that are hard to express in a picture. In other words, a few lines of code are worth a thousand pictures.

So, now that we have a high-level data and control flow diagram, we can begin the process of creating an architecture that supports it. There are a lot of decisions that need to be made. The first step is to decide which decisions are fundamental and will never need to change, and which decisions need to be flexible. Let's assume that the partitioning of the system into modules that pass data using packets is fundamental. The SHDS currently has four such modules, but if we needed to add another or to split up one of the existing modules, that should be easy.

Almost all the other decisions need to be flexible. For example, we know that there is a packet, but what is the form of the packet? And what data does it carry? Is it different for Input Prep compared to Gem Synthesis? If so, how many types of packet do we need? We don't know at this point, so it is critical that we design something that can accommodate a wide range of possibilities.

Another decision is how to deploy this architecture. Do we build an executable with one process running in one thread, or multiple threads or multiple processes? We can't answer that question until we have something in hand that we can measure to see if we need more performance. So, it's best if we design something in which we can start with a single thread and easily add parallelization later if we need it.

Now I'm going to make another fundamental decision – all of the modules will use the same packet communication interface. This doesn't need to be a fundamental decision; each pair of modules could decide on their own version of the interface. That would be more flexible. But if the interface is common, then only the interface will need to change as we add parallelization to the system. In addition, we remove the coupling between adjacent modules in the flow. The Nutrient Extraction team and the Gem Synthesis team only need to negotiate the contents of the packets they pass, not the mechanism for passing them. The benefits of commonality far outweigh the loss of flexibility.

Once we've made a fundamental decision that locks us into an inflexible part of the system that many modules will depend on, we need to make sure that that decision does not increase the temperature of the system. We do this with abstraction.

163

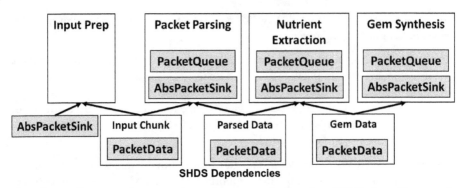

SHDS Dependencies

The above diagram shows a dependency graph for the SHDS. InputPrep and PacketParsing both depend on InputChunk, which implements the PacketData interface. This is how the two modules agree on the form of the data passed between them. The other two modules do not need to know about this data and therefore are immune to any changes in the data.

Three modules instantiate a PacketQueue and implement the AbsPacketSink interface. Each could decide to use a different way of storing its inputs as long as the new method can support the same interface.

Except for the data passed from module to module, there is no coupling in the system. So, it is unlikely that a change made to GemSynthesis will cause a bug to be seen in InputPrep code. However, it is quite likely that some bad data that gets past InputPrep could cause a problem in GemSynthesis. This is the curse of the tail – bugs at the start of the pipeline often don't show up until much later in the pipeline, and the last stage, the tail, gets the blame for a lot of problems caused by earlier stages.

5.9   SHDS Prototype

You will find the C++ code for an SHDS prototype together with unit tests at

https://GeodesicManifesto.com.

The point of the prototype is not to create something useful, but rather to create something that can validate the architecture and demonstrate how coupling is minimized using the abstraction techniques described above. A better emulation of digestion would require more realistic input and output, a lot more analysis of the data while processing it, and a more complete interaction with the control and security subsystems.

A brief description of the implementation choices follows:

- The input is a text stream. The unit tests use Hamlet's soliloquy.

- Input Prep reads the input stream and outputs Input Chunks, a few words from the input stream with non-alphanumeric characters removed.
- PacketParsing separates the chunk into individual words. ParsedData is a single word from the chunk.
- Nutrient Extraction looks for specific characters in the ParsedData words and extracts them as nutrients or toxins. For example, 'l', 'L', 'f', and 'F' are lipid (i.e., fat) nutrient characters. It outputs the nutrients to a text stream. What's left of the input word after all the nutrient characters are removed is sent to GemSynthesis.
- GemSynthesis aggregates a few GemData words and pseudo-randomly creates diamonds, emeralds, rubies and sapphires of various sizes, which it outputs to a stream.

5.10 Evolvable Infrastructure

Software systems need to evolve – that's 'evolve' in the pre-Darwinian sense: to gradually transform and improve. We need to be able to change the implementation of the atomic components without major changes to the code that uses them. We need to develop new capabilities without worrying about breaking the current capabilities.

Suppose that one of the bright young PhDs in research figured out how to extract nutrients from silica. (Nutrition from rocks would be a boon for the Simplified Boy Scout.) We should be able to add a SilicaExtract module to NutrientExtraction, make sure that the security implementation permits silica input, and with some additional testing, the enhanced SHDS would be ready to ship.

The collection of the atomic components and the most common re-usable modules is the infrastructure (literally, "under-structure") of the system. The infrastructure is like the roots of a great oak tree, providing support for the system, and also providing a conduit for nourishment that encourages growth of the system. If the infrastructure is strong, the system will prosper. If the infrastructure is weak, the system may have an unexpected catastrophic failure.

The real HDS depends on enzymes, hormones and other infrastructure chemicals. These are constructed in cells that use DNA as their "program" for construction. The same infrastructure is used across all the body's subsystems. It's a beautifully simple mechanism that can create incomprehensibly complex systems.

In the SHDS, the PacketQueue and the Nutrient Extractor architecture are part of the infrastructure. If you look at the prototype code, you will also see a utilities module that includes implementations of commonly used constructs. In C++, the STL library of data structures is part of your infrastructure. You may also use infrastructure capabilities provided in the Boost libraries or other open source code.

In a software development organization, there are some tasks and capabilities that should always be done in the same way. For example, there should be only one way for developers to report errors to users – developers, documentation writers, and support staff all need to interact with the error subsystem, and a single method makes it easier for everyone. The consistency of infrastructure support for common tasks and capabilities makes it easier to write and maintain software.

If you are using third party frameworks as part of your infrastructure, it is important to create guidelines for use of these frameworks. For example, naïve use of the STL set and map data structures can cause performance problems in multi-threaded systems; a guideline for their use will help avoid such problems. If you are not careful, frameworks can lead you into a series of architectural decisions that are difficult to unravel. They often encourage creation of dependencies that should be avoided.

Consistency and flexibility are the most important design principles for infrastructure. A good infrastructure uses the same atomic components throughout the system and has a rich library of utilities that operate on those components. When infrastructure is done well, the system can evolve quickly and reliably. Enhancements and bug fixes in the infrastructure are shared across all the modules of the system. When new requirements lead to changes in the infrastructure, those changes can be made with minimal impact on rest of the system.

When infrastructure is done poorly, entropy begins to take over. Every change to the infrastructure is a threat to the system. Enhancements and bug fixes in the infrastructure cause bugs in the rest of the system. To avoid these bugs, the infrastructure starts to fork, with options and modes and parallel implementations that are only used in parts of the system. The forking makes the infrastructure worse and leads to more forking. And so it goes. System evolution becomes a slow, tedious process with more effort applied to avoiding problems with existing code than to improving the system.

Software systems often start out with a clean, comprehensible architecture like the SHDS. The original architecture was probably designed by one developer or a small group of developers who had a clear understanding of the subsystem and how it should work. But over time, the infrastructure falls apart.

- Schedule pressure forces expedient decisions instead of long-lasting ones. The design principles are forgotten.
- Developers try to avoid risk by adding modes and options to the infrastructure. Or worse, they create a completely different implementation of part of the infrastructure while keeping the old one around for "compatibility".
- Developers who don't understand the original design objectives make changes that cause parts of the infrastructure to be incompatible. For

example, I've seen cases where there are dozens of ways to get the name of an object; none of them quite alike.

- Code from a third party is integrated into the system. The third-party infrastructure represents the same information, but in a totally different way. Because of schedule pressure, the most expedient way to perform the integration is with data translators. Now there are two completely independent infrastructures in the system, and moving between them is a slow and risky process.

- Difficult infrastructure projects almost never get funded (See the discussion in Managing Change). Managers respond to customer crises by moving resources from infrastructure to more customer-visible development. This move doesn't change the need for infrastructure updates, but instead removes the focus that is needed to keep infrastructure reliable, consistent, and flexible.

As the infrastructure rots, projects that should take a couple weeks now take several months and software quality suffers because there are so many special cases to consider that no one can make changes without breaking something else that seems to be unrelated.

5.11 Real Architectures

The SHDS has a simple clean architecture modeled after a real system that was refined over millions of years of evolution. Most systems do not have a simple, clean architecture. If you ask a typical software developer to describe the architecture of the system, you are likely to get either a blank stare or maniacal laughter.

Real architectures have rotting or incomplete infrastructure with multiple ways of doing the same thing. Real modules have interfaces to many other modules with no clear separation of function. The same functionality is contained in many different modules with completely different implementations. Control is embedded within modules, often in such a way that you can't really tell if it's control. Security is an afterthought leading to multiple ways the system is exposed to danger.

The hope of evolving the mess into a clean, simple architecture is a pipe dream best left to the opioid stupor of Alice's caterpillar. A more reasonable goal is to improve the architecture at a rate that is slightly faster than the rate that it decays. I believe this is possible; but it will require both a methodology, and the discipline to prioritize infrastructure development above the resolution of day to day crises.

As we move on to the methodology chapters, remember this as one of our goals.

5.12 Managing the Architecture

As a manager, you manage your employees, your boss, your peers, your customers and the constant bombardment from your inbox. They will be in your ear, on your back or at your throat. They will demand, cajole and weasel their way into your attention.

As a software manager, you have one more constituent that will never ask for a window cube, or demand a presentation be completed overnight, or backstab, or threaten to sue. Your silent constituent, the architecture, needs you more than the others.

Without your help, the demands of the others will lead to the decay of the architecture. But you and the architecture can deliver more together if you take care of it. With a good architecture and a methodology that supports it, your employees will believe they are part of something enduring; your boss will be off your back; your customers will find new things to complain about; and your inbox will still be full of spam.

Five Stupid Architecture Questions

The manager's role in architecture design is to ask questions, not to make decisions. Let the developers and the architects make decisions. Ask the questions to help them think about their decisions in the right way. Here are a few sample stupid questions. I'm sure you can think of some others that are more germane to your particular problem.

- Where have we had problems in the past where a better architecture could have helped?
- Where do the SOLID principles apply and where are they best ignored.
- What are the parts of the system that are most likely to change? How do we isolate those changes from the rest of the system?
- If there is legacy code that we need to use, how do we isolate ourselves from problems in that code?
- How do we integrate new requirements into the existing architecture?

The Architect

The first step in managing the architecture is to identify the architect. Architecture can be developed by a committee, but one person needs to be responsible for making the final decisions, for enforcing architectural decisions, and for making sure that changes are consistent with the needs of the project. The architect is usually a senior software developer, but the architect could be a manager with a strong software pedigree. Since architecture is hierarchical, complex systems may need multiple architects that each focus on one or more subsystems.

The architect needs:

- Strong software development skills
- A good sense of abstraction and synthesis

- Proficient communication skills
- The respect of the rest of the team
- Enough assertiveness to hold their ground, but enough openness to recognize and adopt good ideas from others

As you might guess, great architects are hard to find. When you find them, pay them well.

Abstraction and Synthesis

Most of the above list is self-evident, but let me expand on the term, "abstraction and synthesis." *Abstraction* is the ability to generalize, to find the common attributes of diverse things. *Synthesis* is the process of combining diverse things into a coherent whole, of building something simple starting from a complex mass. I'm sure there are many ways to do this, but for me this means mentally scanning the problem, focusing on one aspect at a time, and asking a few questions:

- What information is needed here?
- Where does that information come from?
- How do I represent that information?
- What actions need to happen with that information?
- How do I assure that those actions are successful?

These questions then lead me to other aspects of the problem. I follow this questioning path where it leads, often revisiting the same topics over and over, until a coherent picture begins to emerge of the architecture and of the philosophy that guides the architecture.

A "good sense of abstraction and synthesis" is a talent that some people are born with and others are not. Its application is a skill that needs to be honed by practice, by trying, and failing, and trying again. Many good developers do not have the talent. Some good developers have the talent but not the skill, but all good architects have both the talent and the skill.

Architecture Creation and Evolution

The second step in managing the architecture is to set up processes for the evolution of the architecture, remembering that high creativity tasks, like developing the architecture, need loose processes. But once the high-level architecture is in place, the team needs documentation and more rigid processes for how to implement, validate and change it.

The hardest part of architectural evolution is maintaining the architectural philosophy as more and more people are involved. The philosophy is hard to write down. It consists of simple concrete concepts like, "for every type of data, a manager owns that data". But it also includes abstract concepts like, "separate control from data", and guidance for how to make tradeoffs like memory vs. execution time. The architect probably cannot tell you all the philosophical concepts, but he will certainly know if they've been violated. Nevertheless, it's worthwhile trying to write them down and gradually expand the list as the team discovers them.

Maintaining the Integrity of the Architecture

The third step in managing the architecture is to force continuous improvement that stems the natural increase in entropy. The team will work within the existing architecture to implement the required functionality. They will add gargoyles and buttresses as needed, slowly increasing the entropy of the system. And each of these changes, when considered in isolation, will be the best possible addition to the architecture to solve that isolated problem. But when considered as a whole, there may be a better way. You need to make sure that the better way has a chance to happen. It may mean re-implementing large portions of the code base. It will include the risk that new bugs will be introduced. It will consume valuable resources with no visible benefit. But without that better way, the inevitable perils caused by the increasing entropy will slowly eat away at the team's ability to improve the product until there is no chance to recover.

Architecture Control

Use the four components of a control system to make sure that the architecture continues to improve. You need a plan for how the architecture will evolve. You can measure deviations from that plan and from the Architecture Design Principles. I typically reviewed the architecture once or twice for every major release. Each of those reviews would result in refactoring, re-architecture and subsystem rewrites that kept the architecture moving forward.

5.13 Key Concepts

- The SOLID principles are a commonly used set of techniques for building good architectures.
- A fitness function that measures properties of the architecture can help maintain architecture integrity while adapting to changes.
- Evaluate architectures using four design principles:
  - Modularity evaluates the ability for modules to stand alone. Modular modules:
    - Have a single clear purpose
    - Have no unexpected side effects
    - Are independently testable
    - Have clean dependencies
  - Flexibility is the ease of adapting the architecture to changes.
  - Consistency considers whether conceptually similar modules of the architecture are also concretely similar.

- o Sufficiency is the ability of the architecture to address all the system requirements.
- There is no standard for describing architectures, but they are best described with a combination of diagrams and text.
- While designing architectures, it is useful to treat information as conserved. Evaluate your use of information using these attributes:
  - o Compactness
  - o Flexibility
  - o Completeness
- The architecture design example shows how to evolve an architecture starting from a simple data flow to a complete architecture with module dependencies.
- Infrastructure is the collection of atomic components and re-usable modules that form the roots of the system.
  - o Consistency and flexibility are the most important attributes of an evolvable infrastructure.
  - o Maintaining the integrity of the infrastructure while the system evolves is essential to good software development.
- Managing the architecture is one of the most important roles of a software manager.
  - o Choose a good architect who has a good sense of abstraction and synthesis.
  - o Ask questions to make sure the architecture is meeting the needs of the software and conforms to the design principles.
  - o Put processes in place to make sure that the architecture continues to improve.

6 CHALLENGING PROBLEMS

At the heart of almost every system is a <u>challenging</u> problem, from the upper left quadrant of the Complexity Model, a problem where the right solution can make a huge difference to the system. The optimizer in a C compiler determines how fast the compiled program runs. The 3D graphics engine is the key to the user's gaming experience. Audio signal processing algorithms provide necessary data for voice recognition. Numerical equation solvers are the foundation of machine learning. The list goes on and on.

Although it's difficult to generalize how to approach a challenging problem, in this chapter I will offer some guidelines for making key decisions about challenging problems. And then I will go into more depth about approaches to solving a class of challenging problems – the NP problems.

6.1 *Non-Sequitur* – Software and the Scientific Method

> We embrace change through constant measurement, analysis and improvement of the software and methodology.

Principle from the Geodesic Manifesto

When I think of science, the first science that comes to mind is physics whose goal is the understanding of the fundamental laws that govern the universe. Physics is a science of discovery. The fundamental laws are out there and all we can see are the effects of those laws. The scientific method has furthered learning in physics from Archimedes' bathtub to Galileo's ball drop experiment to Newton's apple to the Large Hadron Collider. Pose a question; propose a hypothesis; design an experiment to prove or disprove the hypothesis. Rinse and repeat, leveraging all the proven hypotheses that have come before.

Engineers apply the fundamental laws to construct things: bridges, engines, automobiles, computers. When possible, they analyze the problem using the fundamental laws: the forces that support the bridge, the efficiency of an engine, the wind resistance of an automobile, the power requirements of a computer.

But often, the problem defies analysis: bridge girders become riddled with micro-cracks, the gaskets in the engine degrade over time, the front tires wear out too fast, the computer chip fails because the metal that connects transistors moves over time. Then the engineers become scientists: posing questions, proposing hypotheses and designing experiments.

At its most fundamental level, computer science is not a science of discovery; it is a science of construction. There are no fundamental laws of computing hidden in the universe. Turing's machine, Von Neumann's computers, Shannon's information theory and Knuth's algorithms all were pulled out of thin air by geniuses with strong imaginations.

But at the practical level, software developers must be scientists. Every system is its own universe with its own Big Bang, its own galaxies and its own laws of motion. The system defies analysis because of the complex, opaque and sometimes chaotic nature of software. When faced with a problem – a bug, slow execution time, unsatisfactory results – the solution is hidden in the thousands of lines of code that make up the system. Developers must propose hypotheses, design experiments and analyze the results until the solution to the problem is revealed.

This is why the Geodesic Manifesto emphasizes measurement and analysis. We all need to be scientists.

6.2   Make vs. Buy

You have many choices for how to solve a challenging problem. Sometimes you can adapt an open source or commercial solution to your specific problem. Sometimes you can find publications that describe a solution. Sometimes you need to develop the solution from a blank slate.

The Make vs. Buy decision will set the stage for how you develop the system for years in the future. It will be a very difficult decision to change, so it is important to make it carefully.

When you are faced with the decision to leverage an existing third-party code package or to build from scratch, some will tell you to always use the third-party package – using it will save time, and it's probably implemented by developers who are experts in the domain. Others will tell you to always develop from scratch – you control the implementation, so it will always do exactly what you want, and if you need to fix a bug you have both the source code and the required knowledge. The truth lies somewhere between.

Leveraging a third-party package is often the best answer if the package is widely used, has ongoing support, has acceptable licensing requirements (see Managing Intellectual Property), and you are sure it will be flexible enough to meet your needs.

Advantages	Disadvantages
No coding necessary	Learning the interface to a complex code base is a significant effort

| Developed by domain experts | It may be difficult to get it to do exactly what you want |
| High quality solution for the domain | Even if you have the source code, it may be difficult to address bugs or limitations. |

Leveraging a Third-Party Package

Advantages	Disadvantages
Complete control over architecture and implementation	Significant coding and testing time required
Your team develops expertise in the domain.	While you develop expertise, your solution may be inferior to the third-party solution.

Building from Scratch

In a recent project, we used the sqlite (sqlite.org) database engine which integrated seamlessly, worked perfectly and made it very easy to add database capabilities to our product. Sqlite has a very liberal license (actually, the code is in the public domain). Support for the code is available from the authors. It was a perfect candidate for leveraging third-party code.

We also leveraged several of the libraries from boost (www.boost.org), which also met the above criteria.

On the other hand, I have tried to use other third-party packages and struggled to get what I needed from them, either in functionality or performance. Sometimes I would have liked to use the package, but the license terms were unacceptable for our needs. In many commercial organizations, the copyleft clause of the GNU General Public License (GPL) or its derivatives makes it impossible to use the packages.

I have also seen groups leverage complex software from universities to build new products. Synopsys leveraged the MIS project from the University of California at Berkeley to build its Design Compiler product in the late eighties and early nineties. It worked for them because Synopsys hired several of the MIS developers.

I have also seen this approach yield mediocre results. The rigor required for developing software for PhD dissertations is quite different from the rigor required for a product. The university code can lock you into an architecture that is non-modular and inflexible. You may spend more time fighting the infrastructure than improving the product. In this case it is often better to build from scratch using the published concepts but with an architecture that's designed for evolvability.

There are several factors you should consider.

- Is the solution delivered by the third-party code a differentiating technology for your product? If yes, then I would bias toward building from scratch. You need to have domain knowledge in your team, and you need to improve on the third-party code to sufficiently differentiate your product. You can't be better if you're using the same solution.
- Does your team have the capability to develop the required solution? If no, then unless you believe that you can hire someone quickly, you should use the third-party code.
- Are the licensing terms acceptable for your product? If not, then you have no alternative but to build from scratch or to find a different third-party solution.
- Is the solution known to be robust or is there high-quality support available? Packages like sqlite, the machine learning library TensorFlow™ (tensorflow.org), the file compression library zlib (zlib.net), and many others, have thousands of users and a network of developers who actively improve the package. You will have a hard time doing better.

On the other hand, stay away from a package that implements an obscure algorithm developed by a student who was just learning C++, and that is out there on Github because he thinks it improves his resume.

- If the third-party package accesses the internet, make sure that you can validate the security of the specific version of the package that you are using.

6.3 Staffing

Regardless of whether you choose to make or buy, finding the right person to lead the project will be critical to its success. The leader needs to have domain knowledge and a deep understanding of the implementation, and of how the challenging problem relates to the whole system.

Evaluating the capabilities of a job candidate is a challenge even if you have a reasonable understanding of the field, but if you don't have that understanding, then find someone who does. Even if you have to hire a consultant to help with the technical screening, you will be better off than if you hire the wrong candidate.

Beware that the ability to solve one challenging problem does not necessarily carry over to other problems. I have implemented solutions to many graph problems, and could probably come up to speed quite quickly on a different graph problem. But if you asked me to implement a 3D graphics engine, I would have a couple years of learning curve.

6.4 Metrics

Whether you choose make or buy, the solution to a challenging problem needs to be measured to evaluate the quality of the solution. I will discuss metrics in more detail in the Software Quality chapter, but metrics are so important for challenging problems that I want to go over a few key points here.

Early in the development cycle, determine what parameters you need to measure. It may be obvious, for example, that you want to measure execution time, but maybe you also want to measure some internal parameters that correlate to execution time.

Overcoming the inherent opacity of software is essential to getting a good solution to the problem.

- As you develop the solution, make sure that tests can easily access the parameter values.
- Make sure that you can isolate the solution to the challenging problem so that it can be tested independently from the rest of the system. This may mean that you can run the system in a mode that tests the solution, or even that you create a separate system whose only purpose is to test the solution.

In parallel with the development of the solution, create a metrics benchmark suite. The developers will need a few test cases as soon as the solution starts to function.

Determine a way to establish a benchmark standard (the best-known value) for each parameter of each test case that you intend to measure. Ideally, the standard should come from an independent implementation of the solution. If that's not possible, then comparing against previous versions of your solution may be the only option. Keeping track of the best value of a metric over time at least establishes an upper (or lower) bound for the parameter.

Decide how to manage the tradeoffs that are inherent in challenging problems. The parameters are not independent. Spending more execution time, for example, may improve the results, but is the improvement enough that users will tolerate the waiting? One way to manage tradeoffs is to come up with a global figure of merit for the solution – goodness = a*(execution time) + b*(results). Another way is to establish thresholds for key parameters – execution time may not exceed five seconds. Even if you don't come up with a formula, having the discussion up front will improve awareness of the tradeoffs as the solution evolves.

Benchmarks drive results. An algorithm execution time of 25 seconds may seem pretty good until you hear that your competitor can complete the same task in 4.6 seconds. I have often seen metrics languish at mediocre values for months or years until a competitive benchmark shows that a better result is possible. When faced with losing a benchmark, the team often responds with a breakthrough that improves upon the competitor's result.

6.5 Integrating a Third-Party Package

If you choose a third-party package, you still have work to do to integrate the package into your system, and to coax it to solve your version of the problem. There are two approaches: you can treat the package as a black box, or you can treat it as a starting point for your development.

Black box integration is easier, but still not trivial. Most packages have complex interfaces. You might expect that file compression/decompression would be easy to integrate because the file system interface is simple – just zip and unzip. But the file compression library, zlib, has about twenty pages of documentation. Many other packages have more extensive documentation – some have entire books dedicated to their use. You will need to understand the API, adapt your data to the form that the package requires, and you will need to experiment with the options to see which ones give you the results you need. The metrics you have set up will be invaluable in achieving the best possible integration.

If you intend to modify the package, first make sure that you have the legal rights to do that. Please refer to the upcoming chapter Managing Intellectual Property for details.

Some packages were designed to be modified. If this is the case, then your problem is not so different from using it as a black box, except that, to be effective, you need to understand at least part of the internal architecture. If not, then your first step is to do enough software archaeology to understand the architecture and to determine which parts of the package you need to modify to get the results you're looking for.

6.6 Building from Scratch

Every developer faced with a challenging problem will approach it differently, but there are four parts to every development.

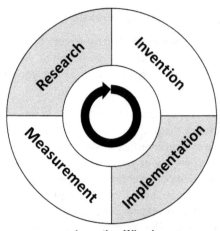

Invention Wheel

- Research how other people have approached this problem and similar problems. (When I think back to how we did this in the 70's and 80's compared to today, all I can think of is: you guys are so lucky. You won't be spending long hours in the library not finding the article you're looking for. A quick internet search will give you more information than you can reasonably process.)
- Invent an approach to the problem.
- Implement your invention.
- Measure your implementation.

Improve it as much as you can. Then do more research, more invention. Implement and measure and go around the loop as many times as necessary to get the results you need.

My approach is to start with invention rather than research. I know this sounds backward, but let me explain why it works better, at least for me. Let's assume I need to develop a new algorithm.

First, I spend time trying to understand the problem in detail. I formulate some simple problems and solve those problems manually. I might create a simple prototype solution using a spreadsheet, just so I can more easily visualize what's going on.

Next, I invent a simple solution to the problem, knowing that there are probably better approaches to the problem.

Next, I implement my invention. At this point, I have a good handle on what data is needed, so I can create a quick and dirty prototype architecture, and a prototype implementation of the algorithm.

Next, I measure my implementation, fully expecting that the results will be terrible. I analyze the results, trying to understand why my approach didn't work as well as I hoped.

Now, I go on the internet and start doing research. With the prototype implementation already done, I understand what I'm reading much better and I'm able to differentiate between good approaches to the problem and approaches that won't work for the specific variation of the problem I'm trying to solve.

I can now start a new invention/implementation/measurement cycle using a synthesis of my original approach and the approaches I researched. If I'm lucky, I can reuse some of the prototype architecture, but if not, then I can throw it away because I didn't spend too much time on it.

My invent-first approach gives me a deeper understanding of the problem so I can better understand the literature, and it provides a fast path to measurement, letting me quickly evaluate my initial implementation and prepare tests to evaluate the future, better implementations.

6.7 *Non-Sequitur* – Managing Intellectual Property

> The first thing we do, let's kill all the lawyers.

Henry VI Part 2, Act 4, Scene 2, William Shakespeare

When Dick the Butcher suggests killing all the lawyers, he's lamenting how hard it is for a criminal to make a living with all those laws around. Lawyers are not evil, unless they're the lawyers for the party that's suing you. The key to good relations with lawyers (and doctors) is to get to them before there's an emergency.

First, a disclaimer: I am not a lawyer and before you make any decisions about legal issues you should consult one. The purpose of this section is to give you enough background that you can understand what your lawyer is talking about when you ask questions about intellectual property.

This section is here in the Challenging Problems chapter because challenging problems are the most likely problems that will require getting software from someone else, and solutions to challenging problems are most in need of protection. And I couldn't find anywhere else to put it.

6.7.1 What is Intellectual Property?

When I buy TurboTax™ I own the disk it came on, but I don't own the software. The disk is tangible property. I can touch it, break it, write my name on it, scratch it or give it to a friend. The software encoded on that disk is intellectual property. When I bought the disk, Intuit granted me a license to use the software, but Intuit owns it. My rights under that license are set forth in the license agreement that we all click through but never read. I can use the software to do my taxes, but, for example, I don't have the right to give a copy to a friend.

Intellectual property (IP) comprises "intangible creations of the human intellect[1]." It's anything you invent. It includes documents (like this book), names (like Coca Cola™) and software both in its source form (C++, Java, etc.) and its compiled form (the bits on the TurboTax disk). Since an IP thief can fit a lot of IP in a backpack, it's important to protect it. Physical locks provide no protection. (The formula for Coke is locked in a safe, but that's more for show than for protection.) The protections are intangible legal protections, as ethereal as the IP itself. You protect documents with copyrights, names with trademarks, and software with patents, trade secrets and legal agreements.

6.7.2 Ownership and Licensing

Copyright

You (or, more likely, your employer) own the code you write. You can add a copyright notice to your code to make it clear who owns it and that you intend to enforce your claim to the code. The notice should be in the form: "Copyright <date> <owner>", like "Copyright 2019 Robert J. Erickson". Your lawyers may want you to add additional text to clarify your rights. The notice should appear in every source code file.

License

Once you claim ownership through a copyright notice, you can decide later how you want others to use the code. That's the license you grant others. The license is a legal agreement that specifies rights granted by the licensor, and the obligations of the licensee. Here, for example, is the text of one of the simpler open source software licenses, the MIT License.

> Copyright <YEAR> <COPYRIGHT HOLDER>
>
> Permission is hereby granted, free of charge, to any person obtaining a copy of this software and associated documentation files (the "Software"), to deal in the Software without restriction, including without limitation the rights to use, copy, modify, merge, publish, distribute, sublicense, and/or sell copies of the Software, and to permit persons to whom the Software is furnished to do so, subject to the following conditions:
>
> The above copyright notice and this permission notice shall be included in all copies or substantial portions of the Software.

---

[1] https://en.wikipedia.org/wiki/Intellectual_property

> THE SOFTWARE IS PROVIDED "AS IS", WITHOUT WARRANTY OF ANY KIND, EXPRESS OR IMPLIED, INCLUDING BUT NOT LIMITED TO THE WARRANTIES OF MERCHANTABILITY, FITNESS FOR A PARTICULAR PURPOSE AND NONINFRINGEMENT. IN NO EVENT SHALL THE AUTHORS OR COPYRIGHT HOLDERS BE LIABLE FOR ANY CLAIM, DAMAGES OR OTHER LIABILITY, WHETHER IN AN ACTION OF CONTRACT, TORT OR OTHERWISE, ARISING FROM, OUT OF OR IN CONNECTION WITH THE SOFTWARE OR THE USE OR OTHER DEALINGS IN THE SOFTWARE.

MIT License https://opensource.org/licenses/MIT

The copyright notice claims ownership. The first paragraph specifies the rights granted to the licensee. The second paragraph specifies the responsibilities of the licensee, in this case requiring the licensee to include the MIT license notice in all copies. The final paragraph disavows any responsibility that the owner has for how the licensee uses the software, and the licensee agrees not to sue the owner. Commercial license agreements (and other open source licenses) will be more complex, but they will still contain these three parts in some form.

Not all source code licenses are alike, and few are as simple and unrestrictive as the MIT License. For example, the GNU General Public License confers serious responsibilities (see below) on the licensee.

As a developer of software you have to decide on the terms for licensing your software products. There are so many different models, that I can't help you. You need to consult with your management and your legal advisors. Most likely these decisions are not in your control anyway.

As an individual licensing a commercial product like TurboTax, you probably don't need to understand the terms of the license. As long as you act reasonably, Intuit is unlikely to sue you. But as a software developer licensing the source code for the solution to a challenging problem, you really need to understand your rights and responsibilities under the license agreement. If you build the software into your code and you suddenly find that the licensor is terminating your rights because you breached the license agreement, you're doomed.

When licensing third party[1] IP, it's important that you have the right to create derivative works. The MIT License, above, confers the right to "modify" the Software. If you get source code, modify it, and use it in your product, you have created a derivative work – a work that is derived from the original. Many open source licenses confer a responsibility on the licensee to make public any changes to the original. If you

---

[1] I understand that the first party is me, but who is the second party?

fix a bug in the software, this give the owner the option to include that bug fix in a future version of the software.

It's also important that you have the right to sublicense the software. Since you are not the original author of the software, when you provide it to your users, you are sublicensing it to them.

GNU General Public License

The GNU General Public License (GPL) and its relative the GNU Lesser General Public License (LGPL) (http://www.gnu.org/licenses/licenses.html) are among the most popular open source software licenses. They were written and are maintained by the Free Software Foundation, a group that advocates that all software should include source code. They are both "copyleft" licenses. Before you use a copyleft license, you should be aware of the implications for your code.

In a copyleft license, one of the responsibilities of the licensee is to distribute source code for the software whether or not the licensee has modified the software. The problem with copyleft is that it applies to the entire program, not just to the licensed software. So, if your million-lines-of-code program links in a hundred-line piece of copyleft software, then you must distribute all million-plus lines of source code. You can question the fairness of it, or the utility of it (who is going to read the million lines except your competitors?), but there is enough legal precedence to believe that the copyleft provisions of GPL may be valid.

(see https://en.wikipedia.org/wiki/GNU_General_Public_License).

If you care about maintaining your trade secrets, then avoid GPL-licensed software. If you are OK with distributing your source code, then go ahead.

6.7.3   Protecting Your Inventions

Suppose that you invented a unique and powerful solution to an old problem. The improvements over the previous approaches are compelling, and you're convinced that there is no better solution. You want to build a company to leverage that invention. How do you make sure no one else can use the same idea for themselves?

Trade Secrets

The simplest way to protect your invention is by keeping it as a trade secret. You and your employees know about it, but you don't let anyone outside the company know about it. The invention is "Confidential Information."

The formula for Coke is a trade secret. Only a few people within Coca Cola know the formula and they take extraordinary precautions to make sure it is not disclosed to anyone else.

Your trade secret is protected because employees have signed agreements not to disclose confidential information, and because you have been careful to mark all information about the invention as confidential.

But since you're depending on the honor of the employees, and because those agreements have time limits (typically a few years), your secret will eventually be known to everyone who cares. That's the fate of all secrets.

NDAs

Because most IP is protected as a trade secret, you need legal protection to slow the inevitable leaking of the secret. Non-Disclosure Agreements (NDAs) essentially say, "I will tell you a secret if you promise not to tell anyone until it's no longer a secret." Lawyers know how to turn those nineteen words into several pages that define what you mean by 'secret', how to know when it's not a secret any more, and what happens if you tell.

The purpose of an NDA is let honest people know what you expect from them. A handshake would be good enough, but making them sign an agreement makes it clear that they were actually listening when you shook hands. An NDA won't stop dishonest people and chances are, unless a breach is blatantly obvious, you won't be able to do anything about it. Most people who have no intention of keeping your secrets won't sign an NDA. Venture Capitalists are notorious for spreading secrets and most of them will not sign an NDA.

Disclosure is a risk-reward tradeoff. If the benefit of telling the secret is high enough, go ahead. But don't rely on the NDA. Assume that anything you disclose will be spread around.

Patents

Patents are nearly the opposite of secrets. When you patent an invention, you tell the world exactly how to reproduce that invention, and in return you get the exclusive right to use the invention for twenty years.

There are two reasons to patent an invention. First, you can use the patent offensively to stop others from using the invention. Second, if someone asserts a patent claim against you, then you can use your portfolio of patents defensively, to counter-assert claims against them. This only works if you hold a patent that they are infringing. If you have a good patent portfolio, then most of the time, you can stay out of court in a cold war of mutually assured destruction.

I'm not going to go too deep into patents, but there are a few high-level things you should know.

- The invention needs to be new, useful and non-obvious.

- o New means you're the first to invent this. A previous invention is called "prior art." If the patent examiner finds prior art, your patent will not be granted.
  - o You wouldn't have bothered to invent it if it weren't useful.
  - o Non-obvious means not obvious to someone knowledgeable in the field. The fact that it's not obvious to your grandmother isn't a high enough standard. If almost anyone in the field, faced with the same problem, would come up with the same or an essentially similar solution, then it was obvious.
- You need to apply for the patent in a timely manner – before public disclosure of the invention for international patents, or within one year of disclosure for US patents. Disclosure means telling someone about the invention without NDA protection, and it includes delivering software that includes the invention to users. The patent process can take a couple years, but it's the date of the application that matters.
- You can't patent something someone else invented. This sounds obvious, but I can't count the number of times that developers came to me with a paper someone else wrote, asking to patent the ideas in the paper.
- A patent is only as good as its enforceability. To enforce the patent, you need to prove that someone is using the invention. If the invention is an algorithm deep inside a product, it's going to be hard to prove infringement without looking at source code.
- If you lose a patent infringement case and you knew about the patent before you infringed, your damages are tripled. So if you lose and the judge tells you to pay $1M, you will have to pay $3M if you willfully infringed. The trouble is that if you personally wrote the code that infringed and didn't know anything about the patent, you may still have triple damages if someone else in the company knew about the patent. That's why I always forbade employees to use online patent databases; the records of who used them are discoverable.

6.7.4   Other People's IP

From time to time you will get IP from someone else; often it's a test case from a customer or user. Your commitment to protect the customer's information is a sacred trust. You should treat it better than you treat your own IP.

The information probably came with an NDA that includes restrictions on how you can use the information, and limits on the time you can use it. The NDA may also restrict who can see the information. So, it's important that you keep track of that IP and can always link it to the NDA that it came with. It may require an elaborate system of network firewalls and procedures to ensure that you can comply with the restrictions. But if you can't comply, then don't accept the data.

6.8 *Non-Sequitur* – NP Problems

Some problems can't be solved, but that doesn't stop us from trying. I will leave peace in the Middle East to diplomats, and will leave eliminating poverty to humanitarians. In this section, I will discuss NP Problems, computer science's own intractable problems.

Managers are often frustrated with the development process and the results when they encounter their first NP problem. They don't understand why results change from day to day, why the algorithms sometimes take so long to run, why the development never seems to end. My goal in this section is to provide enough context that you can understand why these problems are difficult, and that you have an idea of what to try next when the solution is not meeting its goals.

The NP problem is the archetype for all challenging problems. I discuss it here to exemplify the complexity and depth that are inherent in challenging problems. Even if your challenging problem is different, you may gain some insights by understanding the approaches to NP problems.

Entire books have been written on the subject of NP problems. This discussion is a very high-level overview. If you are interested in the mathematics behind NP problems, or if you are interested in a specific NP problem, you can find a lot of material to help you. I will avoid most of the math and will attempt to provide an intuitive understanding of the problems, and will discuss some ways to approach them.

NOTE: I have labeled this section *non-sequitur* because it doesn't directly relate to better understanding of the Geodesic Philosophy. If you are likely to encounter an NP problem in your work, I recommend that you read through section Constraints; the optimization sections that follow that are mostly for developers who might need to solve an NP problem.

6.8.1 Definitions

We use big-O notation to describe the **complexity** of an algorithm. The complexity gives you a relative indication of how fast the algorithm will execute depending on the problem size. A naïve sorting algorithm, like bubble sort, is $O(n^2)$. That means that, in the worst case, sorting a list of 200 elements will take 4x longer than sorting a list of 100 elements. A better sorting algorithm is $O(n \log n)$, meaning that sorting the 200-element list will take 2.3x longer. For an algorithm that is $O(n)$, processing the 200-element list will run 2x longer.

Sorting a list is a P problem, meaning it can be solved in polynomial time. Matrix inversion is $O(n^2 \log n)$; it is also a P problem. Not all P problems are tractable – inverting a one million by one million matrix can take a very long time – but their intractability grows relatively slowly compared to NP problems.

NP problems cannot be solved in polynomial time, hence the abbreviation NP for Non-Polynomial. Many NP problems are $O(n!)$. 10! is about 3.6 million. 100! is about 10^{158}. If you have an $O(n!)$ problem with one million elements, the number of possible solutions is unimaginably large. In these problems, you need to make n decisions, and every decision depends on all the decisions that have come before. In the most naïve approaches, to find the best solution, you need to look at every possible combination of the decisions. This is often called combinatorial explosion.

You will hear the terms NP-Hard and NP-Complete. These terms refer to certain classes of NP problems that are mathematically equivalent. If you can find a P solution to one of these problems, then all of them have a P solution. Most computer scientists believe that a P solution will never be found, and that searching for it is akin to searching for a perpetual motion machine.

Some NP problems must be solved exactly. I will call these *satisfiability* problems. The goal of a satisfiability solver is to find a solution that satisfies the problem constraints. Satisfiability problems have two possible answers – 1) there is a solution, or 2) there is no solution. The Sudoku puzzle is an NP satisfiability problem. Sometimes a Sudoku solver will encounter a puzzle that it can't solve in a reasonable time. Usually, it's better to inform the user of the failure to answer the question rather than to present a solution that's not valid; in that case, there is a third possible answer – 3) I don't know.

Other NP problems have many valid solutions and the objective of the solver is to find the best solution. I will call these *optimization* problems. The Traveling Salesman Problem described below is an optimization problem. The rest of this discussion of NP problems will focus on optimization problems.

6.8.2 NP Problem Example – The Traveling Salesman Problem

In order to better understand NP problems, let's consider the Traveling Salesman Problem. Our itinerant vendor, Nora, gets a list of customers she must visit today. Her problem is to travel the shortest total distance to reach all the customers and then come back home. Luckily, she has a drone, or maybe Mary Poppins' umbrella, so she can travel on a straight line between any pair of customers.

In the discussion that follows, I will use the terms *segment* to mean the distance between two customers, and *path* to mean the ordered list of segments that starts and ends at home. I will use a customer's *index* to refer to its position in the path. Home will always have index 0.

I use the Traveling Salesman Problem as an example to illustrate key concepts that apply to all NP problems. There has been extensive research on the best ways to approach the Traveling Salesman Problem. The state-of-the-art optimizers can find solutions to very large problems within a few percent of optimal. Please note that I am making no attempt to describe the best approach to the Traveling Salesman Problem. I am only trying to illustrate the challenges inherent in all NP problems.

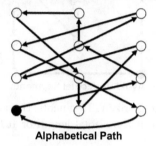

Alphabetical Path

In the above figure, home is the red dot in the lower left, and the customers are arranged on a grid with the north/south distance of one mile, and the east/west distance of two miles. The lines represent the segments of the path Nora must take if she visits the customers in alphabetical order. There's got to be something better.

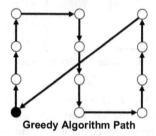

Greedy Algorithm Path

First, Nora tries a greedy algorithm. The next stop is always the closest stop that's still available. This path looks pretty good, but at the end of the day she has a long way to travel home. The total distance is 18 miles (nine vertical routes of length 1.0, two horizontal routes of length 2.0, and the diagonal segment of length $\sqrt{4^2 + 3^2} = 5.0$).

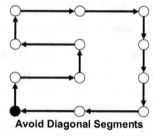

Avoid Diagonal Segments

She draws another path that avoids the diagonal segment, but realizes that this also has a total length of 18 miles. It's not better because there are six long horizontal segments.

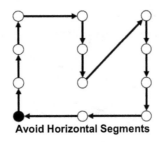

Avoid Horizontal Segments

She tries a path that minimizes horizontal segments. This path only has three horizontal segments and one diagonal. It has a total length of 16.8 miles. Now she's making progress.

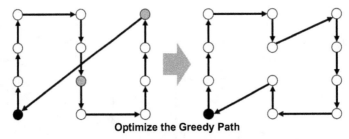

Optimize the Greedy Path

Finally, she goes back to the greedy algorithm's path. She knows that there's a simple optimization she can apply. Whenever two segments cross, she can improve the result by swapping the end-point of one segment with the start-point of the other, and reversing the order of the intervening customers. In the rest of this section, I will refer to this optimization as the *line-crossing heuristic*. This path has a total length of 16.5 miles. There might be a better path, but she has to get going, so she finishes her coffee and starts the drone.

6.8.3   Properties of NP Optimization Problems

This example illustrates a few things about NP optimization problems.

- It's virtually impossible to know if you found the best possible solution.

This simple problem has forty million (11!) possible paths. Most of them look something like the first one, the chaotic one, above. To prove that Nora's path is the best one, she would have to evaluate all of them. In this case, with the stops on a regular grid, she probably found an optimal solution, but it's clear that she could put the two diagonal segments in other places and get the same total path length. If we move all the stops a little off the grid, then probably one of those other equivalent paths will be better than the one she chose.

- You might need to try several heuristics to get a good result.

You can think of a heuristic as a set of rules to apply to a decision. The greedy heuristic rule is "always take the shortest segment that's available".

The intention of a heuristic is to guide the solver to find solutions that are likely to have good results. If you try multiple heuristics, maybe one of them will find a solution that's a lot better than the others.

- A good solution could benefit from a global view of the problem.

Humans are pretty good at solving the Traveling Salesman Problem if the number of stops is small. Their visual processing abilities quickly identify global issues, like lines that cross, and the long homeward segment, but they can't get the details of the length calculation accurate enough to find the best solution. The third solution above with no diagonal segments looks best, but it's not the shortest. Computers are much better at evaluating the details, but not so good at getting the big picture. Just figuring out if there are crossing lines means that I need to compare every line with every other line. (Of course, there are tricks to avoid a lot of the irrelevant comparisons.)

Simple algorithms, like the greedy algorithm, make one decision at a time. More complex algorithms might look at pairs of decisions. It's very difficult to see the global impact of a decision. Instead, we come up with heuristics to guide us. For example, avoiding horizontal segments got us to the fourth solution, with one diagonal, that was pretty close to the best result.

- If you have a solution, you can try to improve that solution.

The best solution to Nora's problem was found by starting with the greedy solution and applying a simple optimization heuristic.

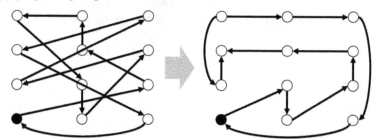

Line-crossing Heuristic Starting from Alphabetical Solution

You can imagine applying that line-crossing heuristic repeatedly to the first, chaotic, solution to get something better. My manual attempt at doing this, shown above without the intermediate steps, resulted in a solution that's pretty far from the best solution.

But it is unlikely that a simple heuristic alone can find the optimal solution starting from a bad solution. However, there are optimization strategies, like simulated annealing, that are much better at finding good solutions. In some sense, they "learn" the global impact of local decisions based on previous decisions.

I'll discuss optimization in a little more detail later in this section.

- Real-world problems are a lot harder than the problems we choose to solve.

The assumption that Nora has a drone so she can fly in a straight line is a nice simplifying assumption, but not practical. Nora probably has to drive a car, navigating a network with one-way streets and traffic congestion. The 'optimal' solution to the simple problem could be far from optimal when used in the real world.

Our hope is that the solution to the simpler problem is good enough when used in the real world. When we see that hope fail, then we start trying to solve a harder problem that is a closer approximation to the real world. Usually, this means that the real-world result is better, but at the cost of increased execution time. But eventually we find some other aspect of the real world, like finding a parking place, that causes a problem.

6.8.4 Approaches to Solving NP Optimization Problems

For most classes of NP optimization problems, you can find publications that describe the state of the art for approaching that problem. In many cases, you can track the approaches over time as researchers struggled to find a good way to solve the problem. At some point in time, a breakthrough occurred and publications stopped. That doesn't mean that the problem is solved, only that the breakthrough gives good enough results most of the time that university researchers stopped caring about finding a better approach. In many cases, the research moved to corporations whose goal is to create a product, not a publication. The corporate research often focuses on doing a better job of solving the real-world problem rather than on finding a completely different approach.

6.8.5 Cost Functions

The optimizer needs a way to decide if one solution is better than another. To make this comparison, it uses a cost function. For the Traveling Salesman Problem described above, the cost function is simply the total distance of the path.

The cost function is the way we model the real world. When you want to model problems that are more like the real world, then you need your optimizer to make tradeoffs. That will require a more complicated cost function.

Suppose that Nora is willing to travel a little more distance if the path puts her in a good location for lunch. She knows that there are good restaurants near three of the eleven customers, and she likes to eat lunch for thirty minutes between 11:30 and 1:30.

If Nora were choosing her path manually, she would probably choose a restaurant and try to arrive at that location about noon. If she thought it required too much extra traveling, she might choose another restaurant or decide to pack a lunch.

To have the optimizer make the decision will require a two-part cost function:

$$C = C_D + W_L C_L$$

where C is the total cost, C_D is the total distance, C_L is the lunch cost, and W_L is the weight of the lunch cost. The weight translates the units of C_L to miles, and determines how to tradeoff miles of distance vs. having a good place for lunch. (Conceptually, there is also a weight for the distance cost, but I almost always make the weight of the primary cost equal to 1.0.)

Although it seems like a reasonable request to have the optimizer consider lunch, that simple request can add enormous complexity to the cost function. It needs to calculate arrival times in addition to the total distance. The arrival time estimates will be inaccurate because unpredictable winds will affect her drone's speed, and the customer meetings might take longer than expected. The cost function will need to figure out what to do if more than one restaurant location falls in the 11:30 to 12:30 window. But most importantly, the execution time of the optimizer will increase by a lot.

For the purposes of optimization, there will always be a way to calculate the cost function from scratch. If your optimizer is making discrete changes (usually called *moves*), like swapping the path order of two customers, then recalculating the cost from scratch for every move will be too slow. You need an efficient way to calculate the change in the cost function for each move. This is the delta-cost calculation.

Delta-cost calculations can be fast if a move only causes local changes. For example, if a move affects the path location of customers A and B, then the delta-cost calculation is local if the delta-cost calculation only needs to look at A and B and their nearest neighbors. If delta-cost calculations are local, then the complexity of the optimizer is $O(m)$, where m is the number of moves.

The arrival time calculation is not local. Any change in the path that happens before noon will affect the arrival time for all customers later in the path, and it will affect the choice of lunch location. Now the complexity of the optimizer is $O(mn)$ where m is the number of moves and n is the number of customers. For large problems it will not be feasible to consider lunch in the cost function.

I chose this example to illustrate the difficulty of modeling the real world in a way that coaxes the optimizer to make the decisions that a human might make. The best we can practically do is to model with a gross approximation to reality. If lunch is important to your customers, I'm sure you will find another way to solve the problem. The solution will be far from optimal, but it will be good enough so that no one goes hungry.

6.8.6   Constraints

In addition to the cost function, most NP problems also have constraints. A constraint is a condition that must be met to have a valid solution. For satisfiability problems, the constraints define the problem. If you find a solution that meets all the constraints, then you are done. For optimization problems, you must find one of many possible solutions that meet the constraints, and that solution should have a near-optimal cost function value.

For the Traveling Salesman Problem described above, the requirement that the path start and end at home is a constraint. Nora might also want to add a constraint that the path may not contain a segment whose length is longer than 4.0 miles.

When it's not practical to model the real-world requirements with a cost function, you can often use constraints as a back-door method to model the real world. For example, Nora might decide to solve the lunch problem with a constraint: the fourth customer on the path must be near a good restaurant.

A solver must understand constraints and be able to generate solutions that meet them. Early in a project that solves an NP problem you need to understand what kind of constraints you need to support. You need to design how you will 1) represent them in your architecture, and 2) how you will satisfy them. It can be very messy to add support for new constraints to a system after the solver is written.

6.8.7   Exploring the Solution Space

NP optimization problems have a lot of solutions. For practical purposes, you can think of them as having infinite solutions, because it's not practical to evaluate them all. For each one of those solutions, it's possible to calculate a value for the cost function. The set of all solutions together with their cost values is called the solution space. You can think of it as an n-dimensional space, where n is the number of decisions.

The goal of an optimizer is to find the solution with the smallest cost. (For the purposes of this discussion, we will assume that there is only one solution with that cost.) That solution is called the global optimum. From the global optimum solution, any move will increase the cost.

We can't visualize an n-dimensional space. So, to illustrate concepts about exploring the solution space, we define an *optimization sequence* to be a series of moves (local changes to the solution) that transforms one solution into another. We can think of the sequence as a function with the cost on the y-axis and the index of the move on the x-axis. In the figure below, we see a series of moves that transform the original alphabetical solution to the final solution. Each move swaps the sequence order of the two yellow nodes. The optimization sequence is shown in the chart.

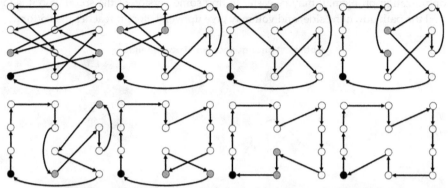

A Sequence of Moves from the Alphabetical Solution to the Best Solution

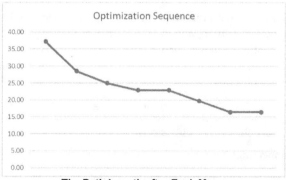

The Path Length after Each Move

An optimization problem is *convex* if you can start at any solution and always arrive at the global optimum through a monotonic optimization sequence. In a convex problem, any move that decreases the cost gets you closer to the optimum solution. In many cases, you can prove that a problem is convex, even though it may be impractical to find such a sequence.

Any optimization technique that never makes moves that increase the cost is called a *hill-climbing* algorithm. It was named for problems that are trying to find the maximum benefit rather than the minimum cost. Maybe it should be called a valley-descending algorithm, but we will stay with the standard term.

For convex problems, hill-climbing algorithms can sometimes find the global optimum, but there's no guarantee. Think of the problem as a cereal bowl. You can get to the bottom by taking five moves that go straight down the side, or you can get there by taking five thousand moves that spiral around the sides of the bowl. Both sequences will get you to the bottom, but one sequence is much more efficient. In an NP optimization problem, it may be easier to find some version of the spiral than it is to find the path down the side, and you may give up well before it reaches the bottom.

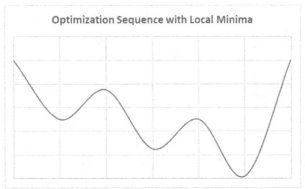

Non-Convex Optimization Sequence

Non-convex problems have multiple local minima, only one of which is the global minimum. At a local minimum, any move will increase the cost. In the figure above, you can see an optimization sequence that shows three valleys. In non-convex problems, the optimizer needs to explore lots of valleys hoping that one of them contains the global optimum.

Some optimization techniques, for example, Tabu Search

https://en.wikipedia.org/wiki/Tabu_search

and simulated annealing

https://en.wikipedia.org/wiki/Simulated_annealing

have built-in strategies for moving from one valley to another. Other techniques try lots of different initial solutions and use an efficient hill-climbing algorithm to find the local minimum for the valley that the initial solution put them in. With any technique, there's an element of luck involved in finding the right valley.

6.8.8   Constructive Optimization

A constructive algorithm starts with nothing and then proceeds to make decisions, one by one, until a candidate solution is found. The greedy algorithm described above is a constructive algorithm.

Stochastic construction uses a stochastic process to make its decisions. Each decision is made by choosing a random number and using that number to make a decision based on a probability distribution. For example, instead of choosing the shortest available segment, choose a segment randomly from the set of all available segments, with higher probability of choosing short segments.

A Constructive optimizer uses a series of stochastic construction processes, learning from the results of previous constructions, and adjusting the decision probability distributions based on its learning. From the previous solutions, it learns the global impact of local decisions.

Many optimization algorithms are modeled after biological or physical processes found in nature. Genetic Optimization

https://en.wikipedia.org/wiki/Genetic_algorithm

and Ant-Colony Optimization

https://en.wikipedia.org/wiki/Ant_colony_optimization_algorithms

are two of the many constructive optimization techniques that can be applied to the Traveling Salesman Problem.

Genetic optimization is modeled after the evolutionary principle of survival of the fittest. The optimizer keeps a gene pool of the most successful solutions generated so far. It then "mates" pairs of solutions to generate new solutions by choosing parts from each parent solution, and occasionally introducing mutations.

Ant Colony Optimization is modeled after how ants find food. In the Traveling Salesman Problem, a group of ants are sent out in search of a good path. The most successful ants mark the path they chose with "pheromones". The next bunch of ants are more likely to follow the pheromone trail of previously successful ants.

Constructive optimizers can sometimes give good results, but they are often slow, and they can be susceptible to chaotic behavior. What appear to be minor changes to the problem or to the algorithm can have major impacts to the results.

6.8.9 Initial Solution Generation

Solving an optimization problem usually happens in two phases. In the first phase, you use some simplification of the problem to find one (or more) initial solution that's pretty good. In the second phase, you use a heuristics-based optimizer to improve that solution. A good initial solution must provide some global context to the optimizer, which typically will only be able to make local optimizations.

The simplest way to generate an initial solution is with randomized construction. You can also use a constructive optimization technique to generate initial solutions that have much lower cost than a random solution.

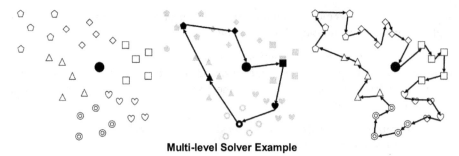

Multi-level Solver Example

Another common way to generate an initial solution is to break the big problem into a bunch of little problems. This approach is called a *multi-level* solver. In the left part of the figure above, you see a Traveling Salesman problem with thirty customers and home (the slightly larger black dot). First, we create six clusters, each with five customers, represented by dots with the same shape. Then we find the best path using pseudo-nodes that represent the clusters, as shown in the center part of the figure. Finally, we find a path through the customers in each cluster, as shown on the right of the figure. Each one of the sub-problems is small enough that it can be solved exactly. The resulting path, on the right, looks pretty good, although it is probably not optimal. You can apply this technique recursively to handle even bigger problems. For example, each of the thirty dots might represent a cluster of five customers to handle a problem with one hundred fifty customers.

Another common way to generate an initial solution is the *analytical* approach. The cost function as described above is only valid if every decision is a discrete yes/no decision. In the analytical approach, you create an approximate cost function that uses a continuous variable for each decision. Essentially, each variable represents some value of maybe. If you can come up with an analytical cost function, you can solve the continuous problem using standard mathematical techniques like Lagrangian multipliers (sorry, that's more math than I promised). The hope is that after rounding to yes/no decisions, the continuous solution will be close to a good solution to the discrete problem. The analytical technique has been very successful in electronic design for deciding where to place each logic gate in a complex chip. Unfortunately, I don't know of an analytical solution to the Traveling Salesman problem, so I can't provide a simple example.

When generating an initial solution, you may want to generate lots of candidate solutions and then choose the best one(s) to continue with. To get fast enough execution time, it is tempting to use a simplified cost function or to ignore some of the constraints. The hope is that you can fix any problems later. In many cases, however, repairing the problems that were not considered while generating the initial solution will cause the optimizer to move far away from the initial solution. For example, ignoring the lunch constraint may require significant reroutes that add a lot of total length to the solution.

So, if you need to simplify the problem for initial solution generation, do it in a way in which any problems can be solved with local optimizations.

6.8.10 Incremental Optimization

Once you have an initial solution then you need to improve it. An incremental optimization algorithm starts with an initial solution and then makes a series of moves that, ultimately, finds a better solution.

You can build your own optimization strategy using an *ad hoc* heuristic – one that is specific to your particular problem. For example, in the Traveling Salesman Problem you could use the line-crossing heuristic described above. Or you might create a special heuristic that addresses the lunch problem.

There are lots of incremental optimization strategies that can be applied to NP problems. They typically have a few common aspects.

- Move generation – Here we determine what moves are possible. For the Traveling Salesman Problem, we might allow any move that swaps the path indices of two customers. In many cases, move generation will need to be aware of constraints and will not generate moves that violate constraints. Depending on the optimization strategy, move generation may generate a large set of moves, or it may generate one move at a time as requested by move selection.

- You might need more than one type of move for your optimization. For example, the line-crossing heuristic requires a sequence of swap moves to get the order right. You may also want to include a three-way swap. Beware that each type of move will need support in the cost function for incremental cost calculations.

- Move selection – Out of the set of all possible moves, choose one move. Some optimization strategies choose from a large set of pre-calculated moves using the delta-cost of the moves as a criterion. Other strategies randomly select moves based on some other criteria. For example, in the Traveling Salesman Problem, you might be more likely to move customers that are attached to long segments.

- To some extent, move selection needs to understand the history of moves to avoid getting stuck in a loop. We need to avoid sequences like: generate move A; execute move A; undo move A; generate move A; etc. Sometimes it's adequate just to limit the number of times that a particular move is allowed.

- Move acceptance or rejection – Most strategies will accept any move that reduces the cost or leaves it unchanged. Strategies differ on what to do with moves that increase the cost.

- Hill-climbing strategies always reject moves that increase the cost, and therefore cannot move to a different valley in the solution space.

- Some strategies, such as Kernighan-Lin's strategy for graph partitioning, always accept the move (up to some limits), hoping that a bad move will enable a sequence of good moves that will more than make up for the loss. Note that you can always remember the best solution ever found, so a bad search won't hurt you.
- In simulated annealing, the move is accepted based on a random number and the current "temperature". A move is accepted if a random number between 0.0 and 1.0 is less than $e^{\frac{-\Delta Cost}{Temperature}}$. At high temperatures, early in the optimization process, many cost-increasing moves are accepted. As optimization proceeds, the algorithm reduces the temperature, making it less likely to accept a cost-increasing move, until at the end, when the temperature is near zero, no cost-increasing moves are accepted.
- Stop criteria – In most cases, you can't practically know if your optimization has found the global optimum, so deciding when to give up is something of an art. Usually you will set a limit for how long you are willing to let the optimization run, or you will run until the optimization stops improving.

6.8.11   One more property of NP Problems

- NP problems are chaotic and subject to the butterfly effect.

A butterfly flapping its wings in Kathmandu can trigger events that lead to a hurricane in Jamaica. Changing the rounding strategy for part of the cost function calculation can change the sequence of accepted moves in such a way that the optimizer can no longer find a good solution.

The butterfly effect occurs because of the way that optimizers explore the solution space. They depend on cost increasing decisions to move from one solution-space valley to another. Sometimes when you improve the optimizer to make more cost-decreasing decisions, the one cost-increasing move the optimizer needed gets rejected. Or, a change in the sequence of moves doesn't give the optimizer the opportunity to make the critical move.

The butterfly effect is perhaps the most frustrating property of NP optimization problems for users, who just want to get the same result they had last week, and for software managers who just want things to improve monotonically. It means that every time you change the software, someone is going to have a negative surprise.

You can manage the negative surprise two ways. First, you need to measure across a broad set of tests, and understand what caused the negative outliers. Second, you need to provide a way for users to overcome your automation. If nine out of ten users' results improved, you still have 10% of users with bad results. If you provide general ways to improve results, like ways to coax the optimizer into the right valley, then those users will have a way to get the results they need.

6.9   Key Concepts

- The decision of whether to use a third-party solution for you challenging problem or to build your own solution from scratch is a far-reaching decision that will have long-lasting ramifications
  - o Integrating a third-party package to solve your challenging problem comes with its own work.
  - o You can't be better than your competitor if you are both doing the same thing.
- Regardless of the make vs. buy decision, set up a good measurement system. Make sure you plan for measurement early in the development cycle.
- When building your own solution, follow the Invention Wheel.

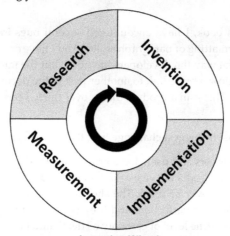

Invention Wheel

- o When starting on the solution to a challenging problem, do enough invention and prototyping to thoroughly understand the problem before diving into the literature.
- Protect your Intellectual Property
  - o Use copyright notices in all source code.
  - o Understand the license agreements of any third-party code you use, in particular understand your rights and obligations.
  - o Protect your inventions with patents, or with trade secrets and NDAs.
  - o Treat the IP that's entrusted to you by others as well or better than you treat your own.
- NP Problems are the archetype for challenging problems.
  - o Since they cannot practically be solved exactly, we resort to heuristics that address a gross approximation to the real problem.
  - o Cost functions are the mechanism to approximate the real world.
  - o Constraints limit the range of solutions to the problem.
  - o Optimization algorithms attempt to find a good solution to the problem.

7 SOFTWARE QUALITY

There was a question on Quora recently: What are the biggest challenges in the computer programming field for the coming years? The answers ranged from P vs. NP, tools and languages, formal methods, overworked developers, functional programming, and the ethics of privacy and security. But none of them mentioned quality.

When I first read the Agile Manifesto, I was shocked that the word 'quality' did not appear.

In the writing of this book, I have encountered several bugs in Microsoft Word™, mostly around the formatting of paragraph styles. And I have encountered other areas where Word works the way the developers intended, but the intention is just wrong. For example, I can follow a hyperlink to another part of the document, but there is no easy way to get back. This is in a product that is over thirty years old with millions of users.

To my mind, quality is the biggest challenge in software.

I think that both developers and users have grown so accustomed to bad quality that we have stopped trying. Products I've worked on have had hundreds or thousands of reported bugs that will never be fixed. The sheer number of bugs makes developers lose hope of ever achieving perfection, and they've stopped trying to improve. Bad quality has reached the same level of certainty as death and taxes.

In this chapter, I discuss the problem of quality, starting with an attempt to answer the question, "What is Quality?" Next, I discuss how to classify bugs, followed by a discussion on testing and other ways to improve quality. I conclude the chapter with a discussion on how to write high-quality code.

There is nothing really new here. But I hope that looking at the problem from a few different angles can help put it in focus. I believe that awareness of quality is our best hope for the future of software. The fact that quality is not on the tip of the tongue of every software developer in the world is the first problem I want to fix. You won't improve if you don't care.

7.1 *Non-Sequitur* – The Bard on Quality[1]

> Who is Quality? what is she,
> That all our swains commend her?
> Holy, fair, and wise is she;
> The heaven such grace did lend her,
> That she might admirèd be.
>
> Is she kind as she is fair?
> For beauty lives with kindness.
> Love doth to her eyes repair,
> To help him of his blindness;
> And, being helped, inhabits there.
>
> Then to Quality let us sing,
> That Quality is excelling;
> She excels each mortal thing
> Upon the dull earth dwelling;
> To her let us garlands bring

Adapted from Two Gentlemen of Verona,
Act 4, Scene 2, William Shakespeare

> What light is light, if Quality be not seen?
> What joy is joy, if Quality be not by —
> Unless it be to think that she is by
> And feed upon the shadow of perfection?
> Except I be by Quality in the night,
> There is no music in the nightingale.
> Unless I look on Quality in the day,
> There is no day for me to look upon.
> She is my essence, and ...
> If I be not by her fair influence
> Fostered, illumined, cherished, kept alive,
> ... I fly away from life

Adapted from Two Gentlemen of Verona,
Act 3, Scene 1, William Shakespeare
(With my apologies to Silvia, wherever she may be.)

---

[1] Actually, the Bard on Silvia, but I asked and she doesn't mind.

7.2 What is Quality?

High-Quality Software is the goal of every software team. No one wants to be the Schlocky-But-On-Time software team or the Does-More-Than-You-Can-Imagine-But-It-Almost-Never-Works software team. They want to bask in the sunshine of Quality, dance to the music of Quality, smell the roses of Quality. But what is Quality? "I know it when I see it," is not enough. Nor is "I know when it's not there," although the absence of imperfections is important.

Corporate quality departments attempt to measure quality with various indicators: weighted defect density, incoming bug rate, test coverage, compiler warning count, etc. Except that they are easy to measure, these indicators provide little value to development teams. They can sometimes tell you if quality is bad, but not if it's good. And once you understand the metrics, you can get corporate quality off your back by fixing your software to get high grades on the indicators without improving the customer's experience.

Let me attempt a definition:

High Quality Software does what the user wants in the way the user expects.

There is no higher compliment for a software product than to hear a user say, "It just works."

Lack of bugs is a necessary part of High-Quality Software. Let's call that *reliability*. Reliable software has few bugs, and no serious bugs. Users will tolerate a few bugs if they are not serious and if it's easy to find a workaround. Users tend to blame themselves for software failures, and if they find something that they did that caused the problem, they feel in control because they can avoid that something in the future. (Most likely they will continue to avoid that something for years after the problem has been fixed.) The bugs where the software fails no matter how much the user tries to change are much harder to tolerate because the user does not feel in control.

But the other part of quality, the part that's not reliability, is equally or more important. Let's call that *functionality*. It's difficult, however, to pinpoint what functionality makes a product high quality. Consider two approaches to user interfaces.

In the intuitive approach, High Quality Software does not need a usage manual because the usage model is so intuitive that it is always clear what to do next. A short demonstration and an online reference manual are all the training that a user needs.

In the highly configurable approach, the learning curve for High Quality Software is very steep, but the reward for learning is that users get exactly what they want. I have seen that some users will tolerate an abominable user interface if the tool gives them the ability to get exactly what they want.

I have used two Verilog hardware description language simulators, ModelSim from Mentor Graphics and VCS from Synopsys. Both products are perceived to be high quality by their users. At the highest level, both products do the same thing: execute a model of hardware to verify that a chip will function correctly. But their approaches are very different.

ModelSim uses the intuitive approach. The ModelSim user interface guides the user through the process of setting up a model and running the simulation. The learning curve for basic operation is short and painless, but if the user needs more capability, ModelSim can handle that as well, but with a steeper learning curve.

VCS uses the highly configurable approach. It requires a series of complex scripts to run. The scripts are often put together with the help of applications support engineers to work for the users' specific problem. VCS is difficult to use for basic operation, but very good at working in complex real-world environments.

Both products are High Quality Software. Each approach works better for some set of users. ModelSim users would be frustrated trying to use VCS, and vice versa. But for each product's users, the product does what the user wants in the way the user expects. And, after all, that's the definition of High-Quality Software.

So, if we can't define the *je-ne-sais-quoi* of Quality, how can you know if you have High Quality Software? And more importantly, how can you know what needs to improve if you don't?

Listen to your customers. The universal truth about customers is that they complain. Make sure that you can hear them. What they complain about and how they complain are the best indicators.

In the last product I worked on before I retired, every quarter the applications support engineers reported problems with the product. I watched as the reports for my part of the product evolved over the first few quarters after the initial release. Every quarter the reported "biggest problem" with my part was different, either because we had already fixed the problem reported the previous quarter, or the users had worked through the learning curve to understand how to address the problem with the features designed into the product. After a few quarters, my part of the product no longer showed up on the problem report, and by the time I retired, several application support engineers had told me that it "just worked."

Customers are not just the best measure of quality, they are the only measure that matters. When customer complaints center around a theme, you need to address that theme. When complaints are evolving with the customers' learning curves, try to stay ahead of them. When customers stop complaining, it's time to work harder.

7.3 Entomology – A Taxonomy of Software Bugs

Life Cycle of a Bug
That can't happen.
That doesn't happen on my machine.
That shouldn't happen.
Why does that happen?
Oh, I see.
How did that ever work?

Internet legend attributed to Mike Cremer

All software developers have had that how-did-that-ever-work moment, when you compare the original code with the "fixed" code and wonder why you've never seen that failure before. Sometimes I am so angry at the bug that I start an archaeological dig through the change history to find the idiot author who wrote that abomination. I will make sure he never does that again. Usually I was that idiot, and unfortunately, I have done that again, and again, and again.

I have seen many bug classification systems. Usually these are put in place to track problems found by customers, and usually they focus only on the impact of the bug on the customer. They are useful for tracking problems for support, but they don't help us improve.

Often these systems avoid using the word 'bug'.

At one place I worked they were 'defects'. The word 'defect' was intended to emphasize the importance of the bug problem to the developers because bugs were so common that the QA department was sure that developers didn't take them seriously. As if changing the name of 'mosquito' to 'annoyance' would make me more likely to slap it. Even vegans will slap mosquitoes if they catch them in the act.

At another place they were 'STARs', probably an acronym whose antecedent is lost in history. The intention here was to obfuscate the problem to customers. Our products don't have bugs; they have STARs, kind of like the ones that grade school kids get for good behavior. If you get stung, you know it was a wasp, even if I tell you it was a cute little bunny.

I will call a bug a 'bug', and present a four-level taxonomy for understanding bugs.

- Manifestation – How do we know that a bug happened? In this taxonomy, a bug only exists if it happened. We can't classify the plethora of potential bugs lurking silently in code, only the ones we can see.
- Locality – Is the cause of the bug near the point of manifestation? Local bugs are much easier to fix than non-local bugs.
- Cause – What mistake did developers make that caused the manifestation? Users cannot cause bugs, no matter how badly they treat the software.

- Test Coverage – Why was this problem not found in testing? Or if it was found, why have we not fixed it?

The taxonomy helps us understand how to improve our processes to eliminate bug causes and improve test coverage for the most important bugs.

7.3.1 Manifestation

Manifestation classifies the bug by how it appears to the user. The following categories are roughly in order of most severe to least severe. In your product, the order may be different.

Silent Killer

The Silent Killer is a violation of the most fundamental agreement between the software and the user. Without any outward sign, it makes an egregious mistake. For a C-compiler, it would be generating code that doesn't work from valid source. For a database tool, it would be losing data. For a map navigation tool, it would be sending the driver the wrong way on a one-way street. You already know what this means for your product.

Crash

The software stops operating, usually because of an invalid operation at the lowest level of the hardware. Typical causes are access of an illegal memory address or execution of an invalid CPU instruction. The program may try to recover, but typically, everything the user was doing is lost. This kind of bug was so common in early Windows® operating systems that it gained the name, "Blue Screen of Death".

Hang

The software is running but not responding. It could be stuck in an infinite loop, or in a very complex problem that will eventually complete after a much longer time than expected.

Assertion Failure

Sometimes, developers add safety checks to detect situations that should not happen. These are called assertions. For example, I assert that the value of variable v will never be less than zero. What happens next often looks the same as a crash to the user. An assertion failure is detected by code you control, while a crash is detected by code you don't control like the operating system.

Requirement Failure

The software fails to meet a requirement. For example, a C-compiler rejects valid source code. This is the most common kind of bug. For your product, you may want to add additional categories under this one.

Parametric Failure

The software operates as intended, but a parameter of the software does not meet the requirements. For example, user interface response time is too slow, or navigation software finds a circuitous route. For your product, you may want to add additional categories under this one for each of your important parameters.

7.3.2   Locality and Extent

Locality classifies the bug by the "distance" between the manifestation and the cause in code space and time. The locality correlates to how hard it will be to debug and fix the problem. You can usually tell within the first few minutes of debugging how to classify a bug's locality.

The Extent of the bug classifies the bug by the amount of change required to fix it. Point failures are limited to a few lines of code. Architectural failures require changes to multiple modules. The first three failures below are point failures.

Local Function Failure

The cause of the bug is near the point of manifestation. For example, if an assertion failure occurs because a value exceeds a threshold, then fixing the calculation of that value in the same function would be a local failure. These are the easiest problems to debug and fix.

Called Function Failure

The cause of the bug is not in the same function as the point of manifestation. For example, the bad value in a threshold assertion may be calculated in a function called several levels down from the assertion check.

Side-Effect Failure

The cause of the bug changed a value in a persistent data structure and that data later triggered a bug manifestation. For example, the bad value in a threshold assertion may have been calculated yesterday and stored in a database. These are the hardest problems to debug. They are often intermittent and difficult to reproduce. Sometimes I have had to write extensive diagnostic code to track down the root cause of a side-effect failure.

Architectural Failure

As opposed to the point failures above, an Architectural Failure has a broad extent. The cause of the bug is an inadequacy of the architecture. This is often the case for parametric failures and for some requirement failures. The fix for the bug may require changes to several modules. Architectural failures require extensive changes that may propagate – each change requiring more changes in other parts of the system. The fixes for these failures trees have the potential of creating many new bugs.

7.3.3 Cause

Cause classifies the bug by the coding problem that caused it. Unfortunately, you can't classify the cause until you have spent the time necessary to diagnose it. Making the effort to classify causes can help you improve your development processes.

The cause we are looking for is the true cause. It doesn't include workarounds and other symptom-hiding changes.

A workaround hides a bug by eliminating the conditions that cause the bug to occur. For example, if there is a bug in a third-party library that only occurs if some conditions are met, the cause is in the third-party library. The workaround is to make sure those conditions never occur.

A symptom-hiding change makes the manifestation of the bug disappear by making a change that is unrelated to the cause of the bug. This can often happen with side-effect failures. If the true cause is writing to a location beyond the bounds of an array, which modifies an instance of a data structure, then a symptom-hiding change might be to pad the data structure so that the array overflow doesn't corrupt any important data. Or if a threshold assertion is failing, a symptom-hiding change might arbitrarily change the value to meet the threshold. Symptom-hiding changes are sometimes required because of the urgency of a problem, but never lie to yourself that you've actually fixed the bug.

The following list of causes is not exhaustive, but it covers the categories that I found most often in my own and others' code.

Programmer Error

A function was implemented incorrectly and does not perform as required. There are many ways that this can happen, including:

- Logical incorrectness – For example, an OR operation should be an AND operation.
- Bad arithmetic – An arithmetic operation was implemented (or algebraically derived) incorrectly
- Sequencing problem – Operations are performed in the wrong order
- Loop condition error – A loop terminates too early or too late
- Missing assignment – The then-clause or the else-clause of an if-statement did not complete all the required operations
- . . . – The list is endless

This class is the most common source of bugs. Code reviews and unit testing are the best way to prevent these bugs. Hiring better programmers helps a lot, too.

Typographic Error

Whereas Programmer Error is a failure of the brain, Typographic Error is a failure of the fingers. I typed function 'inputCount()' when I meant 'outputCount()'.

In addition to typos, there is another category I call Cut-and-Paste-Os. This occurs when I copy some code but fail to make all the required changes in the new copy. This has happened to me so often over my career that I almost always try to use a common function rather than copying code.

Incomplete change

An incremental change was made to the infrastructure or the program flow and the effects of that change were not completely implemented. See the section The Change Tree for a more detailed explanation.

Data Corruption

The data that the code accesses is no longer valid for the current operation. The cause could be in the code that modified the data, or in the code that expects the data to be valid. Data corruption most often occurs in architectures that rely on persistent data and side-effects.

- Invalid memory access – in languages with explicit memory management like C or C++, the data corruption can occur by modification of an invalid memory location, typically by accessing data outside an allocated array
- Stale data handles – A persistent data structure references data that are no longer valid. Maybe the data have been deleted or re-purposed.
- Invalid data state assumption – The data accessed by the code is valid, but not in the assumed state. Maybe an assumed processing step has not yet been performed.

Misunderstood requirements

Either the requirements were incorrect, or the developer misunderstood the requirements. You know this is the cause when the developer says, "Oh. I thought it was supposed to…".

Unexpected input

The input data contains a construct that was not expected.

For example, consider a program that takes a list of rectangles as input. The spec says that rectangles are specified by lower left x and y coordinates followed by upper right coordinates. But you encounter a file that specifies upper left followed by lower right coordinates and suddenly you are calculating negative area. You must accept the file because a competitor accepts it, so you have an Unexpected Input bug.

You often have little control over the input data, and it is difficult to imagine all the ways that users can interpret (and misinterpret) the specifications. You must accept a wide range of inputs and at least give feedback to the user about how to fix the problem.

Unexpected Input failures can also occur with third-party libraries where your expectation of generated data is different from what the library generates.

7.3.4 Test Coverage Failure

The final classification level is test coverage. Ideally, testing should find all bugs, but that is impractical. An analysis of the testing required to identify a bug can help to improve test coverage and perhaps find related problems before they are found by customers.

Bug Found in Testing
The bug was found in the normal course of testing and the bug fix was scheduled for the release. This is the best case other than no bug at all.

Test Failed, But We Didn't Fix It
Schedule pressure will often force you to release software with known problems. If the bug is then found by a customer, then it belongs in this category. Use bugs in this category to improve your judgement for how to triage bugs.

No Test for this Feature
The software failed for a requirement of the system, and there was no test created for the requirement. This is a failure in planning or execution. An untested feature is almost certain to fail. You need to understand how this happened.

Testing Did Not Cover This Case
The situation that caused this bug did not happen during testing. This is probably the most common category for Test Coverage. Even testing with 100% measured coverage will let failures through because validating the correctness of code requires running every line of code with all possible input states.

Test Failed, But Did Not Detect the Bug
Often, after analysis, you will find that the situation that triggered the bug occurred during testing, but the tests did not correctly identify that the results were invalid. Crashes and assertion failures are easy to detect, but incorrect data are much more difficult to validate. You may need to improve the analysis capabilities that are available for testing the product.

Untestable
Occasionally you will find bugs that cannot be found by reasonable testing. These include bugs that are triggered by unusual or difficult to reproduce situations, including:

- An unusual setup of a customer's compute environment

- Real-time interaction between two systems
- A customer's unusual data set

These testing failures provide an opportunity to invent new testing techniques for your product.

7.4 Anatomy of an Automated Test

An automated test validates one or more details of a Module of the system. It has several components that are described below.

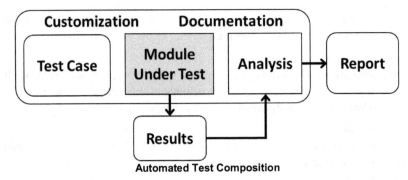

Automated Test Composition

Module Under Test
The *Module Under Test* is the part of the system that this test is verifying. For unit tests, it might be a single function. For real-world tests it will be the entire system. While some full-system tests are necessary, testing is most effective, and debugging is most efficient, when the module is small.

Test Case
The core of the test is the reusable *Test Case*. The Test Case is the set of data and the environment needed to setup the module for testing. In many systems, obtaining or generating test cases is difficult, so it is important to make them reusable and to share them across many tests. Separating the Test Case from the test also makes it easier to manage the intellectual property issues if the Test Case came from outside your organization.

Documentation
Every test needs *Documentation* that states the source of the test case, the purpose of the test, and the history of the test. Stating the purpose of the test makes it easier to understand a failure and to determine whether the module failed or if the test needs to be updated to match recent changes to the module. The history should include a chronicle of test changes (which should be in your revision control system), and a

210

history of failures. Tests that fail often may indicate a problematic aspect of the module, or a problematic test.

Customization

In order to test the specific detail of the module, the test case needs *Customization*. In my experience this has usually been a set of scripts and data files that accompany the test case. Your system may need to do this in a different way. The Customization will include a driver that runs the module to produce the test results.

Results

The test *Results* are the output of the module that include enough detail to decide if the test passed or failed. The results from the module are probably not in the same form as results seen by users of the system. They may need additional diagnostic information. They may need to be in a form suitable for a program to analyze, as opposed to a form that users can understand. I believe that having the module cooperate with the test to improve the analysis of results is more important than having the purity of "black box" testing.

Analysis

Analysis of the results determines if the test passed or failed and may also include evaluation of parametric requirements. Analysis may make use of your team's common analysis engines together with some form of customization for the specific test. For example, if the module outputs a binary data file, you will need an analysis engine that can read the data file and do some interpretation of the data. Developing robust analysis tools is one of the most important parts of a successful Software Validation process.

Test-specific analysis validates that the module performed as expected with the current test case and customization. The validation of the analysis can be exact, for example, checking cell-by-cell that a Sudoku solution matches the expected solution. Or the validation can be inexact, validating the result with high probability, for example, checking that the Sudoku solution is valid without checking cell values.

Testers use inexact validation because exact validation may be too difficult, or even impossible, with the available result data. Inexact validation has the risk of leading to false positives (the test passed because the analysis missed detecting a problem) and false negatives (the test failed, but there wasn't really a problem). False negatives tend to get addressed quickly because they are annoying. False positives often linger until the bug manifests during customer usage.

General analysis validates some attributes of the module that must be valid for every test. For example, the Sudoku puzzle generator must always generate feasible puzzles. General analysis can be embedded in the module's code as assertion checks, or it can be implemented in a separate analysis tool.

Report

Finally, the test generates a *Report*. The report could be as simple as a text file that says, "Passed". Failing tests need enough information for someone unfamiliar with the test to understand why it failed and to debug the problem. Parametric tests need to report the values of the parameters.

7.5 Testing

It's often said that testing doesn't improve quality. It's also often said that if you don't test software, it doesn't work. Both statements are true. The essence of quality comes from developers, but developers need testing to write good code.

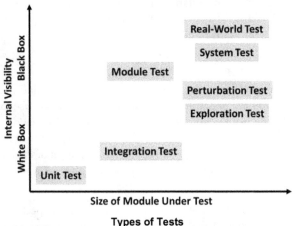

Types of Tests

In this section, I describe the types of testing that I have found most effective for improving quality. The figure above uses the parameters of size of the Module Under Test on the x-axis and the amount of internal visibility on the y-axis to classify the types of tests.

7.5.1 Black-Box vs. White-Box Testing

The first attribute of a test is the amount of access to module internals the test needs: black-box and white-box testing.

Black Box Testing

A *Black Box Test* validates the module using only the public interface to the module. The test does not have access to any private internal state, or private interfaces of the module, or special test modes. The test has to verify the reliability and functionality of the module the same way that a user of the module would do it.

Black Box testing has an aesthetic purity. It seems that you are testing the "real thing".

Because the public interface to a module does not change often, Black Box tests are easy to maintain.

White Box Testing

A *White Box Test* validates the module with knowledge of, and access to, the internals of the module. The module "cooperates" with the testing. The module may have special test modes that do self-checking, or that save intermediate data values. The module may provide analysis tools that not available to normal users of the module.

White Box testing can be more effective than Black Box testing, but it can also be harder to maintain because the internals of the module will need to change more often than the public interface.

7.5.2   Unit Tests

Your first chance to understand your software is through unit tests.

A unit test validates one small piece (the 'unit') of the architecture with minimal dependencies on other pieces. Unit tests are white-box tests that rely on code in the primary language of the system to setup test cases, and to perform customization and analysis. There is no need to dump data to an intermediate on-disk format, or to write independent analysis tools. This makes them ideal for early testing when the code is undergoing rapid change. Developers write better code if they write unit tests simultaneously with writing the functions.

Most of the time, a module developer writes the unit tests for that module, but having an independent tester write them may sometimes improve their effectiveness.

When I was first introduced to unit testing, I was skeptical of its benefits. But now that I've been doing it for several years, I don't know how to develop code without it. Unit testing gives me a way to validate my code in a controlled environment. I can test infrastructure before deploying it – for example, in the SHDS Prototype, I was able to test the Packet Queue before using it in other modules. If there is a problem, debugging a small unit test is much easier than debugging a real test case. This is so true that often I will generate a unit test that reproduces a problem from a real test case just to make it easier to debug. Once unit tests are in place, I can change the implementation of a module and know that the tests are in place to validate my changes.

What constitutes a unit depends on what language you're working in, the common practice in your group, individual taste, and the problem you are currently addressing. Some like to create a unit test for every function. I will do this occasionally for functions that do complex mathematics or use a new algorithm. I generally create one or more tests for every module in the architecture. Sometimes I create a unit test for a subsystem when the modules of the subsystem are highly dependent on each other. This last approach is frowned upon by unit testing purists, who believe that you should isolate each module so it can be tested alone. In practice, it's a tradeoff between the effort needed to create the test vs. the benefit of isolation.

Unit test creation is a lot easier if you use a framework. You can develop your own or use one of the many that are freely available. A quick web search will help you find one that suits your needs for the language you are using. For C++, I have successfully used Google Test (github.com/google/googletest), which is the framework used in the SHDS Prototype.

Spend the time necessary to build tools to help create unit tests. If your tests require data structures to be set up, a tool to do the setup will make you much more productive.

7.5.3   Integration Tests

Unit tests rely on a Unit Test Framework to do consistent checking and to run a suite of tests. Keeping the unit small and independent is an important part of unit testing. However, the same Framework can be useful to test larger subsystems with an environment that is similar to what the subsystem will experience in the full system. These tests are called integration tests because they test the integration of the modules of the subsystem. Integration tests are white-box tests that may rely on external data, and may have longer execution times than unit tests.

Because integration tests have access to private data structures of the subsystem, development of the analysis component of the test is easier and more effective than using a black-box system test to validate the subsystem.

7.5.4   Black-Box Module Tests

The most effective way to test a module (other than integration testing) is to isolate it from the rest of the system and to test it independently with a black-box module test. The challenge of black-box module testing is that most modules are not designed to have independent interfaces for stimulus and for analysis. To be effective, you will need to find a way to get data to the module and to analyze the results of the module's execution.

If the input data is static, then you can capture that data from a System Test. You will need a way to capture the data and write it to disk, and a way for the module to read the captured data. If the interface to the module changes, you will need to re-capture the data and to update the test case. The process for maintaining the captured data needs to be designed up front. Even with a good design, it will need to be honed with learning from false errors caused by test cases with stale data.

If the input data depends on the execution of the module, then you will need to write a test wrapper that emulates the part of the system that the module interacts with. You may also need a way to get the results of the test into an analysis tool. This is probably best done with a test wrapper, even if you decided to use data capture for module stimulus.

7.5.5 System Tests

In a System Test, the module-under-test is the system. A System Test validates the system similarly to the way that a user would use it. A typical System Test will treat the system as a black box for stimulus, but may have access to internal testing modes or special analysis tools that are not available to users.

Most System Tests are targeted at validating a specific aspect of the system. The test case is often artificially contrived because that's the easiest way to isolate that specific aspect. Simplicity also helps speed of execution and ease of debug.

System tests are an important part of any testing strategy. Making sure that simple, targeted tests perform as expected will provide a lot of confidence in the quality of the product. It is often the best way to validate that the interfaces between major modules work correctly.

However, resist the urge to do all your testing as a System Test. Trying to test details of a module with a System Test puts a lot of uncertainty in the test. A problem with the module detail you're trying to test may be hidden by other unrelated problems in the system. For module testing, take the time to build the test wrappers that isolate the module.

7.5.6 Real-World Tests

Real-World Tests are System Tests that use test cases derived from real application of the product. The test cases are complex and the tests stimulate many aspects of the system, however, the analysis component of the test may focus only on a few aspects of the system.

Real-World Tests are perhaps the most important tests in your arsenal. They can uncover a wide range of problems and limitations. Targeted tests, whether at the System or Module level, cannot explore the state space as well as Real-World Tests.

The first problem with Real-World Tests is creating the test case. Creating complex test cases takes time and thought. In projects I worked on, we were often able to obtain test cases directly from customers and we were able to customize these test cases to target specific aspects of the system. This was an ideal situation because customers had high incentive to put time and thought into the test cases. Since every customer used the product in different ways and their test cases emphasized different aspects of the system, we needed a lot of customer test cases to get a high confidence in the quality of the product.

If your system is highly interactive or has real-time requirements, you will need to develop a strategy for capturing real-world stimulus.

The second problem with Real-World Tests is that you can only validate the final results and maybe a few details about a few modules. While running the test, the system may have a corrupt data structure that doesn't manifest as a bug. If you don't validate that data structure, your system has a time bomb. You will not know about the problem that created the corruption until a customer stimulates a similar corruption that does manifest as a bug. Later in this chapter we will discuss self-checks that help find these time bombs.

7.5.7 Perturbation Tests

In quantum mechanics, perturbation theory starts with a known solution to the Schrödinger Equation for a simple system, and then perturbs the system to create a more complex system and uses approximations to find a new solution. For example, starting with an isolated hydrogen atom, apply a weak electric field and you can predict the changes in the states of the atom caused by the field.

In Software Validation, a perturbation test starts with an existing base test, and makes a small random modification to the test case, or to the customization, to create a new perturbed test. Perturbation is a practical way to introduce randomized testing into your software validation processes. There are other forms of randomized testing that randomly synthesize test cases and/or customizations rather than making modifications from a base test. You should consider whether an approach other than perturbation testing will work better for your system.

Most bugs happen not because a function is always wrong, but because a function behaves incorrectly when the inputs to the function, or the persistent data, are in a particular state. For example, $z = 1.0 / (x - y)$ might trigger an error if $x == y$. A perturbed test puts the system in different states than the original base test and might trigger new undiscovered bugs.

The nature of the perturbation depends on the nature of the bug you are trying to find. For example, if your system often fails because of unexpected states of a particular data structure, you will want to make perturbations to the test case that result in differences in that data structure.

Like real-world tests, perturbation tests are only as good as the analysis component. They can't help you find potential bugs that don't manifest. They are good at finding crashes and assertion failures and any bug that can be caught by a self-check or a generic analysis.

You will want to run many (thousands?) of perturbations for a base test. Typically, you will continue to run as long as you are finding new failures. When a perturbed test fails, you will need to capture that test in a form that can be reproduced so that the problem can be debugged.

7.5.8 Exploration Tests

All of the above types of testing use automated tests. There are lots of advantages to automation: the tests don't need to be monitored; they are repeatable; and you can measure test coverage for them. But automation takes a lot of work, particularly if you are going to do a good job of analysis, or if your system is interactive. Automated tests are only as good as the analysis component. They can miss a lot of problems that might be found if a knowledgeable user looked carefully. Automated tests focus almost exclusively on preventing reliability problems; they have almost no impact on improving functionality.

Exploration tests defer automation until a problem is found. An explorer runs the system, observing its operation. The explorer may use interactive analysis tools like data visualization. The explorer will modify the test case or the customization to see what happens. If a problem is found, the explorer might stop to fix it, or to work with a developer to fix it, or create a new automated test that triggers the problem.

Many times, I explored our systems with the intent of monitoring behavior A. But in the course of the exploration, I noticed that behavior B was wrong, and while fixing that also noticed that behavior C was wrong. Then I realized I needed a better analysis tool for behavior C, so I wrote one. Then, after running the new analysis on a lot of tests, I understood how to improve the code for behavior C. Eventually, I would get back to behavior A after fixing several problems on the way.

Exploration testing can have a huge impact on the quality of a system, especially if it's done by developers. Unit tests and integration tests are important, but if that's the only kind of testing that developers do, they will miss a lot of issues.

Exploration testing is the only form of testing that can improve the functionality aspect of quality. When you're exploring, you are the user. High Quality Software does what the user wants in the way the user expects. If it's not doing what *you* expect, what hope does a real user have?

7.5.9 Metrics Testing

Your system requirements will almost always include one or more parametric requirements, like GUI response time, or the system's memory footprint. For many systems, these parameters are among the most important requirements that determine the functionality aspect of quality. These parameters need to be measured and tracked using a suite of real-world tests.

You will want to measure and report each parameter compared to a baseline, usually based on a previous release. You will want to look at the average improvement (or degradation) across all the designs in the suite. You will also want to look at the extremes – and average improvement of 10% may not be good if some test cases degrade by 50%.

I have found that the easiest way to understand the results of metrics testing is with a simple chart that shows the percent improvement/degradation with worst to best sorted from left to right.

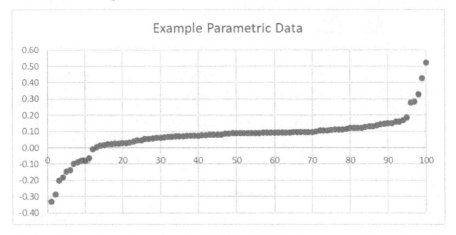

The chart above shows a (simulated) suite of one hundred test cases with a 10% average increase in the parameter with a few outliers up to ±50%. (From a statistics perspective, this is the cumulative distribution of the suite turned on its side.)

You will also want to measure the sensitivity of the parameter to various options. For example, a C-Compiler's execution time may depend on the optimization level.

It's important that the person who is responsible for generating metrics reports has a good understanding of, and intuition for, statistics. I have seen way too many bad reports over the years because the reporter didn't think through the math behind the reports. Bad reports can lead you to bad decisions, or to waste time trying to address a bogus problem.

Also beware that all the metrics you measure are not independent. Compiler execution time and compiled program execution time are related. You need to look at the global picture, not just the independent metrics.

7.5.10 Test Coverage

Many teams measure test coverage as part of their quality processes. There are many ways of measuring test coverage, but for this discussion, let's consider test coverage to be the percent of program statements that were executed during testing. Test coverage can almost never get to 100% because every system contains dead code and diagnostic code that never get executed during a normal run of the system.

Test coverage is a useful metric, but it's important to be clear about what it tells you. High test coverage is a necessary requirement for high reliability. If large portions of the code are not exercised by your test suite, then any bugs in that code will not be detected.

But, high test coverage is not sufficient to guarantee high reliability, for two reasons.

- A statement may succeed in some circumstances and fail in others depending on the state of the data that affects that line. You need to have a test that will satisfy the conditions that cause the failure.
- If a test triggers a failure in a statement, that failure may go unnoticed if the failure is not observed for one of two reasons:
- The failure does not affect the final results. A bad intermediate state will often go undetected because some later processing does not need to look at the bad data.
- The analysis component of the test doesn't look at the specific piece of the results that failed.

So, continue to measure test coverage because 80% coverage is better than 70%. But don't let test coverage lead you into a false sense of security. Even at 95% coverage, you probably have a lot of undetected bugs in the system. And don't let the goal of improving test coverage distract from the real goal of improving reliability. Once you have reached a reasonable level of test coverage, it is better to spend your testing resources on creating more diverse test cases that can trigger new bugs, and on improving analysis tools that can detect a wider range of bugs.

7.6 Developers are Responsible for Quality

I have met developers who thought that it was their job to write the code and someone else's job to test it. They assumed that the role of a Quality Assurance (QA) team was to check what errors developers have made. These developers threw code over the wall and the QA team threw bug reports back at them. Every night QA ran thousands of black-box tests, and every morning they automatically spit out a report that says, "Look what you screwed up yesterday!"

The model in which QA was responsible for quality never worked. First, there were never enough QA people to do all the necessary testing. Second, it was impossible for the QA people to understand what tests were necessary.

In What is Quality? I defined the two aspects of quality:

- *Reliability* is the lack of serious bugs
- *Functionality* is the extent to which the product does what the user expects

The traditional QA process can measure some aspects of reliability, which are necessary conditions for quality, but the process is not sufficient to guarantee a high-quality product. Testing cannot prove that there are no bugs, nor even that there are no serious bugs. This type of testing cannot hope to measure or improve the quality of the software's functionality.

Developers are responsible for quality. They are the only ones who can change quality for better, or for worse. The other members of the team can point out problems, or prioritize issues, or report metrics, or recommend best practices. Developers can fix bugs, improve usability, and find amazing new solutions to problems. They can also create bugs, make inscrutable user interfaces, and make systems that run too slowly.

It's the most important concept in this chapter, so let me say it again. Developers are responsible for quality. They need to make sure that the code they write is correct and has been tested completely. They need to understand the requirements and "think like a customer" to make software that does what the user expects.

Developers are responsible for quality, but they can't do it alone. Developers need help finding situations they did not anticipate. If a developer is the only person developing and testing a module, the same misunderstandings and omissions that are in the code are also likely to be in the testing. Developers need more eyes and more imaginations testing their code.

But testers struggle with setting up test cases and with analyzing the results of their tests. Developers need to help them create better tests by providing setup utilities and analysis tools.

Since developers are responsible for quality, your quality processes need to focus on making developers more successful. Because the term "Quality Assurance" has been used for so long as a process for finding bugs, I call the quality processes I propose in this chapter, "Software Validation." Whereas Quality Assurance focuses on finding problems, Software Validation focuses on helping developers improve quality. It is a cooperative effort between developers and other team members to improve both the reliability and the functionality of the product. Everything you do in software validation is intended to help developers do their jobs better. Anything you do that doesn't help developers should be stopped immediately.

7.7 Beyond Testing

7.7.1 Developer Projects to Improve Quality

Developers are responsible for quality, and most developers take that responsibility seriously. They have pride in their code and want it to work perfectly. But often, the only form of testing that developers do is unit testing, leaving the heavier testing tasks to others with more domain knowledge or automation skills.

In addition to testing, developers can help improve quality in other ways. They can help the testing effort by developing good analysis tools, and can help themselves and their teammates by developing diagnostics and visualization tools.

Test Validation Tools
In the anatomy section above, I discussed test analyses with exact and inexact validation. When exact validation is not practical, then the correlation between the inexact validation and the results needs to be high.

Developers can improve the correlation by providing tools that validate the results of tests.

For example, one common method of inexact validation is the "spot check", which exactly checks a small portion of the results. A tool that makes it practical to check a larger portion of the results will improve the correlation.

In a recent project, we needed to develop a second implementation of an engine that measures the performance of a chip, but that worked on different data structures. To verify the second implementation, we were able to build an analysis tool that could run both implementations and compare the results. Not surprisingly, the analysis tool found problems in both implementations.

Self-Checks
A self-check is a special kind of analysis tool that validates the consistency of internal data structures during the test run.

I have used two kinds of self-checks. You may find other kinds that work well with your system.

A data structure consistency check validates properties of a data structure. For example, if a graph is expected to be acyclic, a cycle check should not find any loops.

An algorithm check runs the same algorithm implemented two different ways and validates that they get the same results. Usually the two implementations are the fast, production version, and a slow but simple version. I have often used this for validation of optimization cost functions, comparing the slow, full calculation with the fast, incremental calculation.

Self-checks may be too slow to run all the time, but they can be enabled during testing to find problems that may not manifest any other way.

Diagnostics

A large portion of developers' time is spent in debugging problems. Improved debug diagnostics can have a major impact on productivity.

A debug diagnostic is code that is invoked while debugging a problem in order to get a better understanding of intermediate states of the program. For example, while debugging problems with Sudoku solver heuristics, I often want to look at the state of the grid before and after the heuristic has run. To see this, I created a text dump of the grid that shows the legal values for all the cells in the grid.

In the graph-partitioning project, I created a mode that could track everything that happened to a specific node: properties, assignments and copies. This caoability was often invaluable in narrowing down the root cause of the problem.

I also created a lot of ad hoc diagnostics that I wrote to debug a particularly gnarly problem, and then deleted when I was done with them. If I found myself creating similar diagnostics for other problems, I would find a way to generalize them and keep them around for future use.

Visualization

A visualization tool is a special kind of diagnostic that shows a graphical view of an internal data structure. It is often much easier to understand the data with a picture than with a text dump.

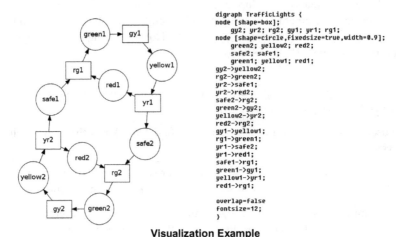

```
digraph TrafficLights {
node [shape=box];
    gy2; yr2; rg2; gy1; yr1; rg1;
node [shape=circle,fixedsize=true,width=0.9];
    green2; yellow2; red2;
    safe2; safe1;
    green1; yellow1; red1;
gy2->yellow2;
rg2->green2;
yr2->safe1;
yr2->red2;
safe2->rg2;
green2->gy2;
yellow2->yr2;
red2->rg2;
gy1->yellow1;
rg1->green1;
yr1->safe2;
yr1->red1;
safe1->rg1;
green1->gy1;
yellow1->yr1;
red1->rg1;

overlap=false
fontsize=12;
}
```

Visualization Example

https://graphviz.gitlab.io/_pages/Gallery/directed/traffic_lights.html

222

For example, it is much easier to understand the picture of the graph on the left than the text description on the right.

There are many free, open-source drawing packages that can help you build useful visualization diagnostics. The table below lists a few.

Package	Purpose
graphviz	Graph drawing (as in above example)
gnuplot	Two- and three-dimensional plots of mathematical functions
xfig	General-purpose vector drawing package

An internet search will help you find other packages that may be more suited to your application.

My typical method of using these packages is to create a generic interface to the package that writes the file format needed by the package, and then to customize the interface for the data I want to visualize. Since I typically use a small subset of the capabilities of the graphics package, the interface I create will be easy to use for the subset of functionality I need. I have never productized these interfaces. If the user needs to see a similar visualization, I would recommend using the GUI that is part of your product.

Every minute I have spent creating visualization diagnostics has paid back many times in debug productivity and in improving the functionality of the products I have worked on.

7.7.2   Processes to Improve Quality

I started this chapter with the statement that testing doesn't improve quality and then proceeded to spend most of the chapter talking about testing. Testing is an important part of a quality strategy; it helps developers improve their code. In addition to testing, you can do many other things to help developers improve their code.

Static Code Analysis

Static code analysis reads the source code of a system and analyzes the code to find potential errors without actually running the code. For example, the analysis may find that function $foo()$ can sometimes return zero, and the expression "$x/foo()$" could yield a bad result. Static code analysis can sometimes find problems that are difficult to find with testing because it does not require a test case to trigger the problem and an analysis that finds it.

Many commercial and open source static analysis tools are available. Search Wikipedia for "List of tools for static code analysis" for a list. My experience is primarily with Coverity™, a suite of code analysis tools from Synopsys. In the early days of our usage,

Coverity reported so many false errors (it said there was an error that I knew that couldn't happen) that it was impossible to find the real problems in that haystack. But after a couple years, with improvements in the tool, and improvements in our customization, when Coverity reported a problem, it was almost always a real problem that needed to be addressed.

Code Reviews

Peer review of code serves two important purposes: it finds problems in code by having another pair of eyes look at it, and it educates someone else about the changes in the code base. Code reviews can take place as a face-to-face review, with two or more people at a monitor going over the change, or as an automated review, with the help of an automated code review tool.

The advantage of an automated code review process is that the reviewer can schedule the review at a time that's convenient, and the author and reviewer don't need to coordinate schedules. The disadvantages are that the reviewers can procrastinate, and that the reviewers may not apply their full attention to the review.

The advantage of a face-to-face review (or more likely over the phone with a shared screen) is that the reviewer is sure to be engaged, and there can be a dialog between the author and the reviewer.

Many commercial and open source code review tools are available that help manage the code review process. Search Wikipedia for "List of tools for code review" for a list. You will need to develop processes and some customization to get the most out of a code review tool. My experience is with Collaborator from SmartBear Software, which worked great for our processes. In the rest of this section, when I say "code review", I mean automated code review.

I used code reviews for education in three ways.

- After fixing a bug in someone else's code, I would often start a code review with the original author and explain why the original code did not work.
- When changing how a central data structure or common function worked, I would start a review with the people most likely to use the changed interface so that they were aware of the changes.
- If I was handing off responsibility for a module to someone else, I would review the code with the new owner.

Finding bugs in other people's code using a code review process requires a big commitment from the reviewer. As an architect, I got a lot of reviews and I had to triage to find the best way to use my time to get the most benefit. When I got a review with changes in twenty files that includes several new classes and new algorithms, I could spend all day understanding and providing feedback. On the other hand, a review with a one-line change to fix a typo was hardly worth the overhead of opening the files. Here are a few guidelines for doing effective reviews.

- Don't review trivial changes. If your code review process requires a review for every change, include a way to skip the review for trivial changes that have been thoroughly tested.
- Review one change at a time. It's often the case that while I was working on problem A, I found and fixed unrelated problem B. If I create two separate reviews for A and B they are more likely to be useful than the combined review.
- When creating a review, point the reviewer to the most important parts of the change.
- Big changes should be reviewed face-to-face.

Whenever I created a major new module, I would schedule a code review with the people who would use that module. I would start with an overview of the architecture, and then go through one, or more, unit test (or automated test) that exercised the module. I would step through the code in the debugger, discussing the implementation and the tradeoffs that I made. This process helped foster a better understanding of the code than throwing a thousand lines into an automated review and hoping the reviewers had the time, the inclination, and the context to understand it. And with better understanding came better feedback.

Test Reviews
Reviewing tests may be as important as reviewing code. Every test has the twofold challenge of stimulating the module to trigger certain behaviors, and analyzing the results to validate that the module behaved as expected. Reviewing tests can lead to improvements in controllability of modules – the ability to trigger behaviors, and to improvements in analysis tools that detect problems.

Usage Reviews
I'm pretty good at using the spreadsheet Excel™. I have a methodology for doing complex calculations and quickly getting results, and I can make the results look good if that's important. Over the years, lots of people have come to me for Excel advice. Watching someone use Excel is often frustrating. I have learned to keep my mouth shut when I see them take five steps to complete an operation that could be done in two steps. I gently suggest changes to the way they have organized the data. But sometimes, they do something I didn't know was possible. "How did you do that?" I ask, and I add another weapon to my Excel arsenal.

Many software products are complex and users find their own familiar paths through the software. Sometimes those paths are not even close to the path that the designer envisioned. Watching someone use my software is always an eye-opening experience. Their usage may seem convoluted, but it works for them, and I may be able to add a few capabilities that make their usage easier.

225

The most important thing I learn from watching them use the tool is often that their goal is very different from the one I expected. They may have constraints I didn't understand, or need to measure a parameter the software doesn't report. Often, I can give them the capability they need with only a short programming effort.

Setting up usage reviews with both novice and experienced users of your product can help you improve the solution. Watching novice users can help you improve the learning curve. Watching experienced users can help you improve many aspects that are important to your customers.

When doing usage reviews, remember that it's not a training session. The person who needs to be trained is you, not the user. You need to observe first and teach later.

Developer Education

A lot of QA organizations attempt, with good intentions, to put rules in place that developers must follow. "All code must compile with zero warnings." "All code must be peer-reviewed." "All bugs older than one year must be resolved." And on and on. Any developer can figure out how to meet the letter of these rules without coming near the spirit of the rules. I admit that I took a few shortcuts when I judged that the spirit of the rule could be met in some other way.

Rules are OK, especially if the enforcement of the rules can be automated, and if there's a way to break the rule when necessary. However, a more effective way to improve developer behavior is to spend time on education. Education can take many forms. Classes and tutorials are effective at teaching the mechanics of programming. Seminars and presentations can make sure the entire team is aware of the team's software development processes and the thinking behind the processes.

Some of the most effective education initiatives I've experienced are informal, self-organized groups that meet to discuss issues. A book club chose a book that covered a topic of interest, and met periodically to discuss chapters of the book. A code review group got together over lunch to look at recent code changes and discuss why they were necessary and how they could be done better. These kinds of groups are great ways for senior members of the team to advise the rest of the team about the practice and philosophy of software development.

7.8 Implementing High Quality Software

To overcome the limitations of requirements:
- We have frequent interaction with customers and users.
- We frequently deliver working software and actively seek feedback.
- Developers must learn to think like their customers.

To overcome the inherent difficulties of software:
- We seek out change from as many sources as possible.
- We plan for change, and change the plan when necessary.
- We embrace change through constant measurement, analysis and improvement of the software and methodology.
- Developers strive for the highest level of technical excellence and assume responsibility for quality.

Principles from the Geodesic Manifesto

Of the two aspects of quality, reliability and functionality, the ways to improve functionality are outlined in the Geodesic Manifesto. If you follow these principles, you are more likely to create software that does what the user expects.

- Developers strive for the highest level of technical excellence and assume responsibility for quality.

Principle from the Geodesic Manifesto

To improve reliability, there is just the one principle that invokes the vague pursuit of technical excellence and the attitude shift of assuming responsibility for quality.

Architectures that minimize interactions between modules have a huge impact on quality, but even with a great architecture and great developers there will be bugs. In my experience, there are three primary sources of bugs.

- Bad implementation
- Invalid assumptions
- Incremental changes

Code review is the best way to combat bad implementation and invalid assumptions. Extra eyes on every change will be more likely to find these problems early.

Software grows like a tree. First you establish the roots, then the trunk and the limbs, then the leaves, and finally the fruit. Clearly, you need to do a good job implementing the infrastructure – the roots and trunk. Bugs and limitations of the infrastructure will multiply as the system grows. You need to design it for robustness and flexibility, and test it to death.

Ideally, when you need to add new functionality, you add a new limb without having to change the trunk or the roots or any of the old limbs. That may be true in a perfect architecture, but reality is seldom so simple. When you developed the infrastructure, you didn't know all the ways it would be used. The limitations of the infrastructure make the process of developing a system extremely non-linear. The development of almost every new limb requires that you go back to the roots and make changes because there's always something you didn't anticipate. Sometimes those changes mean you have to make changes to old limbs that you thought were finished.

All change is incremental. Once some of the code is in place during a system development project, and begins to be used by multiple developers, you have moved from new system development to maintenance development, and you need to manage the *change tree*.

7.8.1   The Change Tree

Every change to the system triggers a set of additional changes. And each of those changes triggers more changes, and so on, creating a tree of changes. Eventually you reach terminal changes that don't trigger others, and the tree is complete.

The change tree is seldom written down; most developers don't even think about it as a thing. A large number of bugs are introduced in incremental change because the change tree was incomplete. Making sure that it's complete and that all the required changes are implemented correctly is the most important part of developing high-quality software.

Great programmers know the entire change tree before they type the first character. Mediocre programmers discover large parts of the change tree after they think they are done.

Does the following scenario seem familiar? Feature A was working fine, but suddenly a few tests are failing. You are baffled because you haven't made any changes that might affect feature A. But Albert was improving feature B and needed to make a minor change to the infrastructure. He made the change and validated that feature B still worked correctly but didn't know that he had affected feature A. You find that Albert's changes needed to propagate to several other places to complete the change tree.

7.8.2   Managing the Change Tree

Most bugs are introduced by incremental changes. This is what teaches senior developers (The Legend of the 10x Developer) to cross the field on their hands and knees triggering land mines with a stick.

What can you do to reduce the risk of introducing bugs with every incremental change?

- Instill the concept of change trees in your team. Just having awareness of them will help.
- Write down the change tree. Even writing it on a whiteboard will help you understand the change, and once complete, the "document" will make it easier to make sure all the changes are completed.
- Review complex change trees with other developers. This is especially useful if you need to change part of the code base that is unfamiliar.
- Make sure there is test coverage, either unit tests or other tests, for changes. If not, then added it now.
- A modular architecture limits the propagation of changes and change trees will be simpler.

7.8.3 Writing Maintainable Code

I often say that the programmer is more important than the program, because as the programmer, you not only write the program, you maintain the program. Straightforward, easy to understand code is more likely to be right, but also, more likely to be changed correctly. Remember that any code you wrote a year ago will look like it was written by a stranger, so you are the primary beneficiary of good code.

Most of the time the code you write is not critical to performance or memory usage or any other metric. It needs to be there (or you should remove it), but the most straightforward, easiest to understand implementation is better than an implementation that tries to optimize a parameter that doesn't matter. You don't need to pack Boolean values into an integer for a data structure that will only occur once. You don't need to optimize floating point arithmetic in a function that is only called a few times.

Refactoring is essential step in writing understandable code. Refactoring means rewriting code to improve its structure and maintainability.

The first implementation of a module is usually completed incrementally. You start with a basic structure and then you add on until it works the way you want. At that point, you want to celebrate with a big whoopee and move on. But you're not done. You need to make it maintainable. You might think that adding a few cryptic comments will get you off the hook, but comments rot faster than code. Think of it as a first draft that will get you a C grade. You need to refactor to get an A.

7.8.3.1 Refactoring Functions
The best way to explain how to refactor functions is to show an example:

Before

```
bool Solver::solveStep()
{
Heuristics(m_grid).clearMustAssigns();
if (! Checker(m_grid).isFeasible())
return false;
Cell *trialCell = nullptr;
```

After

```
bool Solver::solveStep()
{
Heuristics(m_grid).clearMustAssigns();
if (! Checker(m_grid).isFeasible())
return false;
Cell *trialCell = findBestCell();
```

```
int minCnt = m_grid->gridSize()+1;          if (! trialCell) {// all cells were assigned
for (Cell *c : *m_grid) {                    if (Checker(m_grid).isFeasible()) {
if (! c->isAssigned()) {                     m_solution = m_grid;
int cnt = c->numVal();                       return true;
if (cnt < minCnt) {                          } else {
trialCell = c;                               return false;
minCnt = c->numVal();                        }
}                                            }
}                                            vector<int> &values = trialCell->values();
}                                            for (int v : values) {
if (! trialCell) {                           pushGrid();
if (Checker(m_grid).isFeasible()) {
m_solution = m_grid;
return true;
} else {
return false;
}
}
vector<int> &values = trialCell->values();
for (int v : values) {
++m_iter;
if (m_iter == m_gridStack.end()) {
m_gridStack.emplace_back(m_grid);
--m_iter;
} else {
Grid &tmp = *m_iter;
tmp.copy(m_grid);
}
m_grid = &*m_iter;
int r = trialCell->row(),                    assignTrialValue(trialCell, v);
c = trialCell->col();
m_grid->assign(r, c, v);
Heuristics(m_grid).clearAllowed(r, c);
++m_trialCnt;
if (m_trialCnt % 100000 == 0) {
cout << m_trialCnt << endl;
}
if (solveStep()) {                           if (solveStep()) { // a solution was found
return true;                                 return true;
}                                            }
--m_iter;                                    popGrid();
m_grid = &*m_iter;
}                                            }
return false;                                return false;
}                                            }
```

On left you see the core of a Sudoku solver before refactoring, and on the right, after refactoring. (Sorry if C++ is not your native language, but the concepts apply to any language.) Four groups of lines on the left were combined into four function calls on the right. (The function implementations are not shown.) On the right, the main loop (starting with "**for (int v : values)**") reads like pseudocode:

- Push a copy of the grid on the stack; assign value v to the cell in the grid;
- if the recursion returns true, we've found a solution and return true;
- otherwise pop the grid off the stack and try another value until you've tried them all.

Even the intention of the slightly messy **if (! trialCell)...** statement is pretty clear with the addition of one short comment. It's where I handle the exceptional case of finding a complete solution and checking its legality.

On the left, you can understand what's going on, but it takes some effort and you have to figure out what `m_iter` means and why there are special cases. That code still exists, but it's inside a function named `pushGrid()` and that name gives you more context to understand what's happening. This code is more complex than you might expect because it was changed from a simpler implementation to improve performance of the solver.

Most developers will create functions if the function gets used multiple places in the code, but there are advantages to creating functions even if they are only called once. We could make the left side more maintainable by adding comments, but most comments are redundant with the code. We're better off putting the code in a function with a good informative name. That way, the calling routine gets some context, and the implementation is easier to understand because it's only doing one thing. On the left, you need the color coding to see where `pushGrid()` ends and `assignTrialValue()` begins.

In summary:

- Use short functions with good names that act as comments
- Hide implementation details in functions even if the function is only called from one place
- Add comments only where a reader can't easily figure out what's going on purely from context.

7.9   Putting It All Together

This Quality chapter feels like a catechism – you have learned lots of ways to sin, but you have not learned how to live a good life – too much fire and brimstone; not enough Saint Francis. In this short section, I will review the key points of what I've discussed about High Quality Software, and attempt to offer a path to salvation.

High Quality Software does what the user wants in the way the user expects.

There are two aspects of quality:

- Reliability is the lack of serious bugs
- Functionality is the extent to which the product does what the user expects

A bug must manifest before you can count it. To manifest a bug, you need to trigger a failure in a module, and to observe that failure with analysis. Triggering the problem means setting up the conditions that cause the failure. Analysis means understanding that the results of the module do not meet the module's requirements.

You can't measure reliability directly because there is no way to measure how many un-manifested problems are in the code. Instead, you depend on the things you can measure, and hope that they correlate to reliability. You can measure:

- Internal bug discovery rate
- Customer bug discovery rate
- Test coverage
- Test completeness (the extent to which all planned tests have been deployed)

You can classify the bugs you have found and fixed using the taxonomy described in Non-Sequitur: Entomology – A Taxonomy of Software Bugs. Classification may help you determine modules that need additional testing, or that need review or re-writing.

While automated testing is essential to validate that new problems have not crept into previously tested code, it is not the most effective way of finding bugs. Randomized testing, like perturbation testing, can help trigger new problems, but it only helps if you have generalized analysis tools that can detect a wide range of problems automatically. By far the most effective way of finding new bugs is exploratory testing, in which a user modifies test cases and observes the output. While this may seem to be just throwing resources at the problem, I have found many problems this way that could not be found any other way. Exploratory testing is also an effective way to improve functionality.

Functionality can be measured, in a qualitative sort of way (pardon the pun), by listening to your customers and by observing them as they use the software. It would be great if your software had ears and could report to you the number of times users swear at it and what they were doing at the time. Observation and what-if discussions are the best way to improve usability.

Developers are responsible for quality. Only developers can make it better, or worse. To help your developers create high quality software, you need to have processes that enhance the capabilities of individual developers with the knowledge and experience of the entire team. Review processes and co-development processes that start at architecture design and go through code development and test development are the most effective ways to prevent problems.

Developers need to be actively involved in testing. It's not just OK for developers to test their own code, it's essential. In addition to test development, developers can create utilities that help testers trigger bugs, analysis tools that help detect bugs, and diagnostic tools that help themselves find the root cause of bugs.

Creating a perfect module is hard, but not impossible. It's easy to think that a bug is just a bug – let's fix it and move on. But that casual attitude toward bugs leads to a casual attitude toward coding, and requirements, and the rest of the software development process.

When customers buy your software, they think they bought not what it is, but what it should be; and they believe they are entitled to what it could be. Every bug they find, and every glitch they encounter, and every feature they think is missing is a breach of contract.

Developers need to believe that perfection is their goal. Yes, there are barriers to overcome. They never have enough time, or compute resources, or disk space. The APIs they need to use are awkward. The requirements are unrealistic. Some of the people they work with are idiots. But still, if their goal is perfection, I believe they will develop better software than if their goal is good-enough.

A friend and I were debugging a problem. When we got to the root of the problem, it became clear that my friend had made a programming error. He swore loudly.

"It's OK," I said. "It's just a bug. We can fix it."

"I know it's just a bug," he said. "But I'm trying to cut down."

Let's all try to cut down.

7.10 Key Concepts

- High Quality Software does what the user wants in the way the user expects.
- There are two aspects of quality:
  - *Reliability* is the lack of serious bugs
  - *Functionality* is the extent to which the product does what the user expects
- A bug must manifest before you can count it. To manifest a bug, you need to
  - trigger a failure in a module by setting up the conditions that cause the failure
  - observe that failure with analysis, understanding that the results of the module do not meet the module's requirements
- Classify bugs by
  - Manifestation
  - Locality and Extent
  - Cause
  - Test Coverage Failure
- A test consists of
  - Test Case
  - Customization
  - Documentation
  - Analysis
- Tests can be characterized by

233

- o Visibility – white-box or black-box
- o Size of Module Under Test
- There are many kinds of tests, including
  - o Unit tests – white-box tests targeted at a small unit of the code
  - o Integration – white-box tests targeted at small modules and subsystems
  - o Black Box Tests for Modules and the System
  - o Perturbation Tests – generate random variations to find additional problems
  - o Exploration Tests – Use of the system with the intention of finding and fixing problems
- Developers are responsible for quality because they are the only ones who can affect it
- Developers can improve quality in many ways beyond testing
  - o Improved analysis tools and diagnostics
  - o Self-checks
  - o Visualization
  - o Code Reviews
  - o Test Reviews
  - o Usage Reviews
- Many bugs are introduced by incremental changes
  - o Be aware of the change tree and make sure that the change tree is complete for any complex change
- Write maintainable code by constant refactoring

Part 3:
METHODOLOGY

Mammoth Hot Springs, Yellowstone National Park, Wyoming

8 COMMON PROCESSES

Finally, all those seemingly disjoint chapters that preceded come together for the first time. I will use models, management and the Manifesto, architecture, quality and teamwork, and leadership, planning and control. In this chapter, I begin the discussion of software development methodology.

If you've been reading the book in order, it's been a long time since I introduced the Complexity Model. A review is in order.

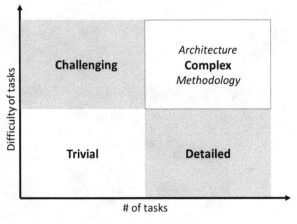

Complexity Model

The Complexity Model categorizes software problems into four quadrants. Trivial is just that. You solve Detailed problems by completing a lot of easy tasks, Challenging problems with a few difficult tasks, and Complex real-world problems by completing many difficult tasks. Complex problems need to be broken down into subtasks in the other three quadrants. You use Architecture, to organize *what* must be done, and Methodology to organize *how* the work gets done.

Software methodology is the set of processes and controls that we use to develop, update and support software. A software methodology needs to be detailed enough and specific enough that routine tasks are well defined. It provides the vocabulary for how we talk about what we do, and it helps avoid the confusion that arises when two people do the same task in different ways. At times, a methodology needs to be flexible enough to encourage creativity and to support our desire to welcome changing requirements. At other times, it needs to be rigid enough to guarantee compliance to the most stringent requirements.

I start this chapter with a general discussion of software processes. Next, I use some of the process concepts to consider what agility means and what are its limits – when can you turn on a dime, and when do you need a traffic circle? Finally, I list the common processes that are needed for most software development.

In the next chapter, I discuss some ways of putting these processes together into a methodology.

8.1 *Non-Sequitur* – Sharpen Thyself

> Give me six hours to chop down a tree and I will spend the first four sharpening the axe.

Anonymous adage often attributed to Abraham Lincoln

If it takes two hours to chop the tree, you should probably be using a saw. Which leads us to . . .

> Habit 7 – Sharpen the Saw

Seven Habits of Highly Effective People, Stephen Covey, 1989

Preparing your tools for the job makes the job easier. Preparation forms the foundation of the Geodesic Philosophy. Planning, Architecture, Methodology and your decision-making ethos all require up-front work to set the path for your development team.

Preparation is the key difference between the Geodesic Philosophy and Agile. In Agile, preparation is devalued, and although not forbidden, just-in-time decision-making is preferred. In the Geodesic Philosophy, preparation is essential to get the highest productivity and the highest quality from your team.

> At regular intervals, the team reflects on how to become more effective, then tunes and adjusts its behavior accordingly.

Principle of the Agile Manifesto

> We embrace change through constant measurement, analysis and improvement of the software and methodology.

Principle of the Geodesic Manifesto

Continuous improvement is a key similarity between the Geodesic Philosophy and Agile. Measure, analyze, improve, repeat. You can always assume that your competitors are improving, so you need to improve to stay ahead.

> This above all: to thine own self be true,
> And it must follow, as the night the day,
> Thou canst not then be false to any man.

Hamlet, Act I, Scene 3, William Shakespeare

Honesty, especially self-honesty, is the most important ingredient in continuous improvement. If you lie to yourself, or, more likely, conveniently ignore the facts that make you look bad, then you are doomed to repeat the atrocities of the past.

> It was the best of times, it was the worst of times,
> it was the age of wisdom, it was the age of foolishness,
> it was the epoch of belief, it was the epoch of incredulity,
> it was the season of Light, it was the season of Darkness,
> it was the spring of hope, it was the winter of despair,
> we had everything before us, we had nothing before us,
> we were all going direct to Heaven, we were all going direct the other way

A Tale of Two Cities, Charles Dickens, 1859

In searching for honesty, there are two sides to every story. Look at both of them.

8.2   Software Processes

An organization is built from many things. There are tangible things like people and computers. And there are the intangibles, like customer relationships and intellectual property. An organization's processes are intangible assets that provide the structure for how the organization keeps doing what it does. For example, Knobs, Inc. has a process for building door handles. Over the course of five years all the people at Knobs who build door handles have changed, but Knobs can still produce the same high-quality door handles because the process has survived.

In software development, we will never get to the same degree of process-completeness as Knobs, Inc., where the methodology can survive independent of the people. A software methodology needs to be flexible enough that it can quickly adapt to changes in the environment or in the organization. You may need to update your processes to support a new legal requirement, like the European Union's General Data Protection Regulation (GDPR). Or, in the early stages of a project, your methodology may revolve around the capabilities of one outstanding software developer, but as the project matures, the methodology must change to spread more of the burden to the rest of the team and to reduce the risk inherent in depending on one person.

8.2.1   What is a Process?

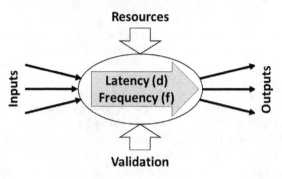

Process Definition

A process is a sequence of actions that achieves a specific goal. A process requires some *inputs*, consumes some *resources* (people, computers, disk space, etc.), and, after a delay defined by the *latency*, emits some *outputs*. The *frequency* defines how often the process may be started. Most of the time, the frequency is 1.0/latency, but there are exceptions. For example, a process that takes a month might be restartable only every two months because the resources can't be free until then. Or it may be restartable every week because some steps can happen in parallel. Many processes include *validation* to make sure that the intention of the process was achieved; for example, the process for completing a software change may include validation that the coding standards were followed.

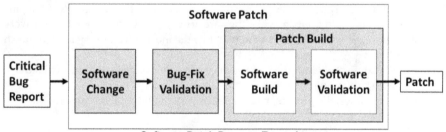

Software Patch Process Example

Processes are hierarchical. For example, the software patch process for getting a critical bug fix to a customer may include a software change process, a bug-fix validation process, and a patch build process. And the patch build process may include a software build process and a build validation process. The hierarchical nature of processes lets us apply a process in different contexts.

Processes are often built around tools like a revision control system, a bug report management system, or a testing system. These tools often provide much more capability than you need, and learning the broad range of capabilities is often daunting. But a couple experts who understand the broad range can define a process for a simplified path through the tool. That process streamlines the training of the rest of the development team who only need to learn the simplified process, and they have experts to rely on for the rare occasions when they need more capability.

8.2.2   Costs and Benefits of Processes

When I was a young software developer, I thought the word "process" was a manifestation of an evil demon. Processes slowed me down, forced me to write specifications that no one read, and constrained my creative freedom. And maybe I was right about those processes. But I didn't understand that by avoiding the prescribed process, I was following a different process. There is always a process, whether it's an individual's process or a common process.

Common processes provide many benefits to a software team. Common processes:

- facilitate automation of tedious tasks like revision control, build, and testing.
- provide a vocabulary that makes it easier to discuss the methodology.
- make it easier to integrate new team members.
- make it easier to work between teams.
- help the team learn from past mistakes and avoid them in the future.

Common processes have costs.

- The mere existence of a common process will cause inefficiencies. Developers will argue about whether the process was followed correctly. They will argue about whether the process is right for their project. And, in case you didn't notice, while they are arguing, they are not writing software.
- For some goals, the process may not be the most efficient way to accomplish it.
- For some problems, the process may cause delays that could be avoided with a different process.
- Sometimes, the process may get in the way of finding the best solution.

8.2.3   Process Rigidity

Because of these costs, we need to consider the rigidity of processes. Some low-level processes will need to be very rigid, because, for example, we can't afford to have developers using two different revision control systems. Some high-level processes may also need to be rigid because the risk and cost of error are too high to allow variation. A process that ensures legal compliance is an example of a process that needs to be rigid. For some processes we may allow developers to occasionally take short cuts, if the benefit is high and the risk is low. Many common tasks will not have a common process – debugging, for example, is so dependent on the problem and the individual developer that it would be nearly impossible to standardize it.

The rigidity of the process needs to increase for tasks with high risk, and to decrease for tasks that require high creativity. This means that two tasks that appear to be the same may follow different processes depending on the state of the project. Early in the development cycle, when only a few developers are involved, flexible processes allow rapid convergence to a solution. Later in the development cycle, when there are many developers, and software validation, and customer support, and customers, more rigid processes are necessary to maximize the productivity of the whole team.

8.2.4 Adapting Processes

A software organization will need to have many common processes, and these processes will change over time. You will find problems that weren't caught by the process and you will update the process to cover that problem. You will find an inefficiency in the process and you will update the process to improve it. You will find ways to reduce delays or increase frequency. And with each change, the process will become more complicated, until eventually, it will look like it was written by a lawyer. When this happens, the development team will start to ignore the common process and do it their own way.

One development team added a twenty-point checklist to the code review template. For every review, the author and the reviewer each needed to click ten boxes. At first, everyone carefully read the ten checklist points and considered them before checking the box. But soon, reviewers checked the green ones and authors checked the orange ones. And then the reviewers checked all the boxes because sometimes the authors hadn't done it yet. And then one developer wrote a little tool that automatically checked all the boxes. And the tool spread to most of the developers. By now no one had read the checklist points for two years, but the checklist was still a required step in the process.

The benefits of a process should always outweigh the costs. Just like the software itself, processes need anti-entropic effort to keep them from becoming burdensome. Since the people who develop processes are often not the people who use them, adding steps is easy. But streamlining processes is just as important. Simpler processes are more likely to be followed correctly, and for many common processes, compliance provides most of the benefit.

8.2.5 Process Automation

One way to streamline a process is to automate the most complex or tedious steps. In the checklist example above, the automatic checker streamlined the process. Unfortunately, its purpose was to subvert the original intention of the checklist. Good automation can streamline the process while strengthening compliance to the intention of the process.

Some of the things that can be automated are:

- Managing the data required by the process
- Checking compliance to standards
- Reporting the results of the process
- Managing use of the compute farm by dispatching jobs to computers

For many cases of automation, commercial or open-source tools are available and can be adapted to your needs. But you will always need to develop some of the automation within your team.

8.2.6 Documenting processes

If a tree falls in the forest, but the falling process was not documented, did it really hit the ground?

You can only have compliance to a process if the process is documented. There are three kinds of process documentation: explicit, implicit and folklore. Each has its advantages and disadvantages.

Explicit documentation means there is a document, hopefully residing somewhere easy to find, that describes the process using text and flow diagrams. The advantage is that it's easy to understand, and the disadvantages are that it's hard to keep up to date as the process changes, and if the document is hard to find it is the same as folklore.

Implicit documentation means that the process has been automated to the extent that the requirements of the next step are clear from context. Usually there will be a message of the form: "Now do this: ..." The advantage is that it's always up to date. The disadvantage is that it may take a lot of work to maintain and to have clear instructions for all the cases that might happen.

Folklore is a nice way of saying that there really isn't any documentation, but that everyone already knows how to do this because it has been done this way since your grandmother wrote code for the Eniac. There are no advantages to folklore documentation, but it's important to admit that this is how most processes are documented. The disadvantages are many, but most importantly, it makes the process very difficult to change.

8.3 Limits to Agility

> Give me forty acres and I'll turn this rig around
> It's the easiest way that I've found ...

> Some guys can turn it on a dime or turn it right downtown
> But I need forty acres to turn this rig around.

Give Me Forty Acres, Earl Green / John William Greene, 1964

One thing that managers want from their software teams is agility – the ability to turn on a dime, to respond quickly to customer requests, and to respond quickly to challenges from the competition. After all, it's software, the most configurable thing in the world – how hard can it be to change? In this section, I will attempt to answer these questions:

- How do we measure agility?
- How much we can expect?
- What does it cost?

As always, please don't confuse agility (small 'a') with Agile (capital 'A').

8.3.1 Software Development is a Low-Pass Filter

Let's start with understanding the limits of agility. Suppose a customer found a bug, and just from the description of the bug (i.e., no lengthy debugging process involved), I realize that in one line of code I need to change a plus sign to a minus sign. Oops! In the organizations I've worked in there is a patch process – the lowest overhead process to get a minor change to a customer as quickly as possible. Here's what would happen (the times for your processes may be different):

- I make the one-line change, build the software, run my standard tests, and get the code reviewed by a peer. Probably about an hour.
- I check in the change and notify customer support. They request a special build and validate that the customer problem is fixed. Probably about a day.
- Customer support requests a patch build from software engineering, who build it and run a full set of tests to verify that my one-line change did not have any unexpected side effects, and to verify other patches that may also have been submitted at about the same time. Probably about two days.
- Customer support notifies the customer that the patch is available.

That's three days to get a trivial patch to a customer. That delay is called the *latency*. Because of the software engineering processes, the *frequency* of patch delivery is one every two days. If your CEO demands that you deliver a patch every day, the most likely short-term result is that no working patches will be delivered until software engineering has time to change their processes, and to acquire more compute and personnel resources. That could take months. Meanwhile, customer support will find some other way to get unauthorized patches to customers, that may be incompatible with other patches, and may only work in limited circumstances, and chaos will ensue.

This illustrates the notion that software development is a low pass filter with two parameters, latency and frequency. The latency of the bug fix to customer process was three days. If the bug diagnosis and fix were more complex, it might be longer. If the frequency of patches is less than one every two days, everything works fine. But if you try to push it past that frequency, nothing good comes out.

8.3.2 Agility Metrics

Latency and frequency are the best metrics for agility. I believe that any other metric is either redundant with these two, or is a red herring. And if you're only measuring latency, you're ignoring a very important parameter of your development team.

Of course, trivial bug fixes are not the only thing that your software team delivers. Each type of development will have its own inherent latency and frequency. As a manager, you need to have a good estimate for these values.

The latency for a feature depends on many factors:

- The capability and experience of the developers
  - Do they work fast?
  - Do they deliver high quality software or does this team depend on Software Validation resources to test?
- The Complexity Model quadrant for the feature
  - A Challenging or Complex problem will be harder to predict
  - A Detailed problem will be easier to predict, but may take a long time or lots of resources.
- The load on the Software Validation team
- The support load on the developers (Are they fixing a lot of bugs at the same time they're developing the feature?)
- Etc.

Software managers get pretty good at predicting the latency for a feature because managers and customers work in the time domain. They are always asking for "sooner!" Software managers learn to predict latency out of self-defense.

The frequency is a more abstract concept. Let's look at an example for a more real problem than the trivial bug fix.

Suppose I have five one-month projects (A through E) in my queue that I can deliver in whatever order you ask. My frequency for these projects is one project per month. From my experience, I can work on two projects simultaneously. Some developers can do more, some only one. Because I often wait for other developers or for software validation, I like to do two projects in parallel, and I decide to work on A and B simultaneously and deliver both in two months, then C and D, and finally E, in a total of five months. But after a month, you decide that you want C and D first. So, I put A and B aside and pick up C and D instead. Assuming priorities don't change again, I will deliver C and D at the end of the third month and then restart A and B. But when I come back to A and B, I need some time to remember what I was doing and to figure out what else changed in the environment and get the software validation group restarted, etc. This "context switch" causes a delay of two weeks, and the five projects now take five and a half months. If priorities change again, then there will be more delays.

Low-pass Filter with High Frequency Input

Priorities are always changing. Customers, competitors, sales, higher-level managers are all high bandwidth inputs. As illustrated in the above diagram, if their high-frequency input goes directly to the software developers, nothing comes out. In the above example, by changing the priorities of two projects every month, you are feeding priorities at twice my frequency, and there is less output.

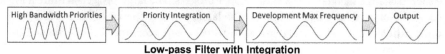

Low-pass Filter with Integration

The software manager can fix this by integrating the priorities so that the software developers see priorities changing at their frequency or below, as shown in the above diagram. The manager listens to the input and responds at or near the input frequency, but only with estimates of when the request will be fulfilled. The manager then puts the requests into the plan according to their priority, but, most of the time, allowing existing work to finish before starting new requests. Obviously, if a change means that current project will never be used, then it should be stopped immediately.

The trick is to do the integration while appearing to be responsive to the priority requestors, which requires some educated guessing about which priorities are going to stick. For most requests, the requestor will be satisfied with a reasonable latency for the development. You can feed the requests to the software developers at the proper rate, and you can feed back expectations to the requestors accounting for the delays caused by integration. Of course, some requests are truly high priority and you will need to sacrifice productivity to accommodate those requests. The judgment needed to make this tradeoff separates the great managers from the good ones.

You will see in the next chapter that some of the methodology frameworks build change integration into the methodology.

8.3.3   Improving Latency and Frequency

The latency and frequency are properties of the development team in its current state, which includes:

* The number and capabilities of the software developers,

- The types of projects in the queue,
- The processes in place for development, quality and release,
- The available compute resources,

and other parameters.

You can decrease latency and increase frequency, but it requires that you change the state of the team. Choosing the right mix of software developers within a budget, improving processes, and convincing management that compute resources that leverage the team are cheaper than delivery delays, are some of the things that managers can do to improve latency and frequency.

8.3.4 Work Parcel Size

Another aspect of agility comes from the size of the tasks involved. Small tasks are easier to change than large multi-developer projects. The large projects require a lot of coordination among the participants. The latency of any change will be large. At the other extreme, it's impractical to manage every keystroke. Somewhere in the middle is the ideal parcel size for maximum agility.

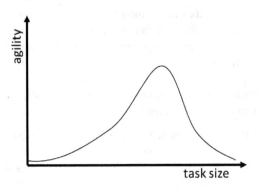

The work parcels need to be small, involving one or two co-located developers. They need to be independent of other simultaneous projects to minimize delays caused by coordination.

Breaking large projects into small, independent parcels requires a good architecture that minimizes interactions between projects, and good planning to coordinate the dependencies among projects without a lot of communication. If you can do that, you will improve your team's agility.

8.4 Recommended Processes and Controls

In this section, I describe processes and controls that need to be in place for nearly every software team. I list them below.

- Requirement Management
  - o Requirements gathering, analysis and prioritization
  - o Bug tracking, analysis and prioritization
- Code and Test development
  - o Definition of done
  - o Coding standards
  - o Source code management
  - o Code review
- Testing
  - o Validation Planning
  - o Test Data Management
  - o Unit and Integration Tests
  - o System Tests
  - o Test Metrics
- Release Management
  - o Build and integration
  - o Branch management
  - o Release processes
  - o Compliance

Every software development team has different needs, uses different tools, and has developed a different internal vocabulary. Your team may not need all these processes, and undoubtedly, your situation will require additional processes beyond those listed here. The list is daunting, but if you are tempted to skip a few steps, remember that you will have a process for these activities whether you document it or not, and an undocumented process is much harder to change.

In the following subsections, I describe these processes at a high level. I cannot define your processes for you. Instead, my goal is to give you some context for defining your own processes and for evaluating the ones you have.

When I say "you need to have" a process, I really mean that your software development and validation team needs to agree on a process. Developing processes happens very early in the life cycle of a development team, but reviewing and updating processes should happen quite often. You can schedule reviews based on the calendar – quarterly or semi-annually – or as part of the review for every major software release.

8.4.1 Requirement Management

8.4.1.1 Requirements Gathering

Understanding what your customers and users need and want is perhaps the most important practice in software development. You may need up to four separate processes for requirements gathering.

- If your customers, who pay for the software, are different from your users, you will need separate processes to gather requirements from each group.
- You may need a process to consider what your competition has and what they are planning.
- You need a process for your own development team to generate requirements for improvements to architecture, infrastructure and quality.

8.4.1.2 Requirement to Project Transformation

Once you've gathered the inputs for each class of requirements, you need to listen to what they say, and then infer what they mean. Customers and users only think about their own problems, not other users' problems, and certainly not yours. For example, suppose that a common theme of the user input is that users are struggling with a certain portion of the user interface. You will hear what's wrong with it, and you will hear suggestions for fixes for the specific problems that each user encountered. You won't hear how to redesign the user interface to change from a single, complex dialog box to a context-sensitive sequence of simple dialog boxes. The transformation of raw input to high-level projects is critical to creating great software.

8.4.1.3 Bug Database

There are countless tools for tracking bugs. Pick one.

8.4.1.4 Bug Prioritization

If you are working on a software system that has no bugs, you can skip this section. ☺

When I first started working on software after years as a hardware designer, I was appalled that there were bugs in the system that hadn't been fixed as soon as they were reported. That was before I understood the difficulty of software development. Every system has bugs that will never be looked at by a developer. If you're lucky, those bugs will die as a side effect of some change in the system. If you're unlucky, they will come back as a swarm of monsters from bad science fiction.

I refer you back to the Entomology section that lists the four traits – manifestation, locality, cause and test coverage – used to classify a bug. The first step in bug analysis is to understand the manifestation of the bug, and the impact that the bug has on the user. The second step is to come up with an effort estimate for a fix. To do this, a developer may need to understand the cause and locality of the bug.

Another useful analysis is to understand trends and themes. It may be more effective to fix a group of bugs with a major architectural or algorithm change than to address each bug individually.

8.4.1.5 Project Prioritization & Estimation

The Agile methodologies that are described in the next chapter – Scrum and XP– have a project queue that provides a prioritized list of projects for developers. The goal of the queue is to help answer the planning question, "What do I do next?" Ideally, when a developer completes a project, he or she takes the next project from the queue. But it doesn't quite work that way because a developer's skillset and availability need to match the project.

The project prioritization process needs to populate the queue with projects that are roughly sorted by importance, and have enough ancillary information so that a developer can understand the skillset and effort requirements.

8.4.2 Code Development

Pulling a project from the Project Queue triggers two parallel sets of processes. Software developers are responsible for the code development track; software validators are responsible for the validation track. These two tracks can share a lot of processes; after all, test development is software development with a different set of requirements. Validation also has some unique processes such as validation planning, handling of test case data, and test infrastructure development. This section covers the coding track; I cover test development in the next section.

Writing code is the most important activity of a software development team. You want to be very careful about the processes and controls you put in place for coding. Developers instinctively rebel against processes and controls, but the ones presented in this section are intended to make their jobs easier. Standardizing the low-level details of coding frees them to think about the high-level problem.

Documenting your code development processes will help streamline onboarding of new developers. Good training can save weeks in the learning curve for a new hire.

8.4.2.1 Definition of Done

All the following contribute to your Definition of Done, which should be explicitly documented.

8.4.2.2   Coding Standards

> Coding conventions are a set of guidelines for a specific programming language that recommend programming style, practices, and methods for each aspect of a program written in that language. These conventions usually cover file organization, indentation, comments, declarations, statements, white space, naming conventions, programming practices, programming principles, programming rules of thumb, architectural best practices, etc.

https://en.wikipedia.org/wiki/Coding_conventions

Coding standards (or conventions in the Wikipedia article cited above) encourage uniformity of the code base. That uniformity makes it easier for any developer on the team to look at any piece of code and understand it.

Coding standards provide the "plan" reference for a control. The identification and feedback of deviations from the standard can be either manual (during code reviews) or automated, and the corrective force comes from a developer modifying the offending code. I strongly recommend automating the identification and feedback for at least part of the standard. If you do this, then it's important to provide a trap door, because sometimes developers have very good reasons for writing code that doesn't comply with the standard.

You can start developing your coding standards with any of the many examples available on the internet, but coding standards for your team need to be dynamic. Coding standards should be reviewed periodically to add new rules and to remove existing rules that no longer apply.

Coding standards need to be customized to address problems specific to your team. For example, in one system I worked with, the team often found problems porting data files across platforms. To fix this, system calls that accessed the file system were wrapped with portability enforcement code. But developers sometimes still used the system calls. We added a rule to our coding standards checker that enforced the use of the wrappers and flagged an error if it found a violation.

8.4.2.3   Source Code Management

I remember when source code management (SCM) was implemented by yelling down the aisle, "I'm going to modify the widget file!" SCM has come a long way since then, with excellent commercial tools and free open source tools available. I make no recommendation on tools, but it seems that most new development teams have settled on git, the SCM tool originally developed by Linus Torvalds for maintenance of Linux.

Whatever tool you use, you need to put processes in place to support its use.

A simplified path for most uses

Most developers will only use a small part of the capabilities of your SCM tool. For them, you need to define a streamlined process with clear criteria for what to do when they need help. Most of the use for a developer is

- Creating a workspace
- Submitting changes to the repository
- Updating a workspace from the repository

Depending on your Branch Management process (see below), you may want to include other activities in the simplified SCM process.

Criteria for commit

You need to clearly define what needs to be done before committing code changes to the repository. The requirements may include unit tests, integration tests, code review, coding standards compliance, and documentation (usually information for an automated documentation tool like doxygen). The criteria may be different for new capabilities vs. incremental updates. For example, you may require new unit tests if a new class is defined, but not for an update that refactors an existing class.

It's best if you can automatically validate that submissions meet the criteria.

8.4.2.4   Code Review

Remember from the Yin-Yang Model that software is vulnerable. Every line of code is a potential bug. Developers make errors. Two developers can read the same requirement and interpret it differently. A developer may not be aware of infrastructure support for a task.

One of the ways you can combat vulnerability is with code reviews. Most code needs to have two developers look at it and understand it. Code reviews have two purposes. The first is to find and correct problems as early as possible.

The second purpose is to educate. Both the author and the reviewer can learn from a code review. Senior developers should use code reviews as an opportunity to reinforce good programming practices for more junior developers. You may think that senior developers should do most of the reviews, but having junior developers review senior developers' code helps them learn how the more experienced developer approached the problem.

Below I list four kinds of code review. You need to have processes in place that specify what kind(s) of code review are necessary for software changes, and the processes that you recommend for performing those reviews.

Automated Review

Static code analysis tools read source code and attempt to find potential problems without executing the code. These tools have come a long way from *lint*, one of the first widely used code analysis tools from 1978. You can choose from a wide range of commercial and open source tools.

Using these tools is not trivial because they will often report a lot of false errors – that is, they will report errors in code that is just fine. They typically require customization to help improve the error reporting. My experience in using a leading commercial tool was that after a few years of customization and tool improvements, it reported more real problems than false problems.

If you choose to make automated review a part of your development process, you need to commit to the customization and to put in place the automation that will assure that developers get timely feedback about the code they are developing.

Pair Programming

Pair programming is the practice of developing code with two developers at the monitor, typically with one typing and the other observing. Pair programming avoids a lot of common programming errors and annoyances, including typos, bad variable or function names, logical errors, etc. It also assures that two people come to a common understanding of the requirements related to the code. In many cases, the productivity improvement more than justifies the use of two developers.

The Extreme Programming (XP) methodology framework recommends pair programming for all development. You may recommend it only for certain classes of development problems.

Post-Coding Review

Post-coding review is an alternative to pair programming. In this process, a second developer reviews the code after the first developer completes it. The reviewer looks at the code and analyzes it for clarity, completeness, logical correctness, interpretation of the requirements, and many other criteria.

The advantage of post-coding review is that the reviewer can schedule the review at a convenient time. One disadvantage is that it's difficult to know how thoroughly the reviewer looked at the code. Another disadvantage is that the 'convenient time' may be far in the future.

Your process for post-coding review needs

- Enforceable time limits for review completion
- Training for how to perform effective reviews
- Measurements of review comments – reviewers who make few comments may be getting a lot of perfect code, or more likely, they are not looking deeply enough

You may also want to have a set of required reviewers for some kinds of code changes. For example, one group I worked with had a set of required reviewers for any change that touched the build system.

Code Walkthroughs

An alternative to post-coding reviews are code walkthroughs in which the developer and the reviewer go through the code changes together after the changes are complete. I have found that big changes, like new subsystems or major refactoring, are better reviewed in person than by looking only at the code differences.

Typically, post-coding reviews are done for every SCM submission. Code walkthroughs are not limited by the quantum of submissions. A major change may comprise many submissions that are difficult to review in isolation. Reviewing them together can improve the quality of the review.

Code walkthroughs give the author and reviewer a chance to discuss the requirements and motivation for the changes.

I believe your processes should encourage walkthroughs as an alternative to pair programming or to post-coding reviews.

8.4.3   Test Development Processes

The processes for developing tests, such as test analysis and test infrastructure, should be almost the same as for production code. You may have different criteria for some aspects of the processes, but do not make the mistake of creating two separate sets of processes for production code and test code.

One likely difference between production code and test code is the language. Test code often relies heavily on scripting languages (Unix shells, perl, python, etc.). I recommend that you minimize the number of languages that can be used, and that you write most of the code in a language that supports complex data structures (such as Python) rather than a shell language (ksh or Perl) that encodes all data as strings.

Architecture, and the principles I proposed for evaluating architecture, are as important for test code as for production code. If your software validation team has a good architect, that's great, but if not, then support the validation team with experienced architects from the development team. Entropy is just as likely in test code, and keeping it low means that developers will spend less time debugging tests and will get better feedback about their code.

8.4.3.1   Validation Planning

Most software needs to be validated by someone other than the author. This is true even though the author is responsible for quality. The author can do a lot of validation through unit tests, integration tests and exploratory testing, but the author tends to test what he wrote rather than to test what was wanted. So the author needs another pair of eyes to validate his code.

Since we have at least two people involved, probably from different departments, and often in different geographic locations, we need some formality in planning the validation of the code. I added an explicit Validation Planning step in the code and test development process. The resulting plan might be as simple as "The existing tests will cover this." Or, it may require a new set of test cases and new test analysis code. The testers may require some diagnostic instrumentation from the author to overcome opacity.

When a bug is found, "I thought you were testing that!" is not an acceptable response. You can avoid that with good validation planning.

8.4.3.2   Test Data Management

Many of the test cases used in real-world tests came from customers. Often these tests are not suitable for SCM systems because they are too big or because they have Non-Disclosure Agreement (NDA) requirements or other legal restrictions (such as privacy). For example, you may be required to delete a test case after two years, but once something is in the SCM system, it is virtually impossible to remove it.

You need to specify processes and policies for dealing with externally acquired test cases. It's probably easiest if you treat all test cases, whether externally or internally developed, in the same manner. You need a secure storage location and you need to document the restrictions for each test case. You need to periodically review the test cases to make sure that you continue to comply with the restrictions.

8.4.3.3   Unit and Integration Tests

Developers write unit tests and integration tests about the same time they write the code that they're testing. For brevity in this section, I will refer to them as development tests.

You need to choose the framework used for development tests. I prefer to use the same framework for both types of tests, but you may choose to use two different frameworks.

By default, development tests should be required, but you may specify when they are not required. If a module integrates a lot of other modules, then the effort of creating development tests may be too high for the benefit they bring.

You need tools and infrastructure that measure the coverage of development tests, and you should set a goal for development test coverage for each module. Be flexible on the goal. Whereas it sounds good to have a goal of 90% coverage, the effort expended to get from 70% to 90% may be large and may be more about fooling the coverage tool than about improving quality.

8.4.3.4   System Tests

For this section, I lump all the tests other than unit and integration tests into the category of system tests. This is a cursory overview of system test processes. When developing processes for software testing, I recommend that you consult the vast body of literature that discusses testing and software validation.

You will need to develop an automation infrastructure for testing. The implementation of the infrastructure should be treated the same as code and should be subject to the same processes as production code. Often, software validators are less experienced coders and could benefit from code and design review by experienced software developers.

The Validation Plan discussed above will include what types of tests are needed for each project. You will also need testing at each level of integration – module, subsystem, system, etc. Each type of test will need standards for how to implement it and when to run it.

The execution of system tests and the analysis of the results is a process that may be the limiting factor in the agility of your organization. If it takes a week to run all the tests necessary to validate a release, you can only release once a week. The tendency for an organization is to add tests and then never remove them. After a few years, you have thousands (maybe hundreds of thousands) of tests that are no longer relevant, but everyone is afraid to prune tests because no one remembers why they were there in the first place.

I recommend that you include processes to combat test bloat. Periodically review tests to see if they are still relevant and remove them if appropriate. Another approach is to categorize tests by relevance, and to run highly relevant tests often, and less relevant tests less often. You can continue to test a release after it's in the field with the intention of patching if necessary. If a low-relevance test finds a problem, you should promote that test.

8.4.3.5   Test Metrics

You need to measure your testing to understand it better.

There are two kinds of test coverage that you need to monitor. The first is code coverage – lines executed, or better, branch condition combinations executed. There are tools to automate code coverage measurement. If you can measure code coverage for each test, then you can use that information to customize test suites to validate software changes based on the code that changed.

The second kind of test coverage is requirements coverage – are all the documented requirements tested? This is harder to automate, and probably needs a manual review. It's also hard because by the third release of the product, you've lost track of the requirements that drove the first release.

If you keep track of test execution time for each test, then you can flag a problem if test execution time suddenly changes dramatically. Also you can use execution time data to categorize tests – long-execution-time tests that seldom find errors should be run less often.

Test failure rates are the best indicator of test relevance. You must be careful in measuring this to consider that there are some days when every test fails, or a large class of tests fail, because of a problem unrelated to the intention of the test. You also need to consider that a test that fails often may have bugs in the analysis or customization code of the test.

8.4.4   Release Management

The goal of software development is to get working software into the hands of people who can use it. Those 'people' may be other developers, validators, internal users, or external users. The process you need for creating a release of working software will depend on the intended audience.

Developers need low latency and high frequency processes for building software; external users need high quality. Development build processes can get by with low rigor, while external releases must go through thorough testing to ensure reliability and compliance with legal and other requirements.

The Build & Integration process provides the primary feedback mechanism for developers. The Module Release process adds rigor to validate that a module is ready for integration into the system. The Internal Release provides a system for internal users for verification and experimentation. The External Release process adds the final rigor to verify quality and compliance.

You will need to support simultaneous release processes for several versions of the system. While you are preparing an external release for version n, you will be doing incremental bug-fix releases of version n-1 and new development for version n+1.

Ideally all the release processes should be independent, but in practice they will be competing for the same resources – people, computers and disk space. You will need to make tradeoffs. Maybe you can't do an internal release and an external release at the same time, so you will try to survive with only the external release, which may cause you to stop new development and focus developers on reacting to problems found in testing the external release. These kinds of tradeoffs will become part of your methodology.

Release processes need to be automated. The code for release automation should be treated just like production code with the same SCM, review and testing requirements.

8.4.4.1   Build and integration

The Build and Integration processes provide the primary platform for developers to assess their work.

The system that you ship to customers will be complex, with code in various forms (compiled C++, Java Jar files, shell scripts, etc.) and data (configuration files, databases, documentation, etc.). Jill Coder needs a copy of that system with the changes she has made to the code and data. (In practice she probably doesn't need the entire system, but I'll use that term for now.) The primary limit to Jill's agility is the time needed to change the system to reflect the changes she has made. That's the Build.

Jill might do ten to twenty routine incremental builds in a day. Incremental builds need to be very fast with minimal additional overhead. Jill will do whatever testing she feels is necessary to have confidence in her changes.

While Jill is developing her code, Jack is developing his code. Most of the time what they are doing doesn't interact. But sometimes Jack and Jill both change the same file – maybe even the same lines in that file, or Jill changes something that Jack's code depends on. When that happens, they need to resolve the changes and make sure that everything works as planned. That's Integration.

Integration happens less often than routine builds, but still frequently. Maybe Jack and Jill need to integrate once or twice a week, but on that day, they may need several integration builds to converge.

Integration builds trigger a subset of tests that can provide good feedback on the integrity of the system with low latency. Typically, the testing will include running all the unit and integration tests, and a selected set of system tests.

Some of the Agile methodology frameworks recommend "continuous integration," which means that Jill is always looking at her changes and everyone else's. In other words, every build gathers the most recent version of every file before building. This is impractical for two reasons. First, such builds are typically slower than incremental builds and will limit Jill's agility. Second, Jill needs some measure of stability to make sure that problems she finds are caused by her own changes, not by changes that someone else submitted.

While continuous integration is impractical, frequent integration is critical to good software development. If Jill waits for more than a couple days before gathering new changes, she will sometimes deliver delayed feedback to other developers and she may miss issues in her own code that the other new code will reveal. A reasonable practice is that every submission is built and verified against the most recent code, and that every developer update to the latest code almost daily (occasionally waiting a couple days is sometimes necessary at times when a lot of changes from other developers need to stabilize, or when the changes Jill is making span a wide range of the code base).

8.4.4.2   Release processes

While the goal of build and integration is agility with reasonable stability and quality, the goal for a release process is stability and quality with reasonable agility. Development builds typically use a stable base of the system and change a few components of that system. Release builds gather the most recent code from the SCM repository, build the system from scratch, and then run a broad set of tests to validate the release and to provide feedback to developers about problems.

If your system deployment architecture is modular, then you can release a module independent of the rest of the system. The Module Release process needs to validate the module itself and its interactions with the rest of the system. Instead of building the system from scratch, the Internal and External Release processes merely assemble all the released modules and perform further testing at the system level. This approach provides more agility than the full-build approach, but requires a robust architecture and refined processes for coordinating changes between modules that need to be synchronized.

You can also use a hybrid approach in which the first release of a major set of changes, version n.0, uses the full-build process, and subsequent update releases, version n.1, etc., use the modular release process.

One goal of internal releases is to provide a testing platform for the new projects that have been pulled from the queue. The processes for testing new features will depend on the feature. The processes should be developed by the team members involved, and should be documented in the Validation Plan.

The second goal of internal releases is to get feedback to developers as soon as possible after a change causes a problem. These are often called regressions – something that used to work fails or no longer works the same way. Internal releases need to be built and verified frequently, daily if possible, but no longer than weekly. Frequency is important, but latency is also important. The results of testing need to be analyzed and fed back to developers within a couple days. I have seen teams focus so much on frequency – getting a daily internal release build – that they lost sight of latency and only looked at the test results once a week.

External Release builds often use the same process as Internal Release builds with a few extra steps to make it suitable for use outside. External Releases need additional testing to validate security and compliance issues that are not relevant to internal releases. If you only do security and compliance testing at the end when you are otherwise ready to release, you will find nasty surprises. It's prudent to start running these tests several weeks before you need to release so that the team has time to resolve them. If your business requires that you be able to release daily or weekly, then you need to run these tests for every internal release.

8.4.4.3   Branch Management

There comes a time for every release when development transitions to maintenance. You need a high-level process for maintaining released software while continuing development for new releases. Maintenance needs to make bug fixes and other minor changes that are safe – meaning they are extremely unlikely to introduce new problems.

You can separate maintenance from development by using a branch policy that separates maintenance changes from development changes in your SCM. I present here an example branch policy that works well, but it's not the only way to do this. Whatever your policy, it needs to be well understood in your development team.

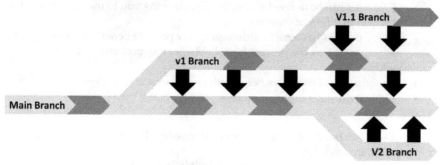

Release Branch Example

The first step in the transition from development to maintenance is to "copy" the code into a stabilization branch using your SCM system – the v1 branch in the above figure – and to limit changes to that branch while testing continues. When the v1 release criteria are met, you can release the software and v1 becomes a maintenance branch where only bug fixes for patches are allowed.

When changes are made in v1, they are merged back into the Main branch and future releases – v2 above – are branched from Main. In this way, all bug fixes made in v1 will make their way into v2. At some point you may decide to make a new incremental release v1.1. Repeat the branching process starting from v1 and merge changes on v1.1 back into v1 and then into Main.

Your code and test policies will be different for every branch. For example on v1, you may require two code reviewers for every change. You may limit who can make changes to critical security or compliance code.

Beware of merges. Modern merge tools are good, but they are not foolproof. A bug introduced by a bad merge-conflict resolution is often difficult to find because usually many merge changes were submitted together.

Beware of not merging. Make sure that you have one Main that always gets the latest changes. If the difference between v1 and Main grows to the point that merging is impractical, you will forever be maintaining two nearly identical code bases with annoying incompatibilities.

8.5   Key Concepts

Software Processes

- A process is a sequence of actions with inputs and outputs that achieves a specific goal by consuming resources.
- Processes can be defined hierarchically, allowing you to use the same sub-process in different contexts.
- Every process has a cost – although it may provide benefits on average, for any specific task the process is probably not the most efficient way to address it.
- Automation of processes helps both compliance and efficiency.
- Explicit documentation of processes is way better than folklore.

Limits to Agility

- Processes have both a latency and a frequency. The frequency might be different from 1.0/latency.
- Software development is a low-pass filter. If priorities change faster than the process frequency, productivity may be significantly reduced.

Recommended Processes

- Recommended common processes standardize how work is done
- They fall into four categories
  - Requirement Management
  - Code Development
  - Test Development
  - Release Management

9 METHODOLOGY FRAMEWORKS

In the previous chapter, I talked about common low-level processes that a software organization needs. These processes form the core of how a development team operates, but you also need a meta-process, one process to rule them all, that oversees the use of those low-level processes.

The word 'methodology' by its structure should mean the study of methods, and there is a branch of learning that does just that. But common usage, especially in high tech, has distorted the word to mean the collection of methods used to achieve a goal, and that's how we use it here. Describing a methodology requires that you know all the processes from the top to the bottom. To avoid the details, proponents of a meta-process often call it a 'methodology framework'. The framework provides a high-level structure into which you can plug the details of your low-level processes.

In this chapter, I will first propose some goals for evaluating methodologies. Then I will review some popular frameworks and assess their performance against the goals. The reviews are necessarily brief because each of the frameworks is the subject of books longer than this one.

As you review the Agile frameworks[1] presented below, it's important to remember an inherent dichotomy. On one hand the frameworks have a goal of improving software development to deliver better software sooner. On the other hand, each of the frameworks is the foundation of a business that provides the livelihood of its proponents. Use the same *caveat emptor* mindset you would use while evaluating any product.

9.1 *Non-Sequitur* – Discrete vs. Continuous, More or Less[2]

Grammarians have pronounced that 'fewer' should be used when modifying countable quantities, while 'less' should be used for continuous quantities.

- After breaking seven windows, there are fewer bricks in my pile.
- After making my sandwich, there is less cheese in my brick.

This seems to be one of the usage rules that most English speakers have been able to remember and to proudly use in common speech.

---

[1] All the frameworks except Waterfall and Asynchronous Project Management

[2] This *non-sequitur* has almost nothing to do with software, but I thought you could use a break.

Clearly the word 'fewer' can only be used to compare countable quantities. However, the word 'less' is much more flexible, and it makes perfect sense to say:

- After breaking seven windows, there are less bricks in my pile.

Or, maybe:

- After breaking seven windows, my pile is less bricky.

But if feels wrong because the discrete vs. continuous distinction has been beaten into us as part of a campaign to save the word 'fewer' from going the way of 'whom', 'well' (the adverbial form of 'good', not the place where Jack and Jill get water), and the dodo. The campaign has been coordinated by the *Académie Grammariénne*, a clandestine group of retired high school English teachers, many of whom are nuns with golden rulers, who keep the Endangered Usage List.

Their campaign to save the word 'fewer' has been successful, but they have lost the battle for 'whom' and 'well'. The word 'whom' hasn't been used this century, except in that phrase above about the nuns. Sister Eucharia[1] is waving her ruler ecstatically, and posthumously.

'Good' is used as an adverb now almost as often as 'well'.

- He made a good play. (adjective)
- He played well. (adverb)
- He played good. (also an adverb)
- He played goodly. (This is the Trump usage)
- A goodly pile of bricks would line the well. (This is nonsense)

How did we get 'well' in the first place? Because 'goodly' was already taken. Let's leave 'well' enough alone and leave the word 'well' for the place we throw the lawyers.

- If we throw a dozen lawyers down the well, will there be fewer lawyers or less lawyers?
- No, because in the time it takes a dozen lawyers to fall to the bottom of the well, a score of lawyers will have passed the bar exam.

Back to 'fewer'. Let's get rid of it. It's inconsistent. We don't say 'more' for continuous quantities and 'many-er' for countable quantities. And in software, a domain where exactitude reigns, we pronounce the phrase "a < b" as "'a' is less than 'b'" regardless of whether we've declared a and b as 'int' or 'float' (or 'double', to be more precise). 'Less' is perfectly well. Let's embrace it. Whom thinks differently?

---

[1] Sister Eucharia was my sixth-grade teacher, a sour, withered old lady in a black habit and a white wimple who wielded a twelve-inch ruler as a deterrent to tomfoolery. A whack on the palm would burn, but a crack on the knuckles could scar you for life.

9.2 Methodology Goals

It's important to understand your goals for a methodology before you choose one. "Being Agile," is not a good enough goal, because there are lots of ways to be Agile, or to achieve agility. And a lot of the things you may want from a methodology, like predictability, may seem to be anti-Agile.

I propose a set of goals based on the Geodesic Manifesto and the Software Management sections on Leadership, Planning and Control. Later I use these goals as a scorecard to evaluate methodology frameworks.

You may have other goals for your methodology, and some of my goals may not apply to your situation. Use these goals as a starting point for your own goals and your own methodology scorecard.

I list a summary of the goals here and then discuss each in more detail.

- Scale
  - o **Diverse Projects** – Support multiple simultaneous projects of new development, infrastructure improvement, incremental improvement and maintenance
  - o **Scale by Size** – Coordinate among many subprojects, potentially across geographies
- Management
  - o **Vision** – Work toward a vision within a high-level plan and an architectural framework
  - o **Context-based Rigidity** – The processes of a methodology have a certain degree of rigidity. It's important that they foster creativity at the right times, and enforce high-quality development practices at others
  - o **Common Processes** – Standardize processes for common development activities
  - o **Low-level Decision-making** – Empower developers to make decisions within their capabilities, with controls that validate key decisions
  - o **Planning** – Always be able to answer the three planning questions: "When will it be done?" and "What will it include?" and "What do I do next?"
  - o **Ease of Implementation** – How difficult is it to master the framework?
- Embrace Change
  - o **Agility** – Maximize the agility of the organization
  - o **Customer Input** – Integrate requirements at a regular interval
  - o **Continuous Improvement** – Periodically assess the methodology, the architecture and the software to find ways to improve.
- High Quality Working Software
  - o **Working Software** – Release working software frequently with frequent measurement of key project parameters

- o **Quality** – Develop high-reliability software that meets or exceeds requirements
- Productivity
  - o **Productivity** – Optimize productivity, especially for the highest contributors
  - o **Skillset Management** – Minimize negative impact of inexperienced and low-skill contributors

9.2.1 Scale

It's important that your methodology continue to work as your problems get bigger.

Diverse Projects
- Support multiple simultaneous projects of new development, infrastructure improvement, incremental improvement and maintenance

A mature software organization always has many kinds of development projects going on at varying stages of completion. You're releasing software, developing new capabilities, fixing bugs, improving usability and enhancing infrastructure. All these projects interact with each other in both obvious and subtle ways because they use the same code base, the same group of developers, the same validation resources and the same compute infrastructure.

Some organizations give in to the temptation to create a different methodology for each kind of project. On the other extreme, an organization may attempt to cram new algorithm development into a methodology that was optimized for fixing bugs. Your methodology needs to encompass all the things you do while maintaining as much commonality as possible.

Scale by Size
- Coordinate among many subprojects, potentially across geographies

Your methodology also needs to scale by size. It's easy to coordinate the activities of five developers in the same room. But as the group grows, organizational boundaries and geographical diversity make the coordination more challenging. The methodology needs to define how groups communicate and cooperate to achieve maximum agility. A methodology based on face to face communication will be difficult to adapt to a global development team.

9.2.2 Management

The role of management in providing leadership, planning projects, and defining processes and controls is the primary difference between Agile and the Geodesic Philosophy.

Vision

- Work toward a vision within a high-level plan and an architectural framework

The vision sets a goal that a development team can rally around. The high-level plan and architectural framework set boundaries that guide the team as they move toward the vision. Any mention of planning or architecture control are often immediately condemned as anti-Agile. But every successful team I've worked with has had them.

Your methodology needs to define a clear role for management to provide these high-level guidelines.

Context-based Rigidity

- The processes of a methodology have a certain degree of rigidity. It's important that they foster creativity at the right times, and enforce high-quality development practices at others

In the section that discusses Software Processes, I discussed the concept of process rigidity – how strictly do you enforce the rules of the process. Some processes need to be rigid, such as release processes and compliance testing, while others can be loose in some contexts.

Your methodology needs to allow for changing process rigidity to help you meet other goals.

Common Processes

- Standardize processes for common development activities

Common processes streamline code development by automating common tasks and providing a common vocabulary to discuss how things get done. See the previous chapter for a discussion on recommended processes.

Low-level Decision-making

- Empower developers to make decisions within their capabilities, with controls that validate key decisions

Most decisions in a software organization should be made by developers who have the best information. But it's important that there are ways to validate those decisions. See the earlier Decision Making section.

Planning

- Always be able to answer the three planning questions: "When will it be done?" and "What will it include?" and "What do I do next?"

The organization needs answers to those questions. Your methodology needs to be able to update the answers as things change, whether from external events from customers and competitors, or from internal events caused by better understanding of the project.

Ease of Implementation
- How difficult is it to master the framework?

Software development methodology frameworks range in complexity from easy (read a book and maybe take a certification class) to difficult (change the way your whole company develops software). I recently saw a post that claimed that a major US corporation was half way on their fifteen-year journey to become Lean, which is perfectly consistent with Lean's principle of "Decide as late as possible," but not with "Deliver as soon as possible."

9.2.3   Embrace Change

Change is inevitable. Change is annoying. Change is the only way to improve. Everyone wants agility and the Agile revolution made it clear that you can get it if you embrace change as an essential part of software development.

Agility
- Maximize the agility of the organization

Minimize the latency and maximize the frequency of the processes you use most.

Do work in small, easy-to-manage chunks.

Customer Input
- Integrate requirements at a regular interval

Understanding the needs of your customers and users, and the capabilities of your competitors is key to delivering the best software. On the other hand, raw customer input is often too high frequency, and needs analysis and synthesis to be useful. A good methodology will invoke a requirements management process often enough to stay in touch.

Continuous Improvement
- Periodically assess the methodology, the architecture and the software to find ways to improve.

All Agile frameworks include learning as part of the methodology. The iterative do-measure-analyze loop needs to be a key part of your methodology.

9.2.4   High Quality Working Software

As the Geodesic Manifesto states, your "goal is to create software-based solutions that do what the user wants in the way the user expect," and to do it frequently. The goals in this group depend on good code development processes, testing processes and release management processes.

Working Software
- Release working software nearly continuously with near-continuous measurement of key project parameters

Developing software and delivering it for evaluation and use is the core job of a development team. Most Agile methodology frameworks are defined around a core release management process. The release management processes are the most important distinguishing features of the methodologies.

Quality
- Develop high-reliability software that meets or exceeds requirements

Quality depends on the code and is validated by testing. Good code development processes are key to quality. Good test development processes provide the feedback needed to continuously improve the code.

9.2.5   Productivity

No team ever has enough resources, whether it's developers, validators, computers or disk space. Your competitiveness depends on getting the most benefit from the resources you have. These goals cover both a Yin and a Yang. The Yang encompasses all the things your team accomplishes. The Yin comprises all those things that you did that you need to throw away and start over.

These goals also consider the wide range of ability in the team. In a typical development team, 80% of the invention is done by 20% of the developers. Any development methodology needs to maximize the productivity of the 20%, while making sure that no one is contributing negative productivity.

Productivity
- Optimize productivity, especially for the highest contributors

Good code development processes enhance productivity by improving communications and improving the maintainability of the code.

The common processes for code development should not be a burden. If every SCM submission requires an hour of documentation, then you've slowed down your team, or given them a reason to subvert the process. As you get feedback on processes to improve them, you should consider the highest contributors' feedback with higher priority.

Skillset Management
- Minimize negative impact of inexperienced and low-skill contributors

The methodology needs to require enough controls to make sure that the code that's developed is suitable for quality and maintainability. You may intentionally develop prototype code that will be removed later. But it's not OK to develop code that will need to be removed because it was poorly designed or poorly implemented.

9.3   Waterfall

In this section, I present the strict Waterfall methodology and its most common modifications. I analyze it against the goals we set in the previous section.

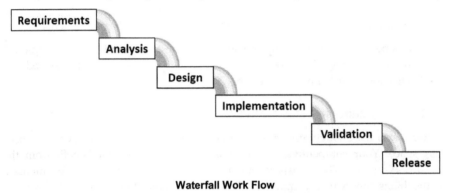

Waterfall Work Flow

In a strict Waterfall methodology, the project is broken up into phases – six phases in the figure above. Each phase must be completed before the next phase can begin. Work always flows downhill and never goes back. This model was inspired by traditional projects, like building a house. You can't put up the walls until the foundation is complete.

Lots of time is spent early in the process understanding and designing the project so that the later stages of implementation and validation have fewer surprises. Each stage generates lots of documentation that can be used by the subsequent stages.

It works great until something changes. A requirement change can set the whole project back to the beginning. A design problem can cause a lot of rework.

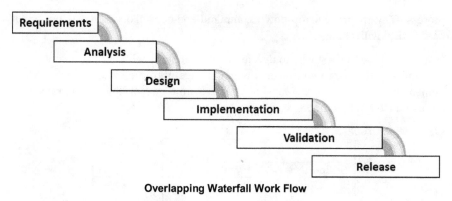

Overlapping Waterfall Work Flow

Strict Waterfall is way too restrictive. The first modification teams make is to allow overlap between the phases because as soon as some of the requirements are defined, someone can start analyzing, and so forth. If you don't allow overlap, you have a lot of people sitting around twiddling their thumbs.

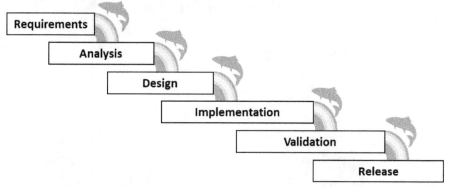

Overlapping Waterfall Work Flow with Iteration

The overlapping model improves productivity, but not agility. If you got the design wrong, you're stuck with it. So most Waterfall methodologies allow iteration between adjacent phases. Think of it as a fish ladder. When I refer to Waterfall beyond here, I assume that the overlapping and iteration modifications are allowed.

At their best, Waterfall projects can deal with the entire project with a global view. The output of the Analysis phase can include a good overall plan with clear milestones. The output of the Design phase can be a good architecture.

Waterfall methodologies are often cited as the least Agile methodologies. At their worst, they make decisions early without enough data to know if they are the right decisions. They require extensive documentation that is quickly outdated and seldom read. They inhibit iteration and that makes it hard to get organizational learning in the

269

process. They are prone to top-down, command-and-control decision making. And it's hard to deal with change.

Waterfall can be the best way to develop new technology where there are not yet any customers, and where requirements won't change until the system is released. But immediately after release, you should move into one of the Agile frameworks discussed later in this chapter.

Waterfall Scorecard

	Waterfall
Scale	
Diverse Projects	▼
Scale by Size	■
Management	
Vision	●
Flexible Rigidity	▼
Common Processes	▼
Low-level Decision-making	■
Planning	●
Ease of Implementation	●
Embrace Change	
Agility	■
Customer Input	■
Continuous Improvement	■
High Quality Working Software	
Working Software	■
Quality	■
Productivity	
Productivity	▼
Skillset Management	▼

Waterfall Scorecard

In the table above you see the first use of the methodology scorecard. The goals from the previous section are on the left, and a rating is on the right. A green circle is good; a yellow triangle is neutral; and a red square is bad.

The Waterfall methodology has several red squares. Too many decisions are made at the high level. The structure of the flow optimizes for projects with unchanging requirements. And it takes too long to get working software which will have a negative impact on quality. As the project gets bigger all those other problems get worse, so it doesn't scale well.

The green circles for vision – good architecture and a high-level plan – and planning do not make up for all the deficiencies of the methodology.

9.4   Water Flow Model

Mackenzie Falls, Granpians National Park, Victoria, Australia

The seeds of improving the Waterfall methodology lie in the waterfall metaphor itself.

In the Waterfall model, the whole project is on a barge floating down one part of the river. The barge goes over the falls to move to the next part of the river. It takes a lot of preparation to get ready for the falls, and once across, it's very difficult to go back.

The barge model makes it difficult to achieve agility. Instead of putting the whole project on one barge, think of the project as a bunch of rubber ducks[1] launched onto the river by the Requirements process. Each duck can then choose its own path down the river. In the photo above, you can see that Mackenzie Falls is composed of many cascades. Some ducks will take the right path on the upper part of the falls and then the left path on the lower part, while other ducks will find different paths.

I call this the Water *Flow* model to distinguish it from Water*fall*. The project follows the flow of the river as it splits and converges.

By breaking up the project into small work parcels, you gain agility. Most ducks can proceed down the river without needing the fish ladder, but if there's a problem, the cost of sending one duck back to the Analysis phase is low. While some ducks are still in design, other ducks have made it through validation and you have working software

---

[1] See https://en.wikipedia.org/wiki/Friendly_Floatees for a description of what happened to a shipping container full of rubber ducks and other floating toys that was lost at sea in 1992.

that you can measure and improve. The early ducks can provide feedback on the process to improve the ride for the later ducks.

With this agility you risk losing the global view that's inherent in Waterfall. Instead of getting the global view at the beginning of the project – at the Analysis or Design phase, you need to accumulate that global view as the project matures. So, instead of starting with a plan, you converge to a plan as the ducks go through the analysis phase. Instead of starting with an architecture, you converge to an architecture as design decisions are validated by implementation.

The simple, go-with-the-flow metaphor is appealing, but you can't just let the ducks wander. You need to make sure that the highest priority ducks are launched first. You need to monitor the ducks to make sure they're not stuck. You need to nudge them along the most productive paths. In other words, you need to get your ducks in a row.

As we review other methodology frameworks in the rest of this chapter, you will see that they are all closely related to the Water Flow model with variations on what phases are needed, how to arrive at the global view, and how to manage the ducks.

9.5   Scrum

Scrum is an Agile framework for managing projects with rapidly changing requirements. Scrum is the most widely used Agile framework. It was developed by Ken Schwaber and Jeff Sutherland in the mid '90s. They have written an excellent summary of Scrum that is available here: https://www.scrumguides.org. They state that it is lightweight, easy to understand, but difficult to master. That last 'but' explains why so many teams that try to use Scrum fail to achieve the productivity and quality gains they hoped for.

Scrum is a methodology framework, not a complete methodology. Scrum does not define common low-level processes that dictate how details of the work get done; that is up to the development team. It does define a high-level, incremental process for managing change, for managing work, and for measuring and analyzing the results. It defines two leadership roles: *Product Owner* who represents the customer and the business to the team and represents the team to the rest of the organization, and *Scrum Master* who coaches the team through the development process and helps them self-organize. A successful implementation of Scrum depends on the whole team committing to the work, contributing to the best of their abilities, and communicating openly. Productive team dynamics is by far the hardest part of Scrum to master.

9.5.1 Overview

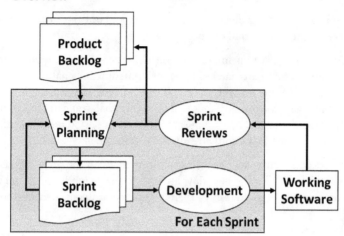

Scrum Model Overview

Here's a brief (and simplified) description of how it works. The Product Owner, together with the rest of the team, creates a Product Backlog – a prioritized list of all known tasks with rough effort estimates. Progress proceeds in intervals called Sprints – short periods of development on the order of two weeks to a month. In most Scrum-based projects, that period is the same for every Sprint. The Scrum Master, together with the rest of the team, creates a Sprint Backlog – the list of items that are planned for the current Sprint. Developers pull items off the Sprint Backlog to implement according to the developers' availabilities and capabilities. Each task is implemented to the team's Definition of Done, including unit tests, integration tests and any other testing that's required. In a daily Scrum "stand-up" meeting, progress is reviewed, and the team may modify its behavior (task assignments, priorities, etc.) to better meet the goals of the Sprint. At the end of the Sprint, the team generates working software that's ready for internal release (and maybe for external release, if possible). The team reviews progress against the Sprint Backlog and measures the resulting software; this review may generate new items for the Product Backlog that will be completed in a subsequent Sprint. The team also reviews the processes they use so that they can continuously improve their behavior.

A Scrum Sprint is schedule-driven rather than feature-driven. Each Sprint has a strict schedule and if items in the Sprint Backlog are not completed satisfactorily to the Definition of Done, they will be deferred to the next Sprint.

9.5.2   The Sprint and the Stand-up

If you ask someone to describe Scrum, they will talk about the two most prominent features – the Sprint and the daily stand-up meeting.

Using a short Sprint has two important consequences. First, it gives a period for requirements integration that matches the development team's natural frequency. If a requirement comes in, the answer, "We will put it in the next Sprint," is a perfectly understandable reply. Most requestors will be aware that you can't insert something into a Sprint once it's started. Second, it sets a minimum period for measurement. We are guaranteed to measure the software after every Sprint.

The daily stand-up meeting keeps everyone informed about the status of the Sprint, is a time to plan the work for the next day, and is a time to identify potential problems and to put actions in motion to resolve them before the problems become too big.

9.5.3   Analysis

Scrum works well if the team is co-located, everyone on the team embraces the values – commitment, courage, focus, openness and respect – and the Product Owner and Scrum Master are committed to inclusiveness. When it works well, the transformation into a super-team happens and both productivity and quality improve dramatically.

Scrum as described by the documents is not always effective.

- The role of the Product Owner is critical to Scrum. This person is responsible for prioritizing requirements, for continually talking to customers and users, for guiding the team in their daily decision-making. It's often difficult to find a Product Owner who is willing and able to spend the time needed to fill the role. If the Product Owner is willing, but not able, then the completeness and priorities of the Product Backlog will not maximize the value of the software. If the Product Owner is not willing, then one or more team members will need to play that role by thinking like a customer, and they are likely to miss some important changes.
- Scrum forces the team to break up development into small chunks that fit in a Sprint. For some tasks, especially early in a project, that just doesn't work. I can think of several projects from my past that took longer than a month to generate something that was measurable by more than a unit test.
- Scrum doesn't scale well. If there are one hundred software developers, you need to break the development into multiple Scrums. Then you need to synchronize all those Scrums some other way. If the team is geographically distributed, daily scrum meetings don't provide the level of communication and openness that's needed. There are several proposed extensions to Scrum to handle larger and distributed teams; I will review one of these, Large-scale Scrum (LeSS), later in this chapter.

- Scrum alone doesn't provide the architectural framework or the architectural decision-making ethos that are necessary for successful self-organization. Although the Product Owner and Scrum Master act as the conscience for the team, they don't make architectural or design decisions.
- The only controls on quality are the Sprint reviews and adaptation and the team's Definition of Done. An effective Scrum methodology needs to include common processes for code and test development. Including continuous integration and testing processes is required to help Scrum teams achieve high quality
- In a real software team, everyone is working on multiple release projects simultaneously. A developer could be working on new features for release n, a patch for release n-1, and planning for release n+1. Balancing priorities across these three releases is difficult to fit into the Sprint framework.

Some of the problems listed above are addressed by the XP methodology, described in the next section, which is why many teams are using a hybrid of Scrum and XP.

9.5.4　It's Agile, but is it Geodesic?

PRINCIPLES

To overcome the limitations of requirements:

- We have frequent interaction with customers and users.
- We frequently deliver working software and actively seek feedback.
- Developers must learn to think like their customers.

To overcome the limitations of people:

- We build synergistic teams that improve the performance of every individual.
- We establish a methodology that fosters creativity and encourages interaction.
- We encourage frequent and open communication among team members.

To overcome the inherent difficulties of software:

- We seek out change from as many sources as possible.
- We plan for change, and change the plan when necessary.
- We embrace change through constant measurement, analysis and improvement of the software and methodology.
- Developers strive for the highest level of technical excellence and assume responsibility for quality.

Principles of the Geodesic Manifesto

If we evaluate Scrum against the Geodesic Manifesto's principles, we see that it is consistent with them. Some of the principles go beyond the Scrum methodology, but Scrum is flexible enough to accommodate them.

PILLARS

Success depends on:

- Leadership that:
  - Creates a vision for the solution we're trying to create
  - Organizes the development team to maximize the contribution of each member
  - Develops dynamic plans that answer three questions: When will it be done? What will it contain? What do I do next?
  - Establishes processes and controls that maximize productivity and creativity
- An architecture that organizes the solution into modules and their interactions that is modular, flexible, consistent and sufficient.
- A methodology that defines common processes and controls that foster innovation, empower the development team to create the best solution, and maximize efficiency while minimizing risk
- A decision-making ethos to guide us as we change the vision, plan, architecture and methodology.

Pillars of the Geodesic Manifesto

However, Scrum is much weaker when evaluated against the Geodesic Manifesto's Pillars, especially leadership and architecture. The Scrum framework depends on distributed leadership within the self-organizing team. If there is a vision, it comes from outside the team. There is no architect, and the responsibility for long-term planning is ambiguous. The only planning question that Scrum attempts to answer is "What do I do next?" The short-term focus of Scrum leads to the common complaint that Scrum teams have trouble committing to delivering features on a schedule.

9.5.5   Scrum Scorecard

	Waterfall	Scrum
Scale		
Diverse Projects	▼	■
Scale by Size	■	■
Management		
Vision	●	▼
Flexible Rigidity	▼	▼
Common Processes	▼	▼
Low-level Decision-making	■	●
Planning	●	■
Ease of Implementation	●	●
Embrace Change		
Agility	■	●
Customer Input	■	●
Continuous Improvement	■	●
High Quality Working Software		
Working Software	■	●
Quality	■	▼
Productivity		
Productivity	▼	●
Skillset Management	▼	■

Scrum Scorecard

Scrum scores low in Scale because it was designed for a single project with a small co-located team. It also scores low in planning because the incremental approach to development makes it hard to get a big-picture plan in place. Skillset Management is often difficult for a self-organizing team; usually management intervention is required to maximize productivity for high performers while minimizing negative impact of low skill developers.

It scores high in the areas that affect agility: Low-level Decision-making, Working Software, and all three Embrace Change categories. It also scores high in Productivity because it is a very low overhead methodology.

The areas rated neutral need to be addressed by additions to your specific Scrum implementation.

9.6   Extreme Programming (XP)

Scrum has rules and a meta-process for dealing with changing requirements and for managing the work of a project, but technical issues like coding, architecture and quality are left to the discretion of the team. XP has more emphasis on how to develop high quality code, and less rigor about how to manage the project. Personally, I find Scrum a little stifling, whereas XP is much closer to the natural way I would develop software, with a few exceptions.

XP's documentation (http://www.extremeprogramming.org) delineates four activities, five values, three principles, thirteen practices and an unbounded set of rules. That's too many lists with too many items. I think you can get the flavor of XP from the values and the practices. I will present these with little editorial comment. That will come later.

The values are:

- Communication – Every team member should have a shared understanding of the system, both from a development view and from a user view. This is accomplished mostly through verbal communication and through the code base.
- Simplicity – XP uses its own non-dictionary definition of 'simplicity'.
- Writing code that is easy to understand.
- Starting with the smallest possible subset of functionality and then expanding from there
- Designing for today's requirements and updating the design later if the requirements change.
- Feedback – Like all Agile methodologies, XP relies on an incremental improvement loop, where feedback comes from measuring the code through testing, particularly unit tests, from users, and from the developers who give feedback to improve the development process.
- Courage – Many of the practices of XP are not natural for many programmers. A developer needs courage to make bold changes to the code, to admit to mistakes, and to persevere in the face of adversity.
- Respect – If simplicity is the Scarecrow's wits, and courage is the Lion's mettle, then respect is the Tin Man's heart. Developers need to write code that others want to work with, to strive for the highest quality, and to trust others to do a good job.

There are thirteen practices – like the Agile Manifesto's principles, more than anyone can easily remember. Luckily, they are organized in five sets. Many of these practices are recommendations for how to implement the Common Processes of the previous chapter.

- Fine-scale Feedback
  - o Pair programming – The thinking here goes as follows: if code reviews are good, then continuous code reviews are better. Always put two people in front of the screen with one typing and one reviewing.
  - o Test-driven development – Write tests before, or simultaneous with, writing production code. The focus is on unit tests, but other tests, such as integration tests, should follow the same practice.

- o Whole team – the team is more than the developers. Include customer advocates and others in the development process.
- Planning
  - o Release Planning – an iterative process of gathering requirements using "stories", and estimating work for each story. Sort the work by value and risk, and make a commitment on delivery date and release content.
  - o Iteration Planning – Like Scrum, the iteration is a short development cycle with working, but incomplete, software available at the end. Choose the stories that will be implemented in this iteration, and assign them to developers.
- Continuous Process
  - o Continuous Integration – developers should always be working with the latest version of the code, and should commit their changes often. This means that changes that will break other code need to be avoided, and incompatible code needs to be encapsulated to maintain compatibility until the changes can be proven.
  - o Design Improvement – The Simplicity value advocates design that does only what's needed today. That means that tomorrow, you may need to make significant changes to the design to maintain the simplicity of the code base. Refactoring and re-writing are an important part of the development process.
  - o Small Releases – The short iteration cycles mean that there are many opportunities to evaluate the software by users and customer advocates.
- Shared Understanding
  - o Coding Standard – Use of a coding standard makes it easier for the development team to understand and enhance the code, no matter who wrote it.
  - o Collective Code Ownership – Everyone is responsible for all the code. Anyone can change any part of it.
  - o Simple Design – Always write the simplest code possible. If you see complex code, make it simpler.
  - o System Metaphor – The team has an ethos for how to evaluate the "goodness" of architecture and design. I discuss such an ethos in section Architecture Design Principles.
- Programmer Welfare
  - o Sustainable Pace – Developers should work at a steady pace with occasional periods of increased intensity.

There is a lot to like in XP. When taken individually, it's hard to argue with most of the values or practices. Test-driven development, continuous integration, collective ownership, and coding standards are all things I have done successfully, and would recommend to any development team.

On the other hand, I'm not a fan of pair programming; it has seldom worked for me. And the release planning method ties down both schedule and content, leaving only quality (or effort) as a variable.

But the biggest problem is incremental design. Incremental design works if I'm coding alone or with a small group of gifted developers. When you add in average and below-average developers it doesn't work. Many times I have seen mediocre programmers "design" modules with convoluted data structures and complex functions that took a long time to develop, and then didn't work. And when a good programmer went in to fix it, the complexity and the problems lingered until we finally gave up and rewrote it. XP proponents say that wouldn't happen if you did pair programming. To which I say, the purpose of pair programming is not to protect us from incompetence. Design needs to be done by developers who have the right complexity limits. Once a good design is in place, developers with lower complexity limits can implement it.

Most programmers need structure before they can be productive, and you need to put that structure in place before they start. Someone needs to look at the whole problem and design an architecture that has a good chance of solving the whole problem, not just the subset problem you're dealing with today. Once an evolvable architecture is in place, and the ethos for how to evaluate a design change is established, then the entire team can contribute productively.

9.6.1   XP Scorecard

	Waterfall	Scrum	XP
Scale			
Diverse Projects	▼	■	■
Scale by Size	■	■	
Management			
Vision	●	▼	▼
Flexible Rigidity	▼	▼	
Common Processes	▼	▼	●
Low-level Decision-making	■	●	●
Planning	●	■	
Ease of Implementation	●	●	▼
Embrace Change			
Agility	■	●	●
Customer Input	■	●	●
Continuous Improvement	■	●	●
High Quality Working Software			
Working Software	■	●	●
Quality	■	▼	●
Productivity			
Productivity	▼	●	●

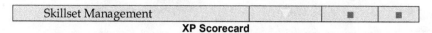

Skillset Management		■	■

XP Scorecard

The ratings for XP are similar to Scrum. XP recommends common processes, which are left out of the Scrum framework. The coding practices are likely to improve quality. The longer-term planning horizon of XP boosts its Planning rating compared to Scrum. XP can scale to larger projects than Scrum.

XP is more of a challenge to implement than Scrum because of the number of recommended common processes.

9.7   Scaling Agile to Large Teams with Diverse Projects

Scrum and XP work best with co-located teams working on a single project. Most software development doesn't fit that restriction. Several frameworks exist that aim to extend the scale of Agile development. In this section, I will briefly review three of these frameworks. Each of them is supported by an industry consortium, or individuals, that maintain documentation about the framework and provide training and certification in its use. I chose these three examples, because they represent the range of available options, from straightforward to very complex.

Frankly, I am not qualified to discuss any of these in detail because I have no personal experience using them. If you are interested in understanding them better, I recommend that you review the materials available at the frameworks' websites. I make no recommendations on the use of these or other frameworks. And I won't be presenting scorecards for these frameworks.

I see a few common themes among these frameworks:

- They are designed to scale to larger teams with diverse deliverables
- The scaling comes at a cost of being harder to implement
- Most of them require leadership to embrace Lean Software Development principles
- They depend on the Leadership, Architecture and Methodology pillars of the Geodesic Manifesto

9.8   Large-scale Scrum (LeSS)[1]

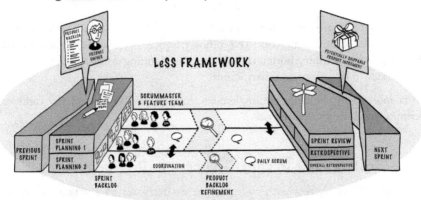

LeSS Framework Overview (https://less.works)

> Complex product development doesn't require complex solutions. It requires a deep understanding of the essence of the problems, which can then be solved with simpler solutions… Note that simpler doesn't mean easier, especially in the short run. Even though LeSS is simple, it is exceptionally hard to adopt well in organizations.

Large-Scale Scrum: More with LeSS, Craig Larman, Bas Vodde, 2015

Large-scale Scrum (LeSS) extends the Scrum framework to scale up to eight teams. A further extension, LeSS Huge, scales to even larger product development. In the following, I focus on the smaller framework. The framework was developed by Bas Vodde and Craig Larman starting in about 2005. They took the thinking behind Scrum and applied that thinking to larger product developments by using a simple hierarchical model.

There is one Product Owner and one Product Backlog for the whole product. The product development is broken up into a few (eight or less) cross-functional, cross-component (full stack), co-located teams. Work proceeds in one multi-team Sprint. The teams plan the Sprint together in two phases: a whole-product planning session, and more detailed team planning sessions. In the first phase, the teams work together to select items from the Product Backlog. Since each team is an end-to-end feature team doing full-stack development in a shared code model, the teams work independently to complete the items for the Sprint, and there is very little coordination needed. At the end of the Sprint, the teams expect to have releasable working software for the product.

---

[1] Some of the material in this section is Copyright The LeSS Company B.V., and is used by permission.

Methodology learning takes place both at the team level and at the product level through team and product retrospectives.

The framework defines principles to guide decision making, and rules that define the bounds of the framework. The principles are similar to the Scrum principles with the addition of a couple principles, like Systems Thinking and Queueing Theory, that apply to the scaled problem. There are twenty-eight rules that define the LeSS framework that have been derived empirically over the time that LeSS has evolved. Here are a few key examples:

- Each team is (1) self-managing, (2) cross-functional, (3) co-located, and (4) long-lived.
- There is one Product Owner and one Product Backlog for the complete shippable product.
- One Definition of Done for the whole product common to all teams.
- There is one product-level Sprint, not a different Sprint for each Team. Each Team starts and ends the Sprint at the same time. Each Sprint results in an integrated whole product.
- Sprint Planning consists of two parts: Sprint Planning One is common for all teams while Sprint Planning Two is usually done separately for each team. Do multi-team Sprint Planning Two in a shared space for closely related items.
- Each Team has their own Sprint Backlog.
- Each Team has their own Daily Scrum.
- An Overall Retrospective is held after the Team Retrospectives to discuss cross-team and system-wide issues, and create improvement experiments. This is attended by Product Owner, Scrum Masters, Team representatives, and managers (if any).

For further information, refer to the LeSS website: https://less.works.

9.9   Disciplined Agile (DA)[1]

The Disciplined Agile Framework (DA), developed by Scott Ambler and Mark Lines, and managed by the Disciplined Agile Consortium (www.disciplinedagileconsortium.org), applies Agile thinking to the entire software development lifecycle, from conception to release and support, and to the entire enterprise. It incorporates the Leadership and Architecture pillars of the Geodesic Manifesto. It was designed to scale to very large projects.

---

[1] Some of the material in this section is Copyright Disciplined Agile Consortium, and is used by permission.

Often, teams that try to implement an Agile methodology do not get the benefits they hoped for. And often, the reason for the shortfall is because limitations imposed by the greater organization keep them from implementing the Agile methodology in its optimum manner. For example, I saw a team using Scrum to develop a product, but the software validation team was in another department, so they were not part of the Scrum. The team made an internal release of the product at the end of each Sprint, and the validation team started working then, finding problems that should have been found much earlier.

DA is called a process decision framework. You won't find tools or process definitions. What you will find is a detailed description of what it means to be Agile. It's based on a set of seven principles (not the Agile Manifesto principles). It defines roles and responsibilities that are necessary for software development. It recommends that you define a hybrid methodology that meets the needs of your software problem. That hybrid may include elements from Scrum and XP, extended with architecture design (Agile Modeling) or other practices. Most importantly, it extends to all the parts of the organization that affect software development to avoid organization-induced failure.

9.9.1 Disciplined Agile Principles

2017 © Disciplined Agile Consortium

Disciplined Agile Principles
(www.disciplinedagiledelivery.com)

The DA principles form the basis of DA's decision-making ethos.

- **Be Awesome**[1] – Set high goals to challenge team members.
- **Delight Customers** – Create high quality software that does what the user wants in the way the user expects.
- **Pragmatism** – Do what's needed, not what's "right". If Scrum, as defined by the Scrum documents, doesn't work for you, do something else.
- **Context Counts** – Your software development methodology needs to work for your problem, within your organization, and with your customer base. You can't just copy someone else's methodology and hope that it works.
- **Choice is Good** – Don't tie yourself down to a single process for every type of task. Your code review process for new feature development may be very different from the process for a critical bug fix. Having process choices can increase the effectiveness and productivity of your team.
- **Optimize Flow** – This principle is a little hard to pin down. It's basically a catch-all for the practices that are common to Agile methodologies – frequent delivery of working software, systems thinking, continuous measurement, and organizational learning.
- **Enterprise Awareness** – It's not enough to optimize your team. You need to contribute to the success of the enterprise, and you need to adapt to, and influence, the context that the enterprise has established. That context may include standard tools and processes, common software modules, and common data management practices.

---

[1] I can't look at this principle's name without being haunted by the vision of an open-plan office full of developers from ten different countries breaking into "Everything is Awesome" from *The Lego Movie*.

285

9.9.2   Scaling Agile

Disciplined Agile Processes (www.disciplinedagiledelivery.com)

DA addresses processes for the entire enterprise from software development (the innermost, bottom box) to the business side of the enterprise. For each of these it provides a decision framework with high-level definitions of roles and processes.

As I discussed in the Yin-Yang and Complexity models, you can't avoid complexity, but you can manage it by applying architecture and methodology to the problem. The developers of the DA framework have extended the ideas of Agile to include the missing aspects of Leadership, Architecture and Methodology. DA can help you develop a methodology that meets the needs of your organization.

9.10 The Scaled Agile Framework® (SAFe®)[1]

The Scaled Agile Framework (SAFe) is a methodology framework aimed at scaling Agile practices to the enterprise. It provides a decision-making framework like Disciplined Agile, and recommends a meta-process that extends Scrum to a much

---

[1] Some of the material in this section is Copyright Scaled Agile, Inc., and is used by permission.

larger scale, and, like XP, it provides a framework for defining common processes that encourage continuous delivery of high-quality software. SAFe is the framework that is the closest match to the Geodesic Philosophy.

SAFe evolved from the book *Agile Software Requirements* by Dean Leffingwell (2011), which describes ways to scale the requirements gathering and management processes within a large organization. Leffingwell partnered with Drew Jemilo to form Scaled Agile, Inc.

(www.scaledagile.com), which has the mission to promote and evolve SAFe (www.scaledagileframework.com).

SAFe defines five core competencies of the enterprise:

- Lean Agile Leadership – the essentials of managing a complex software system
- Team and Technical Agility – the common processes for high-quality software development
- DevOps and Release on Demand – processes for releasing software
- Business Solutions and Lean Systems Engineering – meta-processes for building very complex systems
- Lean Portfolio Management – processes for managing all the software solutions within the enterprise

For the rest of this section, I will concentrate on the first three competencies, the subset labeled "Essential SAFe."

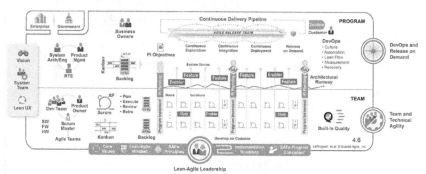

Essential SAFe Overview (www.scaledagileframework.com) ©Scaled Agile, Inc

9.10.1 Lean-Agile Leadership

Leadership forms the foundation of SAFe. Leaders set the values for the organization, build the culture of <u>Lean</u> thinking that's needed for efficiency and organizational change. They provide vision and roadmaps, and they oversee the implementation of a SAFe methodology.

Scaled Agile Principles

The Agile Manifesto provides principles to guide software development. Lean provides principles to improve efficiency. SAFe provides yet another set of principles to guide implementation of a SAFe methodology.

- **Take an economic view** – Consider both the costs and economic benefit of the software you develop
- **Apply systems thinking** – Think about the whole problem; architecture and high-level planning are necessary for success.
- **Assume variability; preserve options** – This is a synthesis of Agile, Geodesic and Lean principles of change and deferred decisions.
- **Build incrementally with fast, integrated learning cycles** – Incremental development with learning are central to all Agile and Geodesic methodologies.
- **Base milestones on an objective evaluation of working systems** – This is a synthesis of the measurement and "plan for change" principles of the Geodesic Manifesto.
- **Visualize and limit WIP, reduce batch sizes, and manage queue length** – As discussed in Work Parcel Size, small tasks increase agility.
- **Apply cadence; synchronize with cross-domain planning** – Cadence is similar to Scrum's Sprint length. Cadence and Synchronization are the core of the SAFe implementation methodology as defined by the Agile Release Train (see below). A cadence-based methodology works well for incremental improvement, but not for major innovation. See Asynchronous Project Management.
- **Unlock the intrinsic motivation of knowledge workers** – This is a restatement of the Geodesic Manifesto's synergistic team principle.
- **Decentralize decision-making** – This is another synthesis of Geodesic and Lean principles.

9.10.2 The Agile Release Train (ART)

SAFe's Agile Release Train (ART) is a cross-functional team who operate on schedule-driven project called the Program Increment (PI). The team is organized into several cross-functional implementation teams that each work on some subset of the system and the task queue. A large organization may have many ARTs that need to work together.

The ART has two clocks: a Scrum Sprint clock of two weeks, and a PI clock of about 8-12 weeks. These two clocks form the cadence of the SAFe methodology. Every two weeks, the implementation teams complete their sprint and the system comes together, forcing evaluation of cross team dependencies and providing feedback to the implementation teams. At the end of the PI period the system is ready for release.

Also running with the PI clock is the Continuous Delivery Pipeline. At any time, one group of people is doing requirements integration that will feed PI n+1, the implementation teams are implementing features for PI n, and the DevOps team is preparing for deployment and release of the solution from PI n-1.

9.10.3 Team and Technical Agility

SAFe's team agility comes from the Scrum-like cadence of the ART and from implementing small work parcels.

Technical agility has three components: architecture, testing and integration.

SAFe recommends defining an architectural "runway" that anticipates how the system will evolve and defines a general strategy for components and interfaces that minimize dependencies among features. SAFe recommends the SOLID principles for developing and evaluating architecture. A good architectural runway facilitates incremental design and improves initial quality.

SAFe uses a test-first methodology to make sure that the system evolves with high quality. The emphasis is on simple unit-level and integration-level tests with system-level tests only as needed.

Continuous integration is the final building block for technical agility. Frequent feedback on the effect of changes makes sure the system is always in a working state.

9.10.4 SAFe Summary

SAFe is a comprehensive framework that can scale to large organizations. The recommended practices have been validated in a wide range of organizations. See

https://www.scaledagile.com/resources/safe-case-studies/

for numerous stories of organizations that have transitioned to SAFe.

Implementing SAFe requires an organization-wide commitment. The required changes can take months or years. Scaled Agile, Inc. provides courses and certification programs that can help an organization with the transition. It also has an extensive network of partners who can help.

9.11 Asynchronous Project Management

The most common Agile methodology frameworks (Scrum, XP and derivatives) move forward in a series of fixed-length intervals, which I will call sprints, adopting the

Scrum terminology. This works well for schedule-driven releases, but reduces efficiency for feature-driven releases (see The Software Uncertainty Principle). If you are using two-week sprints, but you have a three-week task, it's inefficient to stop in the middle of the task, do all the sprint-completion tasks, and then pick up your task again.

Scrum proponents will say you shouldn't have three-week tasks. But if the goal is to see useful improvements after each sprint, it may be impossible to break up a long task because you need that much work to make it useful to someone else.

So, we need a way to manage long tasks. There are two choices: non-isochronous sprints, and asynchronous projects.

The word 'isochronous' (eye-SOCK-run-us) means same time, or in this context, fixed length. To accommodate long tasks, you can make your sprints non-isochronous. If you know that the next sprint includes a long project, you can dynamically change the sprint from two weeks to three weeks. This is a relatively straightforward modification of the common Agile methodologies.

Asynchronous project management proposes a different philosophy for managing tasks. It works toward milestones with the goal of completing each milestone as early as possible. Every programming task is put on a queue when all its dependencies are complete. The queue is prioritized to minimize risk, to maximize productivity and to deliver the milestone as early as possible. Asynchronous project methods can be more efficient than sprint-based methods, but they require more vigilance to keep things working efficiently.

9.11.1 Synchronous and Asynchronous Hardware Design

Most hardware design uses synchronous control. An isochronous clock captures the logical state of the circuit at the end of each clock period, and passes it on to the next period. Clock-synchronized design is easy to think about and straightforward to analyze automatically, but there are inefficiencies in both performance and power usage because every logic value needs to be calculated even if it will not be used. Hardware design teams often use elaborate schemes to avoid these inefficiencies while (mostly) staying within the clock-synchronized paradigm.

Asynchronous hardware design (wikipedia.org/wiki/Asynchronous_circuit) can achieve higher performance and much lower power usage. Instead of capturing the state of the circuit with a clock, the circuit uses self-timed logic. Every logic value consumer asks the logic value producer to generate the value so that values are only produced if they are needed. The producer tells the consumers when it's ready. And the consumers tell the value producer when they're done with it. In a simple mental model of asynchronous design, the data values flow forward in the circuit, and synchronization events flow both backward (requests for values, and done with values) and forward (value ready). The improvements in performance and power come at the expense of increased logic size, and a more complex design paradigm.

Scrum and XP, like synchronous hardware design, use an isochronous period to capture working software. The periodic releases are easy to understand and the methodologies are well documented. But there are inefficiencies. Every sprint has startup and ending costs that don't contribute to the next major goal that might be several sprints away.

To address the inefficiencies, we can use some of the concepts from asynchronous hardware design to improve delivery times and productivity in software development. Our goal for this process is to complete all the requirements defined for a project milestone in the shortest possible time with the highest quality. By understanding the dependencies of the expected tasks for the milestone, the assigned owner of each task can coordinate the synchronization events needed to deliver the milestone in the shortest possible time.

In asynchronous hardware design, each logic value has dedicated hardware to produce it and additional hardware to coordinate the synchronization events. In asynchronous software development, we have many tasks that need to be completed by a few developers. Efficient scheduling of the tasks is the biggest challenge of asynchronous software development.

I present here a rough outline of a process for asynchronous software development. I present the process for one milestone, but in practice, work will proceed in parallel for multiple milestones.

9.11.2 Dependency Graph

The first step is to create a task-dependency graph. Starting from the milestone, work backwards, defining all the tasks that need to come together to meet the requirements of the milestone. Some of those changes will be new modules, and some of them will be enhancements to existing modules. Then, recursively for each module, define all the changes required for that module. As you identify new modules, if two changes are small and related, combine them and merge their requirements. Repeat this recursively until all the changes are small enough to assign as "leaf" tasks. The result of this process is a dependency graph of tasks.

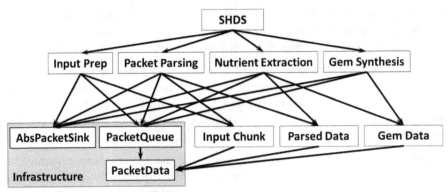

Task-Dependency Graph for SHDS

Above, you see the task dependency graph for the SHDS example from the Architecture chapter. Three tasks, PacketData, PacketQueue, and AbsPacketSink have been combined into one task called Infrastructure. See the simplified graph below.

You can read each edge as "depends on." For example, SHDS depends on Input Prep, that is, SHDS cannot be complete until Input Prep is complete. In the following, I use the terms 'dependent' and 'dependency' to distinguish between the directions of the edge. SHDS is a dependent of Input Prep. Input Prep is a dependency of SHDS.

In practice, you won't need to draw the graph as long as the dependencies are clear to everyone. You can use a Scrum-like task board with a few arrows. Or, you can arrange the tasks in layers where the tasks in the upper layers depend on the tasks in the lower layers.

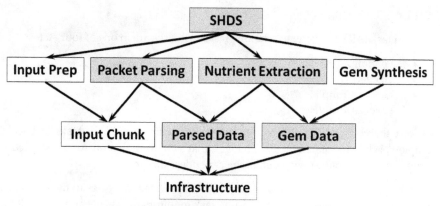

Simplified Task-Dependency Graph for SHDS

9.11.3 Managing the Graph

Assign an owner to each task. You can change the assignment later, but it's important that each task have someone to monitor its dependencies to know when the task can be started. In the graph, the white tasks are owned by Jack and the gray ones by Jill.

Each task will have multiple levels of completion. In the example, I will use two levels, but you may want to add more.

1. Ready for integration – the interfaces to the module are complete and reasonably stable.
2. Done – all the criteria in the project's Definition of Done are complete.

Having multiple levels allows work to proceed on dependent tasks before its dependencies are completed.

Start with the tasks that have no dependencies. In the example, only Infrastructure meets that criteria, but in most cases, there will be multiple start tasks. Once Infrastructure is at completion level 1, then parallel development of its dependents can begin. Jill can start on Parsed Data and Gem Data, and then Nutrient Extraction while Jack finishes Infrastructure.

In the spirit of minimizing risk, it's important to make progress on all the nodes in parallel. It would be a shame to leave Gem Synthesis to the end and then find that it is a lot harder than you thought, or that it requires fundamental changes to Infrastructure. One way to do this is to bring all the nodes up to completion level 1 early in the project.

Be careful not to turn this into a <u>Waterfall</u> project, where you bring everything to level 1, then to level 2, etc. It's important to use a <u>Water Flow</u> model, where each task will proceed through the levels in the way that best benefits the project. Some tasks will be complete before others get started.

9.11.4 Scheduling Tasks

We use a task priority queue to schedule tasks. All tasks are in one of four states:

- Pending
- Queued
- Level 1 Complete
- Level 2 Complete

We start the project with all tasks at Pending, and finish with all tasks at Level 2 Complete. When the state of a task changes, that's an event. Events for a task need to be communicated to the owners of all the dependent tasks.

At the beginning of the project, add the tasks with no dependencies to the queue. As work proceeds, the owner of each pending task monitors the events and when all the dependencies are met, then that task is added to the queue. In a small team, it's probably best to communicate all the events to all the team members.

We prioritize the queue based on task impact. Some of the criteria for prioritization are:

- Number of dependents
- Invention risk
- Ability to enable integration testing or system level testing
- Estimated completion time of the task

You can create a numerical calculation for priority, but it's probably better to let the team members use judgment to order the queue. The task owner and all the dependent task owners should agree on prioritization.

Note that it is possible for tasks to change state in the reverse direction. I call that a regression event. If a task requires a change in a dependency, then the dependency may go from Level 2 Complete back to Queued. For example, if Jill finds that she needs a change in the Packet Queue, then Packet Queue will go back to Queued state until Jack can make that change. Communication of regression events warns team members that their tasks, even their completed tasks, may be impacted by the change.

9.11.5 Communication

Coordinate the project with a combination of meetings and electronic communication. (In the following, I'll use the term 'email' as a surrogate for all forms of electronic communication.)

Status can be reported using email. Meetings are needed when discussion is required.

Task events can be reported using email. Each event communication should include the details of the state change, and some comments about the state of the task. Regression events should include the reason for the change.

Using email to announce that Infrastructure is ready for integration is useful and efficient. But if Nutrient Extraction needs a change to Infrastructure, then Jack and Jill need to talk. I've seen many long email threads with lots of ccs that go on for days, when a short face-to-face or phone discussion would have resolved the problem in a few minutes.

You can use a daily team meeting to ensure that discussion takes place, but in my experience, there are times in the project when you need to meet multiple times in a day, and other times when once a week is sufficient. You need to monitor whether adequate discussion is taking place, and use meetings to augment the natural discussions or to initiate needed discussions.

Asynchronous project management is all about events. Every team member should be familiar with recent events, and with the order of the task queue. The team meeting is the best place to discuss the scheduling of tasks in the queue.

During the standup meeting you need to get answers to the following from each developer:

- What events am I waiting for?
- What events will I generate soon?
- What changes to the existing implementation do I need?

Based on the answers to these questions, you may want to make changes in the order of tasks, or in the owners of tasks. Dynamically changing task ownership is an important practice in asynchronous project management. If Jill is waiting for Input Chunk to be completed so she can start on Packet Parsing, then Jack can pause what he's doing and implement Input Chunk, or Jill can assume ownership of Input Chunk.

9.11.6 Asynchronous Change Management

One of the benefits of Scrum is that its short, periodic Sprints force frequent integration of requirements. When using Asynchronous Project Management, each milestone presents an opportunity to integrate requirements. However, you will often learn of important requirement changes in the middle of a milestone. Then you will need to decide whether to complete the milestone as originally planned, or to modify it to accommodate the new requirement.

It's important to assess requirements changes periodically – biweekly or monthly. If the required change is additive (see Managing Change), you may want to put it into the current milestone. If the change is structural, then the choice is more difficult. If the development team will be writing a lot of new code that will need to be updated after the change is made, then it's better to do it sooner rather than later.

9.11.7 Parallel Development

Asynchronous project management naturally supports parallel development with multiple teams each working toward their own intermediate milestones. While Jack and Jill are working on the SHDS milestone, Bonnie and Clyde are working on the Simplified Human Security System (SHSS), and Victoria and Albert are working on the Simplified Human Control System (SHCS), all with the goal of completing the Simplified Human quickly and with high quality.

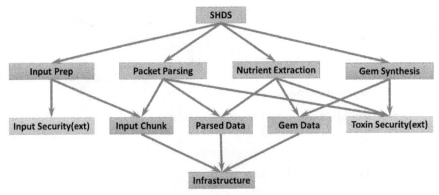

SHDS/SHSS Dependencies

Interactions between teams need to be more formal than interactions within teams. Jack and Jill and Bonnie and Clyde need to agree on the interfaces between SHDS and SHSS. Writing a specification will facilitate and document the agreement.

Each team needs to monitor certain events in the other team's project. The figure above shows the SHSS dependencies in green. The SHSS dependency graph will have similar dependencies on SHDS. Avoiding dependency loops is critical to parallel development. Good architecture design with clean dependencies will make it possible for the two projects to proceed in parallel with incremental integration.

A good build and integration process is required to do effective parallel development.

9.11.8 Summary

Much of the software community has the mistaken impression that Scrum is the only way to be Agile. While Scrum is a good alternative to the Old Way, it isn't the only way to achieve agility.

In this section, I presented a brief outline of how to do asynchronous, event-driven project management. It is a superior alternative to Scrum when you need a content-driven release in which a critical subset of functionality needs to be complete before the project is done. You can also adapt this methodology to schedule-driven releases by adding a Deferred task state and being careful about time.

But the lesson here is not just asynchronous project management. You need to think outside the Scrum. There are better ways to run software projects. Don't get stuck in someone else's methodology. Build the methodology that works best for you.

9.12 Managing the Methodology

Like the architecture, the methodology needs continuous improvement. You need a process for improving development processes, and that process needs to involve the entire team. Even if you are writing code every day, you can only know how the process affects you; you can't know the impact of the process on the entire team. If you're not writing code, you know even less. Maybe something you do every day causes a lot of rework for several junior developers. Or maybe a critical process that works well locally is too burdensome for developers at remote sites, influencing them to find a way to shortcut the process.

The hard part of this is getting developers, especially junior developers at remote sites, to talk to you about their problems. In a meeting, a few vocal individuals will be heard. If you do a survey, many will remain silent because they won't want to rock the boat. So, you are forced into sleuth mode. Sometimes you need to be Sherlock Holmes, finding clues and extrapolating to the logical conclusion. Sometimes you need to be Dr. Watson, gaining the trust of your witnesses so they will spill the beans. Either way, the only way that processes can improve is through a culture of open negative feedback.

You should formally review the methodology periodically, at least once per major release. But in addition, you should continually listen for the clues of ineffective or inefficient processes that are sapping energy from your team.

9.13 Key Concepts

- A methodology framework is a meta-process that sits above the Common Processes you have defined for your organization.
- When evaluating methodology frameworks, it's important to establish goals.
  - ○ See Methodology Goals for a sample set of goals that are used to evaluate some of the methodology frameworks discussed in this chapter.
- The Waterfall model of project management depends on a lot of up-front specification and planning to move the project from phase to phase.
  - ○ Phase overlap and iteration are common modifications to Waterfall methodologies.

- o Waterfall methodologies do not respond well to changing requirements or to discovery of problems in design or implementation.
- The Water Flow model uses the waterfall metaphor, but with small tasks that are moved through the phases independently to achieve greater agility.
  - o Scrum, XP and Asynchronous Project Management all use the Water Flow model.
- Scrum is the most widely used Agile methodology framework.
  - o It uses isochronous sprints to plan incremental development, and daily stand-up meetings to coordinate the activities of team members.
  - o It works well for small, co-located teams doing incremental development.
  - o It depends on good team dynamics.
- Extreme Programming (XP) emphasizes the importance of technical excellence in addition to meta-processes for planning and release.
  - o The principles of XP are mostly consistent with the Geodesic Manifesto and with Lean principles.
  - o The most controversial aspects of XP are pair programming, the prescribed practice of always having two people at a monitor while writing code, and its short-term focused definition of simplicity.
- Large-scale Scrum (LeSS) extends the Scrum Framework to much larger teams using a hierarchical approach to project management.
- Disciplined Agile (DA) is a process decision framework for helping teams develop methodologies that work best for their specific problems.
- The Scaled Agile Framework® (SAFe®) is a methodology framework aimed at scaling Agile practices to large organizations using a synthesis of Lean and Agile principles and practices.
  - o It uses a "cadence"-based approach that synchronizes events across multi-functional teams.
- Asynchronous Project Management presents an alternative to cadence-based approaches to project management.
  - o Its goal is to reach a milestone in the shortest time with highest productivity and quality.
  - o Tasks are managed using a dependency graph, and progress follows events of task completion and requests to expedite tasks.
  - o Asynchronous Project Management works better than the cadence-based approaches for feature-driven releases and new technology development.

10 CREATING A NEW SYSTEM

Creating a completely new system happens very seldom, maybe only once in the life of a company, but the impact of that creation lives forever. All of the good decisions and the bad ones propagate and branch, giving life to new decisions that further propagate and branch. It's hard to make new good decisions based on the old bad ones, but it's easy to make new bad decisions based on the old good ones. So, without intervention, the software rots. I can't stress enough the importance of making as few bad decisions as possible during the creation of the system – and of fixing the bad decisions as early as possible.

Creating a new subsystem happens much more frequently. Although it is tied to the old system and inherits some of its problems, the team embarks on the new mission with hope in their hearts and gleams in their eyes. They have the opportunity to show the world the right way to do it, to solve unconceived problems with just the right mixture of tried-and-true, and of innovation. The thought that in three years they will be fixing bugs introduced in the first week of programming is far from their minds. They are in a blissful euphoria.

Let's let them enjoy their reverie and try to figure out how to help them.

Starting from a blank slate gives you a lot of freedom, but a blank slate provides no guidance. The Agile methodologies presented in the previous chapter are good at improving something that exists, but they don't provide guidance for how to create that something out of thin air.

In this chapter, I will discuss several aspects of new development and make some recommendations on how to proceed. I assume that you are part of a startup and have complete freedom to do the right thing from the beginning. Most likely, you are not in that enviable situation.

NOTE: for this chapter, I will use the word 'system' to refer to the new thing, whether it's a system or a subsystem.

10.1 *Non-Sequitur* – Cinematic Focus

When we think of focus, the first image that comes to mind is of using a magnifying glass to start a fire. The sunlight from across the surface of the glass concentrates onto a small point. As a boy of seven or eight, I used the magnifying glass that came with the dictionary to char holes in pieces of paper and to torture ants as they followed pheromones to their nests.

In software development, there are times when point focus is needed – when you need to get an intricate piece of code just right. You block out all distractions and focus all your light on that one problem.

But more often, we need cinematic focus, where all the images on the screen are sharp and clear. Cinematic focus brings system thinking to the methodology, just as architecture brings systems thinking to the design of the code.

It is much too easy to get lost in point focus, concentrating on one critical piece of the system while losing sight of the big picture. When developing something new, you need to make progress on all the essential parts of the system in parallel. A neglected capability, patched in at the last moment, will suffer from lack of feedback, and will look like an afterthought.

10.2 Case Study

Two teams, A and B, need to develop a similar capability for two different solutions with different high-level requirements. The capability has two modules, Prep and Finish. Each module has a different NP problem at its core.

10.2.1 Team A

While trying to understand the initial requirements for Prep and Finish in Solution A, Team A decides that full automation of the solution with good optimization results is one of the most important requirements.

Team A decides to contract with a third party, P, to provide the Prep module because they think this will save them time and allow them to apply their limited resources to other parts of Solution A. The requirements of Finish are specific to Solution B, so they have to build an interface to P's implementation of Prep and to build their own implementation of Finish.

A couple years later, P is acquired by a competitor. Team A rushes to build their own implementation of Prep, which they complete (I'll call it A-1), but it doesn't perform nearly as well as P's implementation. Team A starts a follow-on project to build A-2, a better implementation of Prep. In parallel a different part of Team A acquires rights to a university implementation of the core algorithms of Prep and starts a project, A-3, to adapt this implementation to their requirements. Both A-2 and A-3 work well in some, but different, situations. So Team A starts a new project A-4 to build a framework into which they can plug A-1, A-2, A-3 and as many new implementations as they want.

Meanwhile it becomes clear that Prep could benefit from having some of the capabilities of Finish as part of the Prep algorithms. But Finish was implemented completely independently, on different data structures, and on a different continent.

There is no way to reuse any of its algorithms directly in Prep, and none of the Prep implementations anticipated that the Finish algorithms might be useful.

A couple years later, Team A's implementation teams for Prep and Finish have grown to over fifty people. Team A still has not met the requirement of good optimization results with full automation; users of Solution A often need Prep and Finish developers to make custom changes to algorithms and parameters to meet their needs. They need to maintain all the previous implementations while they try to meet the requirements.

10.2.2 Team B

Team B starts with two people who have the mission to solve the Prep and Finish problem for solution B.

Team B also has a requirement for full automation with good optimization results for Prep and Finish. But they do not believe that will be feasible in the early releases. Because they know they can't meet, or even know, all the requirements in the first release, they decide to make the Prep module very flexible with a lot of user configuration available. They expect to remove some of the flexibility as the module matures.

In the first week, they sketch out a block diagram of an architecture that identifies the required information needed by the algorithms, the interfaces to the rest of Solution B, and the high-level capabilities that will be needed. They start implementing and testing the infrastructure, the low-level parts of the system that everything else will depend on. Everything they do is tested with unit, integration, system and parametric tests.

They read the papers that describe the university software of A-3. They also read other papers that describe alternative approaches to Prep. They implement a Prep algorithm framework that facilitates quick experimentation, and they start exploring algorithm alternatives, and measuring the results with a suite of test cases.

Pleased with their progress, they start demonstrating Prep to some of the interested parties and find polite nods of approval and a lot of questions about Finish. They implement a quick and dirty prototype of Finish, and new demos find enthusiasm. They add another team member who will be responsible for productizing the prototype of Finish.

They release the software to internal customer advocates and to end users, who complain. Some of the complaints are about capabilities that Team B consciously omitted from the first release. Others are things that the team did not anticipate. They quickly adapt to meet the newly discovered requirements. They add the planned capabilities. They continue to measure and improve the algorithms, constantly improving their measurement techniques.

A couple years later, the team has grown to five people. The architecture has evolved, but when they look back at the original block diagram, it still looks close to the current architecture. Users of Solution B are generally happy with the Prep and Finish modules. Much of the configurability available in the first release has been deprecated because the modules are more automated. Users continue to ask for improvements, which the team is able to implement with extensions to the existing architecture. Team B rarely has to intervene to make customers successful with either Prep or Finish, and most bugs reported in the field have straightforward workarounds by using the built-in configurability.

Team B was able to quickly benchmark Prep-B in solution A and found results comparable to A's results.

10.2.3 Analysis

Disclaimer: As you might have guessed, I was part of Team B, and I merely observed the efforts of Team A.

How do two teams implementing similar capabilities take such different paths? Each team, in retrospect, believes that at each step they made the best decision possible with the information they had. Each team had great developers. Each team used similar common processes. Neither team used an Agile methodology framework, but clearly, Team B, with at most five people, quickly adapting to changing requirements and responding to customer feedback, showed more agility than Team A.

10.2.3.1 Small team

Small teams have more agility than large teams. Communication overhead is lower. It's easier to keep track of what everyone is doing. They are forced to find the most expedient way to get the essential stuff done. Everyone needs to be able to work on the entire project's code. They can quickly make changes to processes that aren't working.

Large teams tend to compartmentalize the work and create boundaries where there should be continuity. Subgroups create political divides that prolong and impair decision making. Large teams often value discussion over measurement.

10.2.3.2 Architecture

Architecture is the embodiment of systems thinking. The initial architecture sketch provided a guideline for how to organize the work. With the big picture in place, it was easier to make incremental architecture changes. The sketch allowed the team to decide which parts of the envisioned solution could not be met in the first release, but it let them develop the essential subset in a way that made it easier to add capabilities later. The sketch showed how Prep and Finish would use the same data structures in a way that would allow them to work together or separately.

I acted as architect, reviewing changes and new design decisions. I initiated refactoring when it was needed. I established the ethos for how to make design decisions, until eventually the role of architect became superfluous because the entire team owned the architecture.

10.2.3.3 Flexibility

One of the dichotomies of the Yin-Yang Model is Rigidity vs. Flexibility. Avoiding rigidity is extremely important in the early days of new development. Early decisions that create rigidity limit your options for eternity.

Team A made early decisions that locked them into rigidity. The initial third-party implementation forced them to create a Finish module that would forever be separate from Prep. And it set off a panic when P was acquired. The use of the university algorithm framework limited their ability to experiment with new ideas. Some of the key algorithmic ideas in B's implementation were virtually impossible to do in A's algorithm framework.

Team B embraced flexibility from the beginning. They knew that they could not meet all the requirements in the first release, so they added user configuration. When a capability was needed by both Prep and Finish, the small team could not afford to implement it twice, so they made sure that one common implementation could be used for both modules.

The quick adaptation of Prep-B to work in Solution A is testimony to the flexibility of Team B's implementation. In addition to Prep and Finish, the infrastructure created by Team B was also used in two other unrelated subsystems.

10.2.3.4 Measurement

Measurement is one way to overcome software's opacity. Deciding what to measure and how to measure it is important to establish early in the life of a system.

Team B created unit tests and integration tests to validate the correctness of the code, but the best information came from the suite of tests created to measure the effectiveness of the Prep and Finish algorithms. Team B continued to refine the measurement capabilities. By the time I left the project, we could run a hundred test cases, each with several options, in less than an hour. Such quick feedback accelerated progress on improving the algorithms.

Continual measurement also helped identify chaotic behavior. Some test cases were susceptible to wide variations after seemingly irrelevant changes. By focusing on those test cases, Team B was able to make its algorithms more repeatable.

10.2.3.5 Lean Thinking

Team B used Lean Thinking without even knowing what it was called. We can look at Team B's behavior for each of the seven Lean principles.

- **Eliminate waste** – small teams with cinematic focus generate a lot less waste than big teams.
- **Amplify learning** – the measurement system they put in place helped them learn about algorithms. Short release cycles that respond to user feedback also helped them learn.
- **Decide as late as possible** – This principle is difficult to follow for new development because "as late as possible" is often yesterday. In new development, that principle needs to be replaced with "Decide, but keep your options open." Making decisions that you know will change means that you will have a lot of unfinished projects and extra features that will need to be purged sometime in the future. They may look like waste, but they were an important part of the learning that you needed before you could build the right thing.
- **Deliver as fast as possible** – Team B created its first internal release for evaluation within a couple months, and then delivered near-continuous updates. External releases were limited by the rest of Solution B.
- **Empower the team** – Management was not involved in technical decisions. Team B gave bi-weekly updates to Solution B's manager. Team B worked directly with user advocates to address user problems.
- **Build integrity in** – Test-driven design played a major role in the quality achieved by Team B. But exploratory testing, using the test cases from the metrics test suite, found more important bugs that would have been impossible to find with unit tests.
- **See the whole** – Architecture provided a guide for technical decisions within the Prep and Finish modules. It wasn't discussed above, but there were a lot of decisions about what Prep and Finish could do to improve the rest of Solution B, and what could be done in Solution B to improve Prep and Finish.

10.3 Common Processes

You may think the Agile Manifesto's devaluation of process in favor of people absolves you from having to define common processes for your organization. You're wrong. You can't develop software without processes, and if you avoid defining good processes, then you will end up with bad ones.

Look at the list of common processes and decide which ones you need immediately and which ones you can defer. For example, you don't need an external release process until you have something to release.

Define the simplest processes possible, and then make them more complex as you encounter issues that need to be resolved. Define a timeframe to review each process – monthly or quarterly, but not longer, and identify the people who need to be involved in the reviews. Managers can own the documentation and enforcement of processes, but the definition needs to come from the people who are using the processes.

10.4 Requirements

The process for defining requirements for a new development is very different from the mature product requirements process I outlined earlier, because you probably don't have customers who can help.

The development team's guess about the initial requirements will be better than anyone else's because they are actually thinking about the problem. Customers are not. Customers can show you the way to incremental improvement, but they are not good at inventing new concepts. If Apple had asked potential customers what they wanted in the first iPhone, they would have answered that they wanted better reception at the basketball game, not that they wanted a phone with no buttons and with simple, inexpensive software applications that interacted through the internet. Customers will be useful later, but not now.

You can come up with your initial requirements in a brainstorming session, by using an email discussion, or by having one person write a draft that everyone reviews. Whatever means you get them, make sure they're written down. That makes them available to the people who need them, makes them easy to clarify when they're ambiguous, and it makes it easy to tell when they change. Once again, despite the Agile Manifesto's misguided values, documentation is not evil.

In a new development, you need to identify which requirements are necessary for the first release. Ask yourself, "What is the smallest viable subset?" Your definition of viability might include a few attributes like useful, competitive, sellable, or others. Like the full set of requirements, the viable subset will change. You need to avoid feature creep; unnecessary features add schedule delay and unneeded complexity. But shipping software that's not viable can be just as bad; you can lose credibility with customers, and with the rest of the organization that depended on this project.

Once you have the initial set of requirements, you're not done. Keep digging for a better understanding of requirements. As the project comes together, start to demo it to users, user advocates and other stakeholders. Listen to their praise, but listen harder for their concerns.

10.5 Architecture Design

You need to have an architecture in mind before you start writing code. But without any code, you have insufficient information to make architecture decisions. Welcome to the world of software!

You will make architecture decisions in the first week of the project that will be nearly impossible to change later. It's worthwhile to spend a little time thinking through the possibilities before you commit.

Most architectures start out looking like architectures you've worked on in the past. If you've always worked with monoliths, you will design a monolith. If you've always worked on client-server systems, you will develop a client-server architecture. Try to bring many kinds of experience into the architecture exploration discussion.

Identify the parts of the system where you have the most confidence. These are places where it's safe to have developers start writing code.

Identify the parts of the system where you have the least confidence. Try to keep flexibility in these parts. For example, in the Case Study, Team B wasn't sure what algorithm would work best, so they built an algorithm framework to facilitate experimentation.

Sketch out the high-level architecture and make sure it's available to everyone on the project. In the early days, it will be changing a lot, so a whiteboard drawing may be best.

Start developing the architecture ethos – the set of rules about right and wrong that will guide design decisions for the team. As the architecture evolves, use the Architecture Design Principles – Modularity, Flexibility, Consistency and Sufficiency – to evaluate changes. You will especially want to enforce good decisions for dependencies and consistency, which are the aspects most likely to diverge early.

The architecture is a statement of intentions. It should guide the team toward a solution. When it stops doing a good job as a guide, you need to change it. Often you can change it by addition – adding a new module, or splitting an existing module. But sometimes you need to detonate large portions of the current architecture and rebuild. It's disappointing when that happens, but it's better to do it now in the early stages of the project than to wait until later when more code has been layered on the wrong foundation. In my experience, big rewrites were scary to start, but they often turned out to be easier than I expected, and the benefits were greater.

10.6 Planning

Remember that the goal of planning is to answer the three planning questions:

306

- When will it be done?
- What will it include?
- What do I do next?

while maximizing productivity and minimizing risk.

The planning processes used in the Agile frameworks works best for schedule-driven releases, where content can be deferred to the next release. New development needs a feature-driven plan, where the smallest viable subset of the requirements must be complete in order to ship, and your goal is to make that happen as soon as possible.

The first step in planning is to determine milestones. It's clear what the final milestone looks like, but what are the early milestones? You need a rough sketch of the planning roadmap as a guide for developers, and to answer the first question, but there's no value in putting too much effort into the later milestones because so much is likely to change between now and then. Concentrate on the next two or three milestones, with a planning horizon of two to three months.

If you think two months is too short, try this experiment. Write down what you expect the state of the project to be in two months. Include predictions of what will work, and what are the most important problems the development team will face. Predict what processes will change. Draw a diagram of the future architecture. Wait two months and compare your prediction to reality. When your prediction comes close to the reality, then you can lengthen your planning horizon.

Once you have milestones, you can treat each one as a mini-release and use standard planning practices.

10.7 Implementing the System

Finally, with the architecture and the plan in place, the team can start writing code!

Hah! The team's been coding for weeks. Anyone who says that they can do design and planning without writing any code is either a liar or a fool.

You have to write code to do design because you can't truly understand anything until you've used it. I didn't understand algebra or trigonometry until I used them in calculus. I didn't understand calculus or differential equations until I used them in physics. The same is true for software, whether you are learning a new language or a third-party library or an algorithm. You have to use it to learn. That's why it is so important that the early stages of the project focus on delivering something that's useful, even if the utility is limited to being used in artificially simple tests.

Deliver something you can measure as soon as possible. That is the core of the Geodesic Philosophy.

307

10.8 Key Concepts

- Cinematic focus, looking at the whole picture, is often more important than point focus.
- Develop new functionality starting with a small team.
- Design an architecture as early as possible and modify it as soon as it doesn't work.
- Build flexibility into the system, especially for parts of the system that you expect to change.
- Measure the key metrics for both reliability and functionality as soon as possible.
- Apply Lean thinking to improve your development methodology.
- Develop key processes as they are needed.
- Gather requirements by whatever means you can, knowing that customers are often not a good source of requirements for new development.
  - Identify the smallest viable subset to focus development.
- Develop a roadmap plan for the release, but pay most attention to the earliest milestones.

Part 4:
TRANSCENDENCE

Birth of Venus, Sandro Botticelli, 1486

11 HOPE

Here I am in chapter eleven, having poured everything I know about software into the first ten chapters. I am bankrupt, empty, depleted. When I started, I wasn't sure I had enough material to fill the pages of a book, but I found enough and only repeated myself a few times.

I started this book by comparing software to bridges and wondering if we could ever bring the practice of software development to the maturity of bridge design and construction. By now you should know that the comparison is unfair. Bridge designers have straightforward, unchanging requirements. Software designers are faced with ambiguous and amorphous requirements that change shape and color and texture every day. Bridge builders have centuries of infrastructure to leverage. Software builders create new infrastructure for every project and throw it away as fast as they develop it. Bridge builders are constrained by the location of the bridge. Software developers are spread around the world.

I titled this last chapter "Hope" because there *is* hope for building better software. Part of that hope comes from the availability of standard infrastructure that the industry calls packages or stacks or libraries. High quality infrastructure removes the burden of infrastructure from developers and frees them to build better applications. But packages still need to be used to do what the user wants in the way the user expects.

Hope does not come from the prevalence of machine learning that moves the problem from coding to data. True artificial intelligence might someday offer hope, but we are a long way from there.

I titled this last part of the book, "Transcendence" because we can only realize our hope by transcending the Old Way, by transcending the Agile way, and by gaining enlightenment with the Geodesic way. The Geodesic pillars of leadership, architecture, methodology and a decision-making ethos are the best way to change hope into reality.

In this chapter, I will go back to the Geodesic Manifesto and annotate it with what we have learned. If we accept its truths, embrace its principles and buttress its pillars, our hope for the future will be a living dream.

11.1 *Non-Sequitur* – Ode to Software

While lines of Python, Java, C
Comprise our system's software,
The function that our users see
Floats rather more aloft where
They cannot see the lines of code
Nor harnesses of testing
Nor architecture arguments
That haunt nocturnal resting.

They see a world that we create
With colors far from nature's
Where laws of physics alternate
Twixt speed of stars and glaciers.
Software has no bounds for us.
We make it cry or sing
According to requirements,
That crown the user King.

We did not know when we began
What shape the system needed.
We did not know the coding plan
Or if we would exceed it.
We committed to an architecture,
With changes sure to come.
We chose a methodology,
But not XP or Scrum.

The system came together soon.
We measured and improved it,
Together chanting teamwork's tune,
Uniting till we grooved it.
And so we found that we could code
To the best of our ability
When we used the Geodesic way
To augment our agility.

11.2 The Geodesic Manifesto – Revisited

The Manifesto of the Geodesic Philosophy of Software Development
Assumptions
We assume these truths:

- Our goal is to create software-based solutions that do what the user wants in the way the user expects.
  - ❖ *I hope that this book will help you to realize your goal.*
- Requirements are an inaccurate abstraction of what customers and users want. Requirements cannot be known completely and will change even after they are known. The only true specification of the solution is working software.
  - ❖ *The ephemeral and amorphous nature of requirements drives the uncertainty of the software development process. Requirements come in the form of text, and conversations and observations. We must translate those into the formality of code. Guess right at the true requirements and you will be successful.*
- People who develop software have a wide range of ability, motivation and temperament.
  - ❖ *Despite Jefferson's assertion, all men (and women) are not created equal. It's not politically correct to say that some people suck at programming, but it's true and we have to deal with it. On the other hand, some people are amazingly good. The first step is awareness, which I tried to help with in the Organization section. (It's also true that some people suck at managing software development; fixing that is the goal of this book 😊).*
- Our problem is to help those people overcome software's inherent difficulties: complexity, opacity, vulnerability, rigidity, and its chaotic nature.
  - ❖ *I created the Yin-Yang Model in the early stages of writing this book when I was trying to understand why software was hard. It has proven to be the most useful of the three models for understanding software. The Complexity Model is useful for management and inspired the Architecture and Challenging Problems chapters. The Software Thermodynamic Model provides insights into how software rots, but was not a useful as I hoped.*

Principles
To overcome the limitations of requirements:

- We have frequent interaction with customers and users.
  - ❖ *Given the importance of customer interaction, I probably didn't spend enough time on this. In the organizations I worked in, customer interaction was never an issue. Customers are vocal, and they have advocates inside the organization.*
- We frequently deliver working software and actively seek feedback.
  - ❖ *Sending out a beta is not enough. "Active feedback" means sitting down with your beta customers and watching them use the software. It means that you need to be open to hearing bad things about your software, and to be ready to fix the problems immediately.*
- Developers must learn to think like their customers.

❖ *This is the best way to translate ambiguous requirements into concrete code.*

To overcome the limitations of people:

- We build synergistic teams that improve the performance of every individual.
    - ❖ *When I was a manager, I always tried to build synergistic teams, but my discussion at <u>Teamwork</u> was my first attempt at understanding how I did it.*
- We establish a methodology that fosters creativity and encourages interaction.
    - ❖ *This is a major difference between the Geodesic Philosophy that encourages common processes that help team members do their jobs, and Agile that shuns processes in favor of "individuals and interactions."*
- We encourage frequent and open communication among team members.
    - ❖ *"To thine own self be true" is one of the themes of this book. Fearless honesty is critical to software development. We will all make mistakes. Admit it and move on.*

To overcome the inherent difficulties of software:

- We seek out change from as many sources as possible.
    - ❖ *Change is the essence of life. The minute we stop changing, we are dead.*
- We plan for change, and change the plan when necessary.
    - ❖ *The Agile Manifesto's value, "Responding to change over following a plan," presumes that you can't do both. A plan that transcends change is another major team of the Geodesic Philosophy.*
- We embrace change through constant measurement, analysis and improvement of the software and methodology.
    - ❖ *Once developers start using the measure-analyze-improve loop, they can't develop software any other way.*
- Developers strive for the highest level of technical excellence and assume responsibility for quality.
    - ❖ *Why settle for less than excellence?*

Pillars

Success depends on:

- Leadership that:
    - o Creates a vision for the solution we're trying to create
    - ❖ *I've been spouting visions for most of my career, but I never understood the importance of the talisman until I wrote the <u>Vision</u> section based on the Arthur legend.*
    - o Organizes the development team to maximize the contribution of each member
    - ❖ *The <u>Organization</u> section focuses on understanding the members of your team, which is the first step toward teamwork.*
    - o Develops dynamic plans that answer three questions: When will it be done? What will it contain? What do I do next?
    - ❖ *I've repeated these three questions over and over. If a plan can't answer them, it's inadequate. If it does more than this, it's constraining.*

    o   Establishes processes and controls that maximize productivity and creativity

   ❖ *The <u>Control</u> section links management control to the control theory I learned as an electrical engineer. One of my favorite insights in this section is this definition of kludge: "a system that solves problem X by creating problem Y."*

- An architecture that organizes the solution into modules and their interactions that is modular, flexible, consistent and sufficient.

   ❖ *When I started this book, I was sure that architecture was the most important part of software development. I now recognize that it's important, but stands equal to leadership, methodology and a decision-making ethos.*

- A methodology that defines common processes and controls that foster innovation, empower the development team to create the best solution, and maximize efficiency while minimizing risk

   ❖ *The biggest failure of Agile is that it got stuck in the existing methodology frameworks. Rather than creating new methodology frameworks that better serve the needs of software teams, they stuck with <u>Scrum</u> and <u>XP</u>. Big software companies like Google, Synopsys, Microsoft and others have avoided Agile because of the link to Scrum and XP. But they still have plenty of agility. <u>Asynchronous Project Management</u> presents a crude outline of a different framework that can provide agility. Feel empowered to create your own.*

- A decision-making ethos to guide us as we change the vision, plan, architecture and methodology.

   ❖ *The ethos – your organization's sense of right and wrong – is another major difference between the Geodesic Philosophy and Agile. I have not said enough about the ethos, and I don't have a formula that can help you create one. Maybe in the second edition.* 😊

12 OBLIGATIONS

12.1 Acknowledgements

I'd like to thank:

- My wife Sally, who both tolerated and encouraged me on this quest.
- Geoff Moore, who encouraged, advised and mentored me through the process of writing.
- My early reviewers, Andy Crews and Joe Marceno.
- Michael Feliz, who always read the early versions the same day and provided insightful and thorough feedback.
- The people who gave me permission to use their IP. They all responded quickly and generously:
  o Emily Gottschalk-Marconi and Julian Hanna for the Manifesto article from *The Atlantic*
  o Craig Larman and Bas Vodde for LeSS
  o Scott Ambler for Disciplined Agile
  o Michelle Stoll for SAFe
- Any reader who made it this far. You are a brave and persevering friend.

12.2 Version History

- 1.0
  o First e-book upload
- 1.1
  o Improve graphics for readability on small and black & white devices.
  o Change form factor to support 6"x9" print layout
- 1.2
  o A few formatting fixes
  o Edited text in the Geodesic Manifest Revisited section.
  o Edited text in LeSS section based on feedback from Craig Larman.
- 1.3
  o Added the Foreword
  o Fixed a couple minor "bugs" in the introduction to the Yin-Yang model and in Software Thermodynamics.
  o Fixed formatting of Agile Principles.
  o Fixed a confusing forward reference in the discussion of the SOLID principles.

12.3 About the Author

Bob with the Birds

Bob Erickson was born and raised in northern Minnesota, where he walked to school in forty below zero weather uphill and against the wind in both directions. He received a BA in Physics and Electrical Engineering from Rice University, and an MSEE from Stanford. After a few years as a hardware designer at HP, he wandered into the Electronic Design Automation industry, working for Silicon Compilers and with Mentor Graphics after the acquisition. He alternated between management roles and development roles for many years before becoming VP of Engineering at startup Synplicity and later VP of Software at startup Tabula. He returned to the Synplicity group after its acquisition by Synopsys, where he worked mostly as a software developer and architect. He was named Synopsys Distinguished Architect before his retirement in 2017.

Bob welcomes feedback and questions. Contact Bob at bob@geodesicManifesto.com.